Understanding the ADA

4TH EDITION

William D. Goren

ABA

Cover design by Amanda Fry/ABA Publishing

Printed in the United States of America.

17 16 15 14 13 5 4 3 2 1

Library of Congress Cataloging-in-Publication Data

Goren, William D., 1960- author.

Understanding the Americans with Disabilities Act / By William D. Goren. — Fourth edition.

pages cm

Includes index.

ISBN 978-1-62722-274-7

1. People with disabilities—Legal status, laws, etc.—United States. 2. United States. Americans with Disabilities Act of 1990. I. Title.

KF480.G67 2013

342.7308'7—dc23 2013034873

Discounts are available for books ordered in bulk. Special consideration is given to state bars, CLE programs, and other bar-related organizations. Inquire at Book Publishing, ABA Publishing, American Bar Association, 321 North Clark Street, Chicago, Illinois 60654-7598.

www.ShopABA.org

Contents

Preface

THERE IS A SAYING: If you are going to write a book, do it because you have to. Any other motive just won't lead to the necessary satisfaction. In other words, to write a book, you have to feel compelled to write it. I had to write this update for several reasons.

First, while there are many Americans with Disabilities Act (ADA) tomes on the market, I still have not seen any, besides the editions of this book, devoted exclusively to making the ADA understandable in an easy-to-use way.

Second, I saw a need for an ADA book that was written from the perspective of a lawyer with a disability. (I have a congenital severe to profound hearing loss but, with the use of lipreading and hearing aids, function entirely in the hearing world. For other reasons, I also use voice dictation technology.) To me, the ADA is not just a law but a way of life. For example, in this book we discuss the concept of reasonable accommodation. Two examples of reasonable accommodations I ask for every day of my life are: 1) asking people on the phone to give examples of the letters they are saying (C as in cat, P as in Patrick, etc.), because without being able to read lips—an impossibility on the phone—I am unable to understand what letter is meant; and 2) asking people not to cover their mouth with their hands. Both of these are examples of reasonable accommodations.

Third, there is a need for an ADA book that discusses preventive lawyering with regard to the ADA.

Fourth, since the last edition of the book was published, the law has evolved. Some issues have come to the fore, while others have receded. Also, the book was in need of bulking up. I took advantage of this update to go into more depth across many of the subject matters covered. Also, there are always new developments in the case law and in regulations that need to be talked about.

In prior editions, the remedies chapter was extremely short. The more I thought about that, the more misguided that approach seemed. After all, without remedies, the law doesn't mean anything. Thus, in the remedies chapter, in addition to some general thoughts, there is now a discussion about standing, when a complaint is sufficient, statute of limitations, and mixed-motive jury instructions, along with expanded discussions of disparate treatment cases, class actions (new to this edition), jury selection, and *Batson* challenges.

The ADA and Sports chapter discusses the recent Office of Civil Rights guidance on § 504 of the Rehabilitation Act and opportunities for students with disabilities to participate in athletics, as well as essential functions of jobs as they apply to athletic endeavors (a recent case involving a deaf lifeguard is discussed).

Chapter 13 has been changed from "hot areas" to "issues on the cutting edge." Issues that are on the cutting edge of the ADA may not always be considered hot areas. However, a good preventive lawyer is always thinking about where the issues with respect to a particular law are headed. In that chapter, the reader will find many of the old standbys that appeared in prior editions along with new ones, such as: negligence and negligence per se actions as an alternative to Title III claims; how *Olmstead* is evolving into other areas (budget cuts and sheltered workshops, for example); and, in the Internet section of that chapter, a discussion of *National Association of the Deaf v. Netflix*. Developments in the area of reassignment as a reasonable accommodation are also covered, as well as a discussion of the Air Carrier Access Act and how it relates to the ADA. This list of additions to the book is not exclusive but is, I hope, indicative of how the book has been expanded from prior editions.

With these goals in mind, a couple of warnings are in order. First, the ADA remains an extremely broad and comprehensive law. This book is not a treatise and is not meant to address every contingency that can arise under the ADA. Rather, the book highlights various aspects of the ADA so that by the end, the reader has an excellent overview of the law as well as a framework for dealing with the ADA in a preventive manner. Second, the ADA is constantly changing; there are new developments every day. Thus, when an ADA issue arises, it is critical that the reader consult a lawyer knowledgeable about the ADA. Finally, keep in mind that the cases cited in this book are for illustrative purposes only and are not meant to substitute for expert legal advice. A lawyer knowledgeable about the ADA should be consulted for the reader's specific legal needs

William D. Goren, J.D., LL.M.,
Decatur, Georgia

Acknowledgments

ON THE PERSONAL SIDE, I WANT TO dedicate this edition of the book to my wife, Susan, for encouraging me to write this update, and all the other updates for that matter, as well as for all her support in so many ways. I would also like to dedicate this book to my daughter, Maya, for enriching my life in ways that are not describable.

On the professional side, I want to acknowledge two attorneys who were incredibly helpful with respect to the litigation forms that appear at the end of this book. With respect to the plaintiff litigation forms, I want to acknowledge Eleanor Mixon Atwood, a partner at Buckley Klein in Atlanta, Georgia. With respect to the defense litigation forms, I want to acknowledge Richard Hunt, a shareholder at the Hunt/Huey law firm, in Dallas, Texas. Thanks to that collaboration, I feel confident that those forms are both of high quality and will be of great use to practitioners regardless of the side of the aisle that they are on. Of course, I would be remiss if I did not thank Richard G. Paszkiet, executive editor of ABA publishing, for his unflagging support, patience, and enthusiasm for all of the editions of this book, including this one.

William D. Goren

About the Author

William D. Goren, J.D., LL.M. (www.williamgoren.com), of Decatur, Georgia, is a nationally known attorney, consultant, and blogger (http://www.williamgoren.com/blog) on all things related to the Americans with Disabilities Act (ADA). His practice focuses on making the ADA understandable so that it successfully works for you—whether you are a business owner, corporate HR professional, higher education administrator, attorney, employer, employee, or government entity. In addition to the four editions of this book, he is the author of numerous articles, most of which pertain to the rights of persons with disabilities.

Mr. Goren is a licensed attorney in Georgia, Illinois, and Texas and is founder, founding member, and current president of the National Association of Attorneys with Disabilities. He is also a member of the Equal Employment Opportunity Committee of the American Bar Association (ABA) Section of Labor and Employment Law, and he is a member of three committees in the ABA Solo, Small Firm and General Practice Division; the Pro Bono and Public Service Committee; Labor, Employment and Civil Rights Committee; and the Technology Committee. Previously, Mr. Goren has served on both the ABA's General Practice and Solo Section Diversity Committee; the Illinois Standing Committee on Disability Law; the Texas Bar Standing Committee on Disability Issues; and was a co-chair of the Civil Rights/Constitutional Law Committee of the Chicago Bar Association. He received his B.A. from Vassar College, his J.D. from the University of San Diego, and his LL.M. in health law from DePaul University.

Concepts Underlying the ADA and Key Definitions

1

CONCEPTS UNDERLYING THE ADA

WHEN DEALING WITH the Americans with Disabilities Act (ADA), it is important to understand the concepts behind it and why the law was enacted. One reason it was enacted was the extreme cost to the federal government of supporting people with disabilities who could be productive members of the work force, especially where employers without undue burden or undue hardship can bear the cost of reasonable accommodations.[1]

It is important to discuss the fundamental premise behind the ADA in order to prevent confusion when it comes to applying the law. The ADA is not an affirmative action statute. Instead, its purpose is to enable people with disabilities to be placed at the same "starting line" as those who are nondisabled. The Equal Opportunity Employment Commission's (EEOC's) phrase is "equal opportunity to attain the same level of performance as his/her colleagues."[2] In the workplace, it is then up to the employee to demonstrate what he or she can do. In the context of using governmental programs and places of public accommodations, getting the person with a disability to the same starting line gives him or her the opportunity to take advantage of the same services, activities, and businesses everyone else uses.

The starting-line analogy is useful in other respects as well. Plaintiff advocates should find it very helpful, since it appeals to Americans' sense of fair play. This concept also works very well in educating employees about accommodating a person with a disability. It is quite common for a person without a disability to believe that a person with a disability who is being accommodated is obtaining some sort of advantage. A true reasonable accommodation does no such thing. It simply gives the person with a disability an equal chance.

Finally, the reader needs to keep in mind that the ADA is an extremely broad law. It affects almost all areas of the legal universe in some way. The ADA applies to private employers of 15 or more employees, nonfederal governmental entities of any size, and places of public accommodations. There are also provisions applying to transportation, relay systems for the deaf, and certain miscellaneous provisions, such as those pertaining to retaliation claims.

KEY DEFINITIONS

Because the ADA deals with discrimination against persons with disabilities, perhaps the key definition is the word *disability*. When people think of disabilities, they generally think of persons in wheelchairs or with severe vision impairments. However, the definition of disability under the ADA is far broader. A person has a disability under the ADA if he or she:

- has a physical or mental impairment that substantially limits one or more of life's major activities;
- has a record of such an impairment regardless of whether he or she currently is substantially limited in a major life activity; or
- is regarded as having such an impairment.[3]

Before the American with Disabilities Act Amendments Act (ADAAA), which became effective January 1, 2009, there was tremendous litigation over whether a person was substantially limited in a major life activity. According to an EEOC regulation, "substantial limitation" referred to an individual who was unable to perform, or was significantly limited in the ability to perform, an activity an average person in the general population can perform.[4] Under this theory, a person who is deaf does not have the ability to hear compared to an average person, so the person who cannot hear has a disability. However, as mentioned in the last edition of this book, the U.S. Supreme Court's decision in *Toyota Motor Mfg., Kentucky, Inc. v. Williams* [5] superseded the EEOC regulations on this issue when it held that to be substantially limited in performing manual tasks meant that the person had to have to have an impairment that prevented or severely restricted the individual from performing such tasks.[6]

The Supreme Court reached that conclusion by relying on a standard dictionary in combination with the principle that the ADA as originally written did not give regulatory bodies the right to implement definitional terms of the ADA.[7] With some exceptions, the courts extended the *Toyota Motor* definition to all disabilities.[8] The ADAAA overruled the EEOC regulation and *Toyota Motor*'s holding as to what it meant to be substantially limited in the major life activity. More specifically, the ADAAA specifically states that the EEOC standard, which was far higher than the *Toyota Motor* standard, was still too high.[9] The ADAAA also states that it specifically rejects the standard *Toyota Motor* set with respect to what it meant to be substantially limited in a major life activity.[10] Finally, as mentioned above, the ADAAA said that regulatory bodies have the authority to implement definitional terms,[11] and the EEOC took advantage of that authority in its final regulations implementing the ADA Amendments Act of 2008. In its final regulations, the EEOC defined "substantially limits" as being a matter of whether the person is substantially limited in a major life activity as compared to most people in the general population.[12] While a person no longer needs to be "severely restricted" or "prevented" or even "significantly restricted" to be substantially limited in a major life activity, the plain language of the term suggests something more than de minimus.

With respect to substantial limitation, the ADAAA also has a couple of other things to say. First, the ADAAA says that to show a substantial limitation, a person does not need to show that an impairment impacts more than one major life activity.[13] Second, an impairment that is episodic or in remission is still considered a disability if it would substantially limit a major life activity when active.[14] This, "episodic" language is very significant for people with certain kinds of disabilities. For example, multiple sclerosis can flare up, causing real problems for the sufferer, while other times it may be quite manageable. There are other disabilities that work that way as well.

Finally, there is one other issue that needs to be addressed with respect to substantial limitation on a major life activity: what if the plaintiff alleges that the major life activity is working? The ADAAA specifically states, as mentioned below, that working is a major life activity. However, there is nothing in the ADAAA stating what it means for working to be substantially limited. *Sutton v. United Airlines* held that in order to be substantially limited in the major life activity of working, you have to show that the person is unable to perform a broad class of jobs.[15] The EEOC, in its proposed regulations, proposed changing the definition of what it meant to be substantially limited in the major life activity of working. More specifically, the EEOC stated in its proposed regulations that it was now a question of whether the impairment substantially limits an individual's ability to perform, or to meet the qualifications for, the type of work at issue.[16] In the final regulations, the EEOC backed down from its proposed regulation. Instead, it took out entirely the discussion of working as a major life activity from the regulations and placed it in the appendix.

In the appendix to its final regulations implementing the ADAAA, the EEOC returns to the *Sutton* standard by saying that for a person to be substantially limited in the major life activity of working, the individual would have to show that the impairment substantially limits his or her ability to perform a class of jobs or broad range of jobs in various classes as compared to most people having comparable training, skills, and abilities.[17] I have long wondered why so many plaintiff lawyers over the years have argued that their client was limited in the major life activity of working, as many times another major life activity could just as easily be argued, especially now with the ADAAA defining disability in such broad terms. In fact, one wonders, in the absence of a very unusual situation—and some do exist—if it would not be malpractice for an attorney to allege working as the major life activity.

It is really not possible to discuss "substantially limits" without also discussing "major life activity." The EEOC, when implementing the ADA originally, never really defined what a major life activity was; they just gave examples.[18] In *Toyota Motor*, the Supreme Court also discussed what constitutes a major life activity. The Supreme Court held that a major life activity was any activity of central importance to most people's daily lives.[19] However, the ADAAA does define a major life activity, as follows:

> 1) including but not limited to: Caring for oneself, performing manual tasks, seeing, hearing, eating, sleeping, walking, standing, lifting, bending, speaking, breathing, learning, reading, concentrating, thinking, communicating, and working; and 2) including the operation of major bodily function, such as but not limited to: Functions of the immune system, normal cell growth, digestive, bowel, bladder, neurological, brain, respiratory, circulatory, endocrine, and reproductive functions.[20]

Considering how broad the definition of a major life activity is now, it's hard to believe that whether a person has alleged a major life activity could seriously be an issue anymore. In the unlikely event that a person alleges a major life activity that is not on the list, the question could arise as to whether its central importance to most people's daily lives is still a standard that is in play. The EEOC, in its interpretive guidance to the final regulations implementing ADAAA, specifically says that the *Toyota Motor* standard of whether the major life activity is of central importance to most people's daily lives is a standard no longer on the table.[21]

If a person takes medicine or uses prosthetic devices to compensate for a disability, does that make him no longer disabled under the ADA? For example, is a person who has a hearing loss and wears hearing aids considered not disabled under the ADA?

It can be argued that, with the rare exception of fully correctable vision,[22] a prosthetic device allows a person with a disability to *compensate* for the disability rather than cure it. For example, does a person with a substantial hearing loss who wears hearing aids and reads lips have a disability under the ADA? What if a person with 20/200 vision wears glasses, which correct her vision to 20/20 or better: Does that person have a disability? I have a congenital hearing loss of 65-90+ dB in both ears, which is in the severe-to-profound hearing loss range. However, I wear top-of-the-line hearing aids, read lips, and, through hard work on my own, have excellent rhetorical skills. Do I have a disability? Certainly, absent the hearing aids, I most certainly do; however, I wear my hearing aids all the time except when I am in the shower or sleeping.

Prior to the ADAAA, mitigating measures had to be factored into the calculus as to whether a person had a disability,[23] and because of *Toyota Motor*'s definition of what it meant to be substantially limited in a major life activity, two other perversions were created. First, the combination of *Sutton* and *Toyota Motor* created a disincentive for the person with a disability to use mitigating measures. The whole idea of using mitigating measures is to compensate for that disability so that the person can function as closely as possible to the way the nondisabled person does. However, if mitigating measures work, then a person would not be prevented or severely restricted with their use in performing a major life activity (the *Toyota Motor* standard).

To discourage people with disabilities from using mitigating measures would seem to be bad public policy. However, it was a conclusion compelled by a reading of *Sutton* and *Toyota Motor*. Second, a plain reading of both cases meant it was entirely possible that a person with a physical impairment using mitigating measures may be protected under the ADA depending on the time of day or the circumstances. For example, a person with a hearing impairment who uses hearing aids may or may not, depending on the nature of his or her hearing loss, be disabled under the ADA prior to the amendments, while he or she wears the hearing aid(s). However, people who wear hearing aids do not wear them all the time. Even people who do wear hearing aids often, such as myself, will take them off when they shower or when they sleep. Thus, during those times that person would most definitely have a disability under the ADA. Accordingly, a person who wears hearing aids and has a job that requires staying overnight would be entitled to various accommodations, such as a flashing light for an alarm clock, flashing smoke alarm, flashing door knock, etc., but under the ADA (as interpreted by the courts) may or may not be entitled to reasonable accommodations during the day depending on the severity of the loss and the type of hearing aids he or she wears. Such a conclusion may not have been intended by *Sutton* and *Toyota Motor,* but nevertheless followed quite logically from the holdings of those cases.

The absurdities raised by the prior discussion have now been erased with the advent of the ADAAA. The ADAAA specifically states that whether a person is substantially limited in a major life activity must be determined without respect to the use of such mitigating measures as:

> 1) medication, medical supplies, equipment, or appliances, low vision devices (not including ordinary eyeglasses or contact lenses), prosthetics including lens and devices, hearing aids and cochlear implants or other implantable hearing devices, mobility devices, or oxygen therapy equipment and supplies; 2) use of assistive technology; 3) reasonable accommodation or auxiliary aids or services [which will be discussed later in this chapter]; or 4) learned behavioral or adaptive neurological modifications.[24]

Note that the ADAAA treats eyeglasses and contact lenses quite a bit differently than any other disability when it says that eyeglasses and contact lenses are to be factored into whether a person is substantially limited in seeing.[25] The ADAAA also states that any tests requiring an assessment of a person's uncorrected vision must be job-related and consistent with business necessity.[26] These provisions of the ADAAA specifically recognize that contact lenses and glasses are unique with respect to compensating for disabilities. In most cases, you could say that contact lenses and glasses generally "cure" the disability. That is simply not the case with other disabilities. In those cases, prosthetic devices and the like only compensate for a person's disability, not cure it. For example, I still have a 40dB hearing loss even with hearing aids. Hence, it makes sense that eyeglasses and contact lenses be carved out for unique treatment.

A person with a "temporary" disability does not have a disability under the ADAAA. However, just how long a temporary disability has to go on to no longer be a temporary disability for purposes of the ADA is far from clear. The EEOC in its final regulations implementing the ADAAA does say it is possible that a disability could arise even if it lasts, or is expected to last, for less than six months.[27] The EEOC's view is that the reference to disabilities that are "transitory *and* minor," (a natural or expected duration of six months or less and therefore not a disability),[28] which appears in the ADAAA, is restricted to claims alleging that the person was discriminated against by an employer who regarded him or her as having a disability.[29]

The second definition of disability under the ADA includes a person who has a record of an impairment regardless of whether he or she is currently substantially limited in a major life activity.[30] This definition commonly applies to people who have records of learning disabilities.

Many students are diagnosed with learning disabilities very early in their education. Some outgrow those disabilities (some studies show that 80 percent of children with Attention Deficit Disorder outgrow it), and others learn to compensate for their learning disabilities without accommodations. Those persons will still be protected under the ADA and should not be discriminated against because of a documented learning disability.[31] The definition of discrimination is met if a record relied on by the employer indicates that the person either has or had a substantially limiting impairment.[32] The information could be found in medical records, education records, and personnel records, although with respect to personnel records, the ADA, due to a requirement that medical information not be contained in a person's personnel records, has lessened the likelihood of such information appearing there.

The final instance of a person having a disability under the ADA involves a person who is being *regarded as* having an impairment.[33] Often, people who discriminate jump to the wrong conclusion about whether a person has a disability. For example, an individual may assume that a gay person has HIV,[34] or a basketball referee association may assume that a person with glasses cannot referee a game because he or she does not see as well as a person without glasses or contacts. Also, while a more in-depth discussion of drug and alcohol abuse will follow later in this book, a person regarded as having a drug or alcohol problem is also protected under the ADA.[35]

To be "regarded as" having a disability, must a person be regarded as having both a physical or mental impairment *and* a substantial limitation in a major life activity? The *Sutton* case answered this question in the affirmative.[36] However, the ADAAA makes it quite clear that the answer to this question is in the negative. For the "regarded as" definition to apply, the defendant only has to perceive that the plaintiff had a disability; it is not necessary for the defendant to also perceive that the plaintiff had a substantial limitation on a major life activity.[37]

The ADAAA represents a sea change on this particular point. From a reading of the case law, it can be argued that the courts prior to the

ADAAA were adopting a subjective standard as to whether the employer perceived a limitation on a major life activity.[38] The ADAAA properly returns the focus to whether a person is perceived as having a physical or mental impairment.

Finally, we come to the issue of *qualified*.[39] A person may have a disability and not be protected under the ADA because he or she is not qualified. *Qualified* has two different meanings under the ADA depending upon whether Title I (which applies to employers of 15 or more employees) or Title II (which applies to governmental entities regardless of size) is at issue. Under Title I of the ADA, a person with a disabling condition is qualified if he or she satisfies the requisite skill, experience, and education requirements of the position and can, *with or without reasonable accommodation*, perform the essential functions of the job.[40] This definition, however, raises questions of its own, such as what is a reasonable accommodation (discussed in Chapter 3) and what is an essential function of a job (discussed in Chapter 2).

With respect to Title II of the ADA, a person is considered to be otherwise qualified if he or she can, *with or without reasonable modifications* to rules, policies, or practices; the removal of architectural, communication, or transportation barriers; or the provision of auxiliary aids and services, meets the essential eligibility requirements for receiving services or participating in programs or activities provided by a public entity.[41] Prior to the ADAAA, "auxiliary aids and services" was not defined. However, the ADAAA does define that term as including:

> 1) qualified interpreters or other effective methods of making aurally delivered materials available to individuals with hearing impairments; 2) qualified readers, taped texts, or other effective methods of making visually delivered materials available to individuals with visual impairments; 3) acquisition or modification of equipment or devices; and 4) other similar services and actions.[42]

As with the ADA, the ADAAA is going out of its way to recognize visual and hearing impairments. However, a close reading of the last two definitions of "auxiliary aids and services" reveals that the phrase arguably applies to much more than visual and hearing impairments. For example, in a Title I context, a person who has difficulty typing due to a disability might be able to argue that these last two definitions of auxiliary aids and services would allow him or her to be qualified because of the employer's obligations to furnish auxiliary aids and services (e.g., voice dictation software).

"Qualified" also arises in another context in ADA jurisprudence: that of direct threat. *Direct threat* is a term that was settled by the U.S. Supreme Court in *School Board of Nassau County, Florida v. Arline*.[43] That case, involving a public school teacher terminated for having tuberculosis, held that whether a person is a direct threat (and, to many courts' way of thinking, "not otherwise qualified" or "qualified") depends upon evaluating:

- the nature of the risk (how the disease is transmitted);
- the duration of the risk (how long the carrier is infectious);
- the severity of the risk (the potential harm to third parties);
- the probabilities that the disease will be transmitted and will cause varying degrees of harm.[44]

The final regulations of the EEOC implementing the ADAAA are very similar to the *Arline* standards. The EEOC regulations state that a person is a direct threat after considering the following factors based on reasonable medical judgment that relies on the most current medical knowledge and/or on the best available objective evidence. Those factors are:

1. The duration of the risk;
2. The nature and severity of the potential harm;
3. The likelihood that the potential harm will occur; and
4. The imminence of the potential harm.[45]

If a person is found to be a direct threat, many courts are finding that the person is not otherwise qualified or not qualified and is therefore not protected under the ADA. This line of reasoning creates unnecessary confusion for someone trying to understand the workings of the ADA, even though the courts are committed to the terminology. I find it helps to think of "otherwise qualified," or what is now called "qualified," and "direct threat" as two different concepts,[46] both of which may result in a finding of not being qualified. Think of "qualified" as referring to whether a person can do the essential functions of the job with or without reasonable accommodations or a person effectively accessing a service with or without reasonable modifications. Thus, to follow this analysis through in the employment context, "direct threat" refers to when a person can do the essential functions of the job with or without reasonable accommodations but that person performing the job would constitute a direct threat.[47]

Finally, is "direct threat" an affirmative defense or something that the plaintiff has to prove as part of his or her case? The answer depends on the Circuit Court. In the 11th Circuit, the case on point is *Moses v. American NonWovens Inc.*[48] In *Moses*, the plaintiff worked in several capacities for NonWovens, including as a product inspector, web operator, and hot splicer assistant.[49] All jobs involved working with exposed machinery, some of which became extremely hot.[50] Moses had epilepsy, and the employer fired Moses because the epilepsy posed a possible threat of an accident.[51] The issue before the court was whether it was up to the employer or up to Moses to show whether a direct threat existed. The court held that the employee—in this case, Moses—had the burden to show that he was not a direct threat, and that he had not produced probative evidence that he was not a direct threat.[52]

The case of *EEOC v. Amego*, a First Circuit case, is slightly different.[53] *Amego* is interesting in several respects, not the least of which was that a provider of mental health and mental retardation[54] services was sued by an employee for violation of the ADA.[55] In *Amego*, an employee who was responsible for overseeing a group home for persons with autism and other mental illnesses developed several serious problems: She became involved with a co-worker who used cocaine; she suffered from clinical depression and eating disorders; and her attempts to treat her depression were unsuccessful.[56] As a result, her work performance suffered, and she attempted suicide twice by overdosing on medications.[57] Finally, there were indications that the medicine at the group home was not being monitored properly.[58] Amego eventually let the plaintiff go because they believed she could not perform an essential function of the job—handling medications for persons in the group home—with or without reasonable accommodations and that she posed a risk to herself and others.[59]

The district court found for Amego, and the EEOC appealed.[60] The EEOC claimed, among other things, that direct threat is an affirmative defense, while Amego claimed that proving direct threat or the lack of was part of the plaintiff's case.[61]

How did the court settle the issue? In a sense, it split the difference. The court concluded that determining who has the burden of proof depends upon whether the essential job functions involve the safety of others. If the safety of others is involved in a job's essential functions, then it is up to the plaintiff to show that he or she is not a direct threat, and doing so would include showing that he or she is otherwise qualified.[62] However, if the safety of others is not involved in the job's essential functions, such as in the case involving the teacher with tuberculosis, then it is up to the employer to prove direct threat as an affirmative defense.[63] This approach was also cited favorably by the 10th Circuit.[64]

There is a third approach the U.S. Courts of Appeals take, and that is they consider "direct threat" to be an affirmative defense, and therefore the burden is on the defense to make the showing of direct threat. This is the approach taken by the Seventh,[65] Fifth,[66] Eighth,[67] and Ninth[68] Circuits.

With respect to "direct threat," the ADA itself does not mention whether "direct threat" applies to not only other people but to the individual plaintiff as well.[69] The EEOC, in implementing the ADA's employment provisions, has said that "direct threat" applies where a person threatens his or her own health as well as the health of others.[70] In the case of *Chevron U.S.A. Inc. v. Echazabal*,[71] the U.S. Supreme Court was directly faced with this question. In *Chevron,* the plaintiff worked for independent contractors at an oil refinery owned by Chevron.[72] He applied for a job directly with Chevron twice and was offered the job if he could pass the company's physical.[73] Both times, the physical showed liver damage as a result of hepatitis C, which Chevron doctors said would be aggravated by his working at the oil refinery.[74] Each time the plaintiff applied, Chevron withdrew the offer.[75] The second time Chevron withdrew the offer, it asked that the plaintiff be reassigned to a job without exposure to harmful chemicals or be removed from the refinery altogether.[76] The plaintiff filed suit, claiming that this conduct violated the ADA.[77] Chevron relied on the direct threat defense as specified in the EEOC regulations.[78]

In finding for Chevron, the U.S. Supreme Court relied upon employers' obligations under the Occupational Safety and Health Act to provide a safe working environment for its employees.[79] The Court went on to note that the "direct threat" defense had to meet a fairly compelling standard.[80] More specifically, the Court said that the direct threat defense must be based on a reasonable medical judgment relying on the most current medical knowledge and/or the best available objective evidence.[81] Further, this assessment must be based on an individualized assessment of the individual's present ability to safely perform the essential functions of the job as described in the EEOC regulations.[82] Thus, it is now clear that "direct threat" applies to threats to the individual as well as threats to others.

All of which is beside the point if an employee is not involved. Just who is an employee under the ADA? The Supreme Court was faced with this very question in *Clackamas Gastroenterology Associates, P.C. v. Wells*.[83] In *Clackamas,* a bookkeeper brought an ADA discrimination claim against her employer, Clackamas Gastroenterology Associates.[84] Clackamas defended on the grounds that it did not have 15 or more employees.[85] The question before the Court was whether the four physician shareholders who owned the corporation could be considered employees.[86] If the shareholders could be considered employees, then the statutory number of 15 would be satisfied, but if they were not employees, then Clackamas did not have the requisite number of employees to be subject to the ADA.[87] The Supreme Court held that whether a person is an employee comes down to just how much control is exercised over him.[88] For example, the Court looked to its prior case law to say that control can be measured by such things as: the skill required; the source of the instrumentalities and tools used to do the job; the location of the work; the duration of the relationship between the parties; the hiring party's right to assign the work to another; the discretion the hiring party has over when and how long to work; the method of payment; the hiring party's role in hiring and paying assistants; the nature of the work insofar as it is a part of the regular business of the hiring party; and so on.[89] Those familiar with revenue ruling 87-41,[90] which the Internal Revenue Service uses to decide whether a person is an independent contractor or an employee, will most assuredly see the similarities. The Court went on to favorably cite EEOC guidelines on how one can determine whether a "partner" was in actuality an employee. Those guidelines lists six factors to use in making this determination: 1) whether the organization can hire or fire the individual or set the rules and regulations of the individual's work; 2) whether and, if so, to what extent the organization supervises the individual's work; 3) whether the individual reports to someone higher in the organization; 4) whether that individual is able to influence the organization; 5) whether the parties intended for the person to be an employee as specified in any written agreements or contracts; and 6) whether the individual shares in the profits or losses of the organization.[91] The Court noted that no one factor was dispositive; rather, the conclusion depends on "all incidents of the relationship."[92] Thus, the Court sent the matter back for further proceedings to see if the four physician shareholders were indeed employees.

So, how should the practitioner deal with the question of whether a person is an employee vis-á-vis the ADA and other federal antidiscrimination laws? A really good preventive approach I have used in the past is Revenue Ruling 87-41, mentioned above. That revenue ruling is eerily similar to some of the Supreme Court case law, also noted above. The practitioner may also want to look at the EEOC guidance cited favorably by the Court in *Clackamas*.

Notes

1. *See* 74 Fed. Reg. 48,431, 48,434–37 (Sept. 23, 2009).
2. EEOC's Enforcement Guidance on Reasonable Accommodations, http://www.eeoc.gov/docs/accommodation.html at 9, no. 9 (1999).
3. 42 U.S.C.A. § 12102(1) (WL, current through Pub. L. 113-9 (excluding Pub. L. 113-4), approved May 1, 2013).
4. 29 C.F.R. § 1630.2(j) (WL, current through May 30, 2013; 78 Fed. Reg. 32,362).
5. Toyota Motor Mfg., Ky., Inc. v. Williams, 534 U.S. 184 (2002).
6. *Id.* at 196–98.
7. Not giving due deference to regulations will be much harder for a court to do now, since the ADAAA specifically gives the authority to the EEOC and the DOJ to implement definitional terms under the Americans with Disabilities Act. *See* 42 U.S.C.A. § 12205a (WL, current through Pub. L. 113-9 (excluding Pub. L. 113-4), approved May 1, 2013).
8. *Compare* Scheerer v. Potter, 443 F.3d 916 (7th Cir. 2006) (holding that *Toyota Motor's* definition of substantial limitation extended across disabilities) *with* EEOC v. Sears, Roebuck & Co., 417 F.3d 789 (7th Cir. 2005) (holding that *Toyota Motor*'s definition of substantial limitation did not extend across all disabilities, but rather was limited to the major life activity of performing manual tasks).
9. ADA Amendments Act, Pub. L. 110-325 § 2(a)(7), (8).
10. *Id.*

11. 42 U.S.C.A. at § 12205a (current through Pub. L. 113-9 (excluding Pub. L. 113-4), approved May 1, 2013).
12. 29 C.F.R. § 1630.2(j)(ii) (WL, current through May 30, 2013; 78 Fed. Reg. 32,362).
13. 42 U.S.C.A. § 12102 (4)(c) (WL, current through Pub. L. 113-9 (excluding Pub. L. 113-4), approved May 1, 2013).
14. *Id.* at § 12102 (4)(d).
15. Sutton v. United Airlines, 527 U.S. 471, 491 (1999).
16. *See* 74 Fed. Reg. at 48,442.
17. Appx. to Part 1630—Interpretive Guidance on Title I of the Americans with Disabilities Act and discussion of 29 C.F.R. § 1630.2(j)(5) and (6), *available at* http://www.gpo.gov/fdsys/pkg/CFR-2011-Title29-vol4/xml/CFR-2011-Title29-vol4-part1630.xml.
18. *See*, 29 C.F.R. at § 1630.2(j) (WL, current through May 30, 2013; 78 Fed. Reg. 32,362).
19. *Toyota Motor,* 534 U.S. at 198.
20. 42 U.S.C.A. at § 12102(2). Also, the EEOC took advantage of the amendments to the ADA that specifically granted them the ability to promulgate regulations with respec to the definitional terms when, in their proposed regulations, the EEOC added to the list of major life activities the activities of sitting, reaching, and interacting with others. *See* 74 Fed. Reg. 48,431–01, 48,440 (Sept. 23, 2009). In the final regulations, these additions from the proposed regulations remained (*see* Appx. to Part 1630—Interpretive Guidance on Title I of the Americans with Disabilities Act and discussion of § 29 C.F.R. 1630.2(i)(1)(i), *available at* http://www.gpo.gov/fdsys/pkg/CFR-2011-Title29-vol4/xml/CFR-2011-Title29-vol4-part1630.xml).
21. Appx. to Part 1630—Interpretive Guidance on Title I of the Americans with Disabilities Act and discussion of § 29 C.F.R. 1630.2(i), *available at* http://www.gpo.gov/fdsys/pkg/CFR-2011-Title29-vol4/xml/CFR-2011-Title29-vol4-part1630.xml.
22. Sutton v. United Air Lines, 527 U.S. 471 (1999).
23. *Id.* at 482.
24. 42 U.S.C.A. at § 12102 (4)(E)(i).
25. 42 U.S.C.A. at § 12102(4)(E)(ii).
26. 42 U.S.C.A. § 12113(c) (WL, current through Pub. L. 113-9 (excluding Pub. L. 113-4), approved May 1, 2013).
27. 29 C.F.R. § 1630.2(j)(ix) (WL, current through May 30, 2013; 78 Fed. Reg. 32,362); *see also* Appx. to Part 1630—Interpretive Guidance on Title I of the Americans with Disabilities Act and discussion of § 29 C.F.R. 1630.2(j)(1)(ix), *available at* http://www.gpo.gov/fdsys/pkg/CFR-2011-Title29-vol4/xml/CFR-2011-Title29-vol4-part1630.xml.
28. 42 U.S.C.A. at § 12102(3)(B).
29. 29 C.F.R. § 1630.2(j)(ix) (current through May 30, 2013; 78 Fed. Reg. 32,362).

30. 42 U.S.C.A. at § 12102(2)(B).
31. *See* Appx. to Part 1630—Interpretive Guidance on Title I of the Americans with Disabilities Act and discussion of § 29 C.F.R. § 1630.2(k), *available at* http://www.gpo.gov/fdsys/pkg/CFR-2011-Title29-vol4/xml/CFR-2011-Title29-vol4-part1630.xml.
32. *Id.*
33. 42 U.S.C.A. at § 12102(2)(C).
34. *See* discussion of 29 C.F.R. § 1630.2(l) in Appx. to Part 1630—Interpretive Guidance on Title I of the Americans with Disabilities Act, *available at* http://www.gpo.gov/fdsys/pkg/CFR-2011-Title29-vol4/xml/CFR-2011-Title29-vol4-part1630.xml.
35. *See* Miners v. Cargill Commc'ns, Inc., 133 F.3d 820 (8th Cir. 1997). This case is discussed in depth later in this book.
36. *Id.* at 489.
37. 42 U.S.C.A. at § 12102(3)(A).
38. *See* Hanson v. Caterpillar, Inc., _F.3d_, 2012 WL 3139946 (7th Cir. Aug. 3, 2012).
39. The term "qualified" and the term "otherwise qualified," which is from the Rehabilitation Act, are conceptually the same.
40. 29 C.F.R. § 1630.2(m) (WL, current through May 30, 2013; 78 Fed. Reg. 32,362).
41. 28 C.F.R. § 35.104 (WL, current through May 30, 2013; 78 Fed. Reg. 32,362).
42. 42 U.S.C.A. § 12103(1) (WL, current through Pub. L. 113-9 (excluding Pub. L. 113-4), approved May 1, 2013).
43. School Board of Nassau County, Fla. v. Arline, 480 U.S. 273 (1987).
44. *Id. at* 288.
45. 29 C.F.R. § 1630.2(r) (WL, current through May 30, 2013; 78 Fed. Reg. 32,362).
46. *See* EEOC v. Amego, Inc., 110 F.3d 135, 142 (1st Cir. 1997).
47. *Id.* at 142–43.
48. Moses v. American Nonwovens, Inc., 97 F.3d 446 (11th Cir. 1996).
49. *Id.* at 447–48.
50. *Id.* at 447–48.
51. *Id.* at 447.
52. *Id.*
53. EEOC v. Amego, Inc., 110 F.3d 135 (1st Cir. 1997).
54. Mental retardation is no longer a favored term. Rather, mental retardation is now subsumed into the category of "intellectual disabilities."
55. *Id.* at 137.
56. *Id.* at 138–39.
57. *Id.* at 139.
58. *Id.*
59. *Id.* at 141.
60. *Id.*

61. *Id.* at 141–42.
62. *Id.* at 144.
63. *Id.*
64. McKenzie v. Benton, 388 F.3d 1342 (10th Cir. 2004).
65. Branham v. Snow, 392 F.3d 896, 906-07, 07 fn 5 (7th Cir. 2004).
66. EEOC v. E.I. du Pont de Nemours & Co., 480 F.3d 724 (5th Cir. 2007).
67. EEOC v. Wal-Mart stores, Inc., 477 F.3d 561 (8th Cir. 2007).
68. Hutton v. Elf Atochem N. Am., Inc., 273 F.3d 884 (9th Cir. 2001).
69. *See* 42 U.S.C.A. § 12111(3) (2005) (WL, current through Pub. L. 113-9 (excluding P.L. 113-4), approved May 1, 2013).
70. *See* 29 C.F.R. at § 1630.2(r).
71. Chevron v. Echazabal, 536 U.S. 73 (2002).
72. *Id.* at 76.
73. *Id.*
74. *Id.*
75. *Id.*
76. *Id.*
77. *Id.*
78. *Id.*
79. *Id.* at 84–85.
80. *Id.* at 85–86.
81. *Id.* at 86.
82. *Id.*
83. Clackamas Gastroenterology Assocs., P.C. v. Wells, 538 U.S. 440 (2003).
84. *Id.* at 442.
85. *Id.*
86. *Id.*
87. *Id.*
88. *Id.* at 448.
89. *Id.* at 445 n.5.
90. Rev. Rul. 87-41, 1987-1 C.B. 296.
91. *Clackamas,* 538 U.S. at 448.
92. *Id.* at 449, n.8.

2 Essential Functions of the Job

IN THE DEFINITION of "qualified" in the employment context, the term *essential function* plays a critical role. How do you determine the essential functions of a job? The EEOC has said it will look at the following factors:

(i) The employer's judgment as to which functions are essential;
(ii) Written job descriptions prepared before advertising or interviewing applicants for the job;
(iii) The amount of time spent on the job performing the function;
(iv) The consequences of not requiring the incumbent to perform the function;
(v) The terms of a collective bargaining agreement;
(vi) The work experience of past incumbents in the job; and/or
(vii) The current work experience of incumbents in similar jobs.[1]

These factors can become complicated when they are applied to a particular case. However, determining essential functions does not have to be complicated. Think of essential functions as any element of the job fundamental to achieving the job's purpose. Those elements that are not fundamental can be classified as marginal functions. For example, consider the job of the lawyer. In order to be a lawyer, one must be able to research legal matters and communicate the findings. Does the person have to be able to appear in court? Most lawyers never see the inside of a courtroom, so appearing in court for those lawyers would not be considered fundamental to their job.

The example above raises another issue: The essential functions of a job need to be accurate. If typing 60 words a minute is required by the job but the person in that position never typed more than 40 words a minute, then 60 words a minute is not an essential function of the job—40 words a minute is.[2]

Finally, two mistakes are frequently made when assessing essential functions of a job. First, essential functions are often confused with major life activities—an entirely different concept. For instance, hearing is not an essential function of being a lawyer. An essential function of being a lawyer is being able to gather and process information and to communicate it to others. Whether the person hears or communicates in sign language doesn't matter. Similarly, hearing is not an essential function of the job of being a softball umpire. Calling balls and strikes and outs quickly and accurately are among the essential functions of that job. Finally, as we will see later in the professional sports chapter of this book, hearing is not an essential function of being a lifeguard either.

What about sight? Is seeing an essential function of umpiring/refereeing? Perhaps surprisingly, the answer is no; calling the game accurately is. Of course, without sight the game cannot be called accurately; therefore, the person would not be protected under the ADA, because he or she could not do the essential functions of the job with or without reasonable accommodations. In other words, the person who can't see and wants to umpire a game does not have a valid ADA claim, not because he can't see (the life activity), but because he can't perform the essential functions of the job—making accurate calls with or without reasonable accommodations.

The second problem area is confusing essential functions of the job with tasks. For example, is 10-key data entry an essential function of a data entry job? The answer is no; 10-key data entry is a task, not a function. The essential function of the job is data entry at a certain rate of speed; how it gets done doesn't matter. The only exception would be if it could be shown that data entry for the particular job could be done only through 10-key. Take another example: Is reading an essential function of the job of an administrator, clerk, or, for that matter, a lawyer? You might think it is, but isn't the essential function of the job the ability to absorb and process information no matter how it is done?[3] For example, it could be done with the assistance of an in-person reader or a screen reader, voice dictation technology, etc.

Finally, in determining essential functions, it is helpful if the particular job has been analyzed to determine the components. That can be accomplished by hiring consultants and talking to the person who does the job. It also means keeping job descriptions current and comprehensive but not overly so. Most jobs are dynamic, and their essential functions change over time. Thus, if a job description is not current and comprehensive but not overly so, the employee may have the opportunity later to allege that her or his essential job functions were different from those contained in the job description. Also, keeping the lines of communication open between employees and employer should help ensure that the essential functions of a job are monitored properly.

In short, determining essential functions of the job does not have to be complicated. If it is handled correctly, the employer benefits by avoiding costly litigation and plaintiff verdicts. The employee benefits by having more freedom to accomplish his or her job in accordance with his or her capabilities.

If a case is in trial, who determines essential functions of the job—the judge or the jury? A case that addressed this question is *Barber v. Nabors Drilling U.S.A., Inc.*[4] In *Barber*, Nabors refused to allow the plaintiff to return to his job as a tool pusher on an oil-drilling rig after he received treatment for a back injury.[5] The plaintiff throughout the course of the litigation maintained that he was capable of performing the essential functions of the job.[6] In determining that the jury should decide a job's essential functions, the Fifth Circuit stated:

> If we venture to second-guess, then we simply usurp the most critical function of the jury in ADA cases, i.e., the injection of some indispensable common sense in the determination of what is or is not an essential function. When a statutory scheme such as the ADA necessitates some seemingly arbitrary line-drawing exercise, courts of law do well to refer the question to the

> jury, and consequently the appellate court must respect the jury's call, unless it is unsupportable by the evidence.[7]

Finally, the court said:

> A highly deferential standard is especially appropriate with regard to the jury's determination of what the essential functions of the job are, since the evidence, as in this case, most often consists of *post hoc* descriptions of what the employee was expected to do and what he actually did, which necessarily requires the jury to judge the credibility of witnesses and the veracity of their testimony.[8]

Since *Barber* was decided, other circuits, such as the Third, Sixth, and Eighth, have also adopted the proposition that essential functions of the job is a question of fact.[9]

With the amendments to the ADA, litigation will now shift from whether a person has a disability in the first place to other areas, such as whether the person is otherwise qualified (Rehabilitation Act) or qualified (ADA). With respect to "qualified," here are some things to think about.

1) Are the essential functions of the job accurate, and comprehensive but not overly so, and current, and do they reflect what actually happens in that job rather than what is on the piece of paper?
2) Does the company have a system by which the essential functions of its various jobs are reviewed on a regular basis?
3) Whenever possible, make the essential functions of the job as precise as possible, though reasonable inferences are permissible. Also, multiple duties associated with essential functions are also permissible.
4) Make sure the company is consistent across the board with respect to those essential functions.[10] For example, if a retail store could show that store managers routinely have certain functions regardless of their location, that would be helpful.

A company that did this just right recently was Walgreen Company. I suppose that is not surprising, as it has been leading the charge recently with respect to hiring persons with disabilities. In *Jones v. Walgreen Co.*,[11] Walgreens played its cards just right. In that case, a long-term employee of Walgreens, some 20 years, injured her knee.[12] One thing led to the other, including surgery, and she was let go for her inability to perform the essential functions of the job.[13] The case eventually went to the First Circuit Court of Appeals, which affirmed the district court's grant of summary judgment for Walgreens.[14] What Walgreens had going for it was its rather precise essential job functions.[15] Also, those functions were capable of reasonable inferences, leading the court to decide its only possible conclusion was that the manager could not perform the essential functions of the job with or without reasonable accommodations.[16] Walgreens also was able to have a variety of different managers come in to explain what those essential functions of the job reasonably meant.[17] Finally—something that you are likely to see more of—Walgreens had a disclaimer in its job description:

> [t]he job description is to be used as a guide for accomplishing company and department objectives, and only covers the primary functions and responsibilities of the position. It is in no way to be construed as an all-encompassing list of duties.[18]

Therefore, the disclaimer gave Walgreens wiggle room so that the essential functions of the job as they were written could be reasonably construed to include a variety of different duties. Any company would do well to read this case and to adapt it if the company wants to successfully set up a system to enable it to adequately defend any litigation arising over essential functions of the job.

ATTENDANCE

Is attendance an essential element of the job? One would think so. However, that isn't necessarily the case. For example, it may depend on the type of job.[19] It may also depend on the employer's practices with respect to that job.[20] A case that illustrates the former proposition is *Samper v. Providence St. Vincent Medical Center*, 675 F.3d 1233 (9th Cir. 2012). In *Samper*, a neonatal nurse had fibromyalgia, a condition that limits effective sleep and causes chronic pain throughout the body.[21] As a result of that condition and how it affected her, she was unable to regularly come to work in accordance with her employer's attendance policy.[22] Eventually, Samper was discharged for, among other issues, seven absences in the 12-month period as well as a general problem with attendance.[23] She then filed suit alleging violation of the ADA.[24]

In affirming summary judgment for the employer, the Tenth Circuit held that regular attendance compromises essential job functions where the job requires attendance.[25] How do you know when that job requires attendance? The court said that a job could require attendance for variety of reasons. Those reasons include: the employee must work as part of the team;[26] or the job requires face-to-face interaction with clients and other employees;[27] or the job requires the employee to work with items and equipment that are on-site.[28] With respect to the neonatal nurse, the Tenth Circuit said that all of these requirements were satisfied considering the nature of the job and the stakes involved for the hospital and its patients when the hospital is not staffed adequately.[29] The Tenth Circuit did note that there were situations where attendance might not be an essential element of the job.[30]

That said, depending on the employer's practice, even a job that satisfies all these criteria at first blush may not be a job where attendance is an essential function of the job. For example, in a case that predates *Samper* but nevertheless illustrates this point, the Fifth Circuit held that a flight attendant for Southwest Airlines may not have been in a job where attendance was an essential function in light of Southwest's extremely lenient attendance policy, and thereby created a question of fact for the jury to decide.[31]

So how does an employer go about figuring out whether attendance is an essential function of the job? For purposes of preventive law, consider using a two-step process. First, is the job one of the jobs mentioned in *Samper* that typically requires attendance as an essential element? If not, does the employer have the data to back up its contention with actual practice that attendance is an essential element of that job notwithstanding *Samper*? Finally, regardless of whether one of the jobs mentioned in *Samper* is involved, it is always helpful if the employer has the data to back up its contention with actual practice that attendance is an essential element of that job.

Notes

1. 29 C.F.R. at § 1630.2(n)
2. *See* EEOC's Interpretive Guidance to 29 C.F.R. § 1630.2(n).

3. Borkowski v. Valley Central School District, 63 F.3d 131, 141 (2d Cir. 1995).
4. Barber v. Nabors Drilling U.S.A., Inc., 130 F.3d 702 (5th Cir. 1997).
5. *Id.* at 704.
6. *Id.*
7. *Id.* at 708.
8. *Id.*
9. Turner v. Hershey Chocolate U.S., 440 F.3d 604 (3rd Cir. 2006); Kiphart v. Saturn Corp., 251 F.3d 573 (6th Cir. 2001); Finan v. Good Earth Tools, Inc., 565 F.3d 1076 (8th Cir. 2009); *see also* Feldman v. Olin Corp., _ F.3d _, 2012 WL 3641774, *4 (7th Cir. Aug. 27, 2012) (holding that enough evidence existed to make essential functions a question of fact).
10. *See Feldman,* 2012 WL 3641774, *4
11. 679 F.3d 9 (1st Cir. 2012).
12. *Id.* at 11.
13. *Id.* at 11–13.
14. *Id.* at 11.
15. *Id.* at 15.
16. *Id.*
17. *Id.* at 15–16.
18. *Id.* at 15.
19. *See* Samper v. Providence St. Vincent Med. Ctr., 675 F.3d 1233 (9th Cir. 2012).
20. *See* Carmona v. Southwest Airlines Co., 604 F.3d 848 (5th Cir. 2010).
21. *Samper,* 675 F.3d at 1235.
22. *Id.* at 1235–36.
23. *Id.* at 1236.
24. *Id.*
25. *Id.* at 1237.
26. *Id.*
27. *Id.*
28. *Id.*
29. *Id.* at 1238–41.
30. *Id.* at 1239.
31. *Carmona,* 604 F.3d at 859–62.

Concept of Undue Hardship and Reasonable Accommodation in the Employment Context

3

WHAT IS A REASONABLE ACCOMMODATION in the employment context? Under the ADA, reasonable accommodation is defined in the negative. More specifically, a reasonable accommodation is anything that does not constitute an undue hardship.[1] Thus, it becomes imperative to know what an undue hardship is. In determining whether an accommodation is an undue hardship, the EEOC will look to several factors:

- The nature and net cost of the accommodation needed. Keep in mind that any reimbursements, tax deductions, and the like are counted against the employer.
- The overall financial resources of the facility or facilities, the number of persons employed at the facility, and the effect of the reasonable accommodation on expenses and resources.
- The overall financial resources of the covered entity, the overall size of the business of the covered entity with respect to the number of its employees, and the number, type, and location of its facilities.

- The type of operation or operations of the covered entity, including the composition, structure, and functions of the workforce of such entity, and the geographic separateness and administrative or fiscal relationship of the facility or facilities in question to the covered entity.
- The impact of the accommodation on the operation of the facility, including on the ability of other employees to perform their duties and on the facility's ability to conduct business.[2]

Other critical points about undue hardship must also be considered. First, the EEOC believes (which may or may not be the view of the U.S. Supreme Court) that undue hardship is measured against the entire operations of the employer and not just one department.[3] Thus, for example, Person X works in the MIS department. Person X has a disability, and everybody agrees that he needs an accommodation that will cost $600. The MIS department is just one division of a multimillion-dollar company. Whether the accommodation will constitute an undue hardship is, in the EEOC's view, measured against the entire operations of the company and not just the MIS division.

Second, a business does not have to make an accommodation when that accommodation would constitute an undue hardship on the operations of its business.[4] Thus, if undue hardship is to be measured against the entire company, the employer generally will be better off arguing that the accommodation needed will result in an undue hardship on its operations rather than argue financial undue hardship. This is especially true because three different studies cited by the EEOC in its proposed regulations implementing the ADAAA estimate that the mean costs of reasonably accommodating a person with a disability range anywhere from $462 to $1,434.[5]

Finally, it bears noting that undue hardship does not equal inconvenience. Undue hardship is a term of art, and unless the accommodation rises to the level of a fundamental alteration in the business or is an undue hardship under the factors listed above, it is irrelevant if the accommodation inconveniences the employer.[6] It is amazing how often one hears that businesses do not have to reasonably accommodate because doing so is not convenient. Also, the rules of reasonable accommodation apply to pre-employment skills testing as well, and any pre-employment skills testing must be established in such a way that the person's abilities are measured and not his or her disabilities.

What steps can an employer take to deal with the issue of reasonable accommodation? First, keep the lines of communication open between the employer and the employee. Open communication is critical to prevent problems from occurring due to a *misperception* of reasonable accommodation: that is, that the employee's requests must be honored at the risk of violating the ADA. That is simply not true. Deciding on implementing a reasonable accommodation is a process subject to negotiation between the employer and the employee. The key is to determine a way to get the employee with a disability to the same starting line as the person without a disability. The employer, through the negotiation process, has the flexibility to determine how.[7]

Second, be creative. What can be a reasonable accommodation is limited only by the parties' imagination. The employee will often know what accommodation he or she needs to do the essential functions of the job. It's not unusual for a company to estimate the cost of an accommodation and proceed through the approval process only to be told by the employee, "All I need is this," at a cost far less than originally contemplated by the company.

Third, remember that no two disabilities are precisely the same, and every case must be analyzed on its own merits (this statement is a truism with, as we will see later in this book, huge implications for class-action litigation). For example, just because a person with one disability needs certain accommodations does not mean that a different person with the same disability needs the same accommodations.[8]

Fourth, the concept of good faith bears discussing. An employer who exercises good faith in dealing with a reasonable accommodation request is protected from damages stemming from intentional discrimination.[9] Some preventive steps to help ensure that a defendant can be found to have acted in good faith might include the following:

- Demonstrate a willingness to try multiple accommodations for the person's disability.
- Document any and all attempts at reasonable accommodations.
- Keep the lines of communication open.
- Have the accommodation process be cooperative rather than adversarial in nature.
- Demonstrate a record of creativity in dealing with the accommodation request.

Preventive steps are critical because an employer can be held liable for refusing to engage in the interactive process. A case that illustrates this is *EEOC v. Sears.*[10] In *Sears*, the EEOC sued on behalf of a plaintiff (the plaintiff intervened in the suit brought by the EEOC) suffering from neuropathy and non-insulin-dependent diabetes.[11] As a result of these conditions, the plaintiff, Keane, eventually could not walk more than the equivalent of one city block without her right leg and feet becoming numb.[12] When that happened, walking became virtually impossible and extremely slow.[13] The plaintiff felt as if she would have to use her hands to lift up her leg to take one step at a time.[14] Sometimes the plaintiff doubted she could make it out of her worksite safely and would have to hold onto the wall for support.[15] The lower court granted summary judgment for the defendant and Keane appealed.[16] The Seventh Circuit disagreed with the lower court grant of summary judgment on whether Keane had a disability under the ADA and remanded it back to the lower court for further proceedings.[17]

After the case had been remanded back to the lower court, *Toyota Motor* was decided by the U.S. Supreme Court.[18] The lower court then revisited the issue of whether Keane had a disability under the ADA and concluded that the *Toyota Motor* standard for what constitutes a substantial limitation on a major life activity was not met by Keane; therefore, Keane did not have a disability protected by the ADA.[19]

The case was once again appealed to the Seventh Circuit.[20] The Seventh Circuit in the second appeal was faced with two issues: first, whether *Toyota Motor* was the proper standard to use in determining whether Keane was substantially limited in a major life activity under the ADA,[21] an issue that has now been superseded by the ADAAA; and second, whether Sears could be liable for refusing to accommodate Keane, assuming Keane was a person with a disability under the ADA.[22]

Before exploring the accommodation issue further, other facts that bear noting here include:

1. Keane asked her immediate supervisor if she could eat lunch in the intimate apparel stock room so as to minimize her walking on the job.[23] Initially her request was granted, but subsequently the supervisor announced a blanket policy preventing all eating in the stockroom.[24]

2. As Keane's condition worsened, she asked her immediate supervisor if she could walk through the shoe stockroom when going between the employee swipe-in area and the intimate apparel department.[25] She was referred to the manager of the shoe department, who denied her request.[26] Keane's immediate supervisor then went to the store manager, David Allen, who also denied the request.[27]
3. At some point, her immediate supervisor gave Keane permission to use the shoe stockroom as a shortcut; however, the first day she attempted to use the shortcut, a superior yelled at her to get out of there and also stated that the person who gave her permission had no business doing so.[28] Subsequently, the store manager posted someone at the entrance to the shoe stockroom and drafted a person to bar anyone from going through the door.[29]
4. Keane also asked the store manager if she could park near the merchandise pickup lot by the employee entrance.[30] The store manager denied that request and suggested that Keane use a parking space reserved for persons with disabilities.[31] However, parking in the persons with disabilities space meant that Keane still had to walk across the store to the employee swipe-in location and then walk back to her work area at the beginning and end of each shift.[32]
5. Eventually, the store manager asked Keane to have a doctor fill out a Sears physician certification form (Sears already had in its possession one doctor's note).[33] Keane's general practitioner completed the form and noted the diagnosis.[34] He recommended that Keane limit excessive walking and be allowed easy, short access to her job site.[35] However, when the store manager received the form, he assumed that the reserved parking space near her department was sufficient to accommodate Keane and informed her immediate supervisor that Keane would not be allowed to cut through the shoe stockroom.[36] The store manager never asked for any additional information.[37]

In finding that Sears could be held liable for failure to accommodate Keane, the Seventh Circuit set forth what is needed to prove a plaintiff's claim for the failure of an employer to accommodate a person with a disability. To prove a claim of disability discrimination based on an employer's failure to reasonably accommodate a person with a disability, a plaintiff has to show that 1) she is a qualified individual with a disability; 2) the employer was aware of the plaintiff's disability; and 3) the employer failed to reasonably accommodate the plaintiff's disability.[38]

The Seventh Circuit said that the ADA imposes on the employee the obligation to initially inform the employer of a disability.[39] Where the notice of a disability from the employee is ambiguous but is sufficient to notify the employer that the employee may have a disability requiring accommodation, the employer has the obligation to ask the employee for clarification.[40] Thus, an employer is not allowed "to shield itself from liability by choosing not to follow up on an employee's request for assistance or by intentionally remaining in the dark."[41] Fourth, the court noted that Keane gave Sears two different doctors' notes of her diagnosis and the recommendation that she be permitted to avoid walking long distances.[42] Finally, the court noted that Keane, all told, had informed three different levels of Sears' management of her disability.[43]

The Seventh Circuit, having found that the plaintiff had a disability and that her employer was aware of the disability, now turned its attention to whether Sears failed to accommodate that disability. The court held that Sears could be liable for failing to accommodate the plaintiff's disability for the following reasons. First, once an employee discloses the disability to the employer, the employer is obligated under the ADA to engage the employee in an interactive process to determine the appropriate accommodation under the circumstances.[44]

Second, this interactive process requires the employer to engage in a give-and-take process with the employee with a disability so that both parties can determine what accommodation will enable the employee to continue working.[45] If this process does not lead to reasonable accommodation of the person with a disability, the responsibility for the failure to reasonably accommodate the employee lies with the party that causes the breakdown.[46]

Third, an employer will not be liable for failure to accommodate where the employer acts in good faith during the interactive process and the employee refuses to participate or withholds essential information.[47]

Fourth, if an employee requests an appropriate accommodation, the employer cannot simply reject that request without offering other suggestions or at least expressing the willingness to continue discussing possible accommodations through the interactive process.[48] That is, an employer cannot simply reject an employee's request for an accommodation without explaining why that request has been rejected or offering alternatives.[49]

Finally, the court concluded that the plaintiff had made several specific requests for accommodations; however, Sears did not engage in the interactive process, and, in fact, Sears disengaged itself from the interactive process altogether.[50] Accordingly, the Seventh Circuit reversed the lower court's award of summary judgment for Sears.[51]

With respect to reasonable accommodations, another question arises of whether a person regarded as having a disability by the employer is entitled to a reasonable accommodation. On this, the various circuits in the U.S. Court of Appeals were split. Circuits holding that reasonable accommodations were not available in such cases included the Ninth Circuit, the Eighth Circuit, the Sixth Circuit, and the Fifth Circuit.[52] Circuits holding that reasonable accommodations were available in such a case included the Third Circuit, the First Circuit, the Tenth Circuit,[53] and the Eleventh Circuit.[54] The ADAAA has definitively resolved this conflict. That is, we now know that reasonable accommodations are not available for a person complaining of "regarded as" discrimination.[55]

Finally, as can be seen from this chapter, the concept of reasonable accommodation and undue hardship overlap. Since reasonable accommodation is something that does not constitute an undue hardship, and undue hardship is an affirmative defense, the real question arises as to what is the burden of proof in reasonable accommodation cases. Unfortunately, the courts have been all over the place on this issue.

In the Federal Circuit, the plaintiff retains the burden of proving that he or she was the victim of illegal discrimination, but the burden of production is on the employer to show that it is unable to accommodate the plaintiff without undue hardship.[56] The Eleventh Circuit places the burden of production and persuasion, presumably as to both reasonable accommodation and undue hardship, on the plaintiff.[57] The D.C. Circuit appears to put the burden of production on the plaintiff, but the burden of persuasion with respect to undue hardship on the defendant.[58] In the Second Circuit, the plaintiff bears the burden of production and persuasion on the issue of whether the plaintiff can perform the essential functions of the job with or without reasonable accommodations, but the defense has the burden of persuasion with respect to whether an undue hardship exists.[59] Finally, in the First Circuit, plaintiffs fully bear the burden of showing that they could perform the essential functions of the job with or without reasonable accommodation, but the defense fully bears the burden of showing any undue hardship.[60]

These cases are terribly confusing, and perhaps the Supreme Court will step in at some point to clear this up. It is true that the Supreme Court cited many of these decisions favorably when it said that for purposes of summary judgment, a plaintiff need only show that accommodation seems reasonable on its face, and once that is done the defendant employer must show special circumstances demonstrating undue hardship.[61] However, that language does not answer the question about who has the specific burden of production and persuasion when it comes to the issue of reasonable accommodations and undue hardship. It also was referencing summary judgment motions and not the burdens that the litigants have at trial. Thus, on this issue, we will have to stay tuned for further developments.

REASSIGNMENT AS A REASONABLE ACCOMMODATION

Does an employer have the obligation to reassign an employee with a disability who can no longer do his or her job with or without reasonable accommodation but who can do another job with or without reasonable accommodation where that other job is vacant? Or, does the employer have the option to allow that person to be part of the competitive bidding process?

These questions were addressed by the Seventh Circuit in *EEOC v. United Airlines, Inc.*[62] In that opinion, the U.S. Court of Appeals for the Seventh Circuit initially held that United Air Lines was under no obligation to guarantee a reassignment to a vacant position for an employee who could no longer do the job they currently held because of a disability, but who could, with or without reasonable accommodation, do the job of a vacant position. The Seventh Circuit relied on a prior case from 2000, *EEOC v. Humiston-Keeling, Inc.,* saying that the ADA was not violated where the company had a competitive transfer policy.[63]

In this case, United Air Lines had a reasonable accommodation guideline that said an employee who, because of disability, could no longer do the essential functions of their current job even with reasonable accommodation could be transferred to an equivalent or lower-level vacant position as a reasonable accommodation.[64] However, that process at United Air Lines was competitive.[65] That is, while employees needing accommodations were given preference (they could submit an unlimited number of transfer applications, were guaranteed an interview, and received priority consideration over similarly qualified applicants), the reassignment was not automatic.[66] That is, United Air Lines was free to hire a different individual should there be a superior applicant to the person with a disability.[67]

In essence, the Seventh Circuit said that its hands were tied because of prior precedent from 2000.[68] However, this panel of judges invited the entire Seventh Circuit to hear this case, a rehearing en banc, because the panel had doubts as to whether the decision relied upon here was still good law in light of *United States Airways Inc. v. Barnett*, 535 U.S. 391 (2002).[69] Accordingly, the EEOC did petition for rehearing en banc.[70] Once that happened, every member of the court (Seventh Circuit) in active service approved overruling *EEOC v. Humiston-Keeling, Inc.*, which had found that competitive bidding was consistent with the ADA and was the basis for the aforementioned panel decision.[71] Accordingly, the original panel opinion was vacated and a new panel opinion was circulated to the full court.[72] When that new opinion was circulated to the full court, no member voted to rehear the case en banc.[73]

In short, a new panel decision of the Seventh Circuit was issued which threw out its prior decision in *EEOC v. United Airlines* and also overruled *EEOC v. Humiston-Keeling, Inc.*[74] In doing so, the court adopted a variation of the approach in *Barnett*. First, the Seventh Circuit directed the district court to consider if mandatory reassignment was ordinarily a reasonable accommodation.[75] If the district court then found on remand that mandatory reassignment was ordinarily reasonable, then it must determine if there were fact-specific considerations particular to United's employment system that created an undue hardship and rendered the mandatory reassignment unreasonable.[76]

The question arises as to who has the burden of proof with respect to proving the *Barnett* factors as applied to a mandatory reassignment case. In the Seventh Circuit's opinion vacating their original opinion and overruling *EEOC v. Humiston-Keeling, Inc.*, they cited favorably another case, *Shapiro v. Township of Lakewood*,[77] which described how the burden of proof works. First, the employee must show that the accommodation is the type that is reasonable in the run of cases.[78] Second, if the accommodation is shown to be reasonable in the run of cases, the burden then shifts to the employer to show that granting the accommodation would impose an undue hardship under the particular circumstances of the case.[79] Finally, if the accommodation is not shown to be reasonable in the run of cases, the employee can still prevail by showing that a finding that the accommodation was reasonable was warranted under the particular circumstances of the case.[80] The Seventh Circuit concluded that it agreed with other U.S. Courts of Appeals that had already determined that the ADA requires employers to appoint disabled employees to the vacant position provided that such accommodations either do not create an undue hardship or run afoul of collective bargaining agreements.[81]

Thus, in light of all this, the critical question becomes what did *United States Airways Inc. v. Barnett* have to say about whether an assignment of a person with a disability to another position is something mandated by the ADA. The problem is that *United States Airways Inc. v. Barnett* is all over the place with respect to whether an employer with a seniority system has the obligation to reassign a person with a disability to another position he or she is otherwise qualified to do within the company. Depending upon which opinion you read in *Barnett,* you get different answers. For example, Justice Breyer's majority opinion, in which Chief Justice Rehnquist, Justice Stevens, Justice O'Connor, and Justice Kennedy joined, said that it would be a very unusual set of circumstances that would require an employer to override a seniority system and mandate that the employer transfer an individual with a disability to another position that they could perform with or without reasonable accommodations.[82] It is not clear how the majority view applies to this case being discussed here, since *EEOC v. United Airlines* did not involve a seniority system.[83]

Justice O'Connor and Justice Scalia have opinions that are a bit broader in scope than the majority opinion. Justice O'Connor's concurring opinion with respect to determining when an employer would have the obligation to reassign a person with a disability to a position that he or she could do with or without reasonable accommodation focused on whether that position was vacant.[84] That is, if a position was vacant, a position that no employee currently worked in and to which no individual had a legal entitlement, then to Justice O'Connor the employer would have the obligation, despite a seniority system, to reasonably accommodate the person with a disability by the transfer.[85] Therefore, application of this rule to the case being discussed here would result in the person with the disability being able to transfer into that position as a matter of right, assuming that position was vacant.

Justice Scalia's dissenting opinion in which Justice Thomas joined has another view on the matter. In his dissenting opinion, he said that the ADA envisions the elimination of the obstacle of the current position when there was an alternate position freely available.[86] That is, if the person with a disability was qualified for the position he or she was seeking reassignment to and no one else was seeking it, or no one else seeking it was better qualified, then the ADA demanded that the person with the disability be given that position.[87] In other words, an employer does not have to reassign a person with a disability to an open position if another person has superior qualifications.[88] In short, if Justice Scalia's view prevails, then United Air Lines' competitive transfer policy, which gives a preference but not an entitlement to the person with a disability, would be upheld.

Judging from a CLE seminar I attended in June of 2012, the EEOC's view is that a person with a disability seeking reassignment who is otherwise qualified would not have to compete for a job if the job was equal to or lower than their current job. We will see if the courts go along with this.

So where does this leave things? The latest opinion of the Seventh Circuit raises two questions. First, what does "the run of cases" mean? Second, the burden shifting at first seems to be reversed. That is, in *Barnett* the presumption was that a seniority system will prevail,[89] whereas here the assumption is that mandatory reassignment is reasonable. The difference is attributable to the U.S. Supreme Court saying in *Barnett* that it assumed that such a request is reasonable in the absence of the seniority system.[90] Regardless, the best preventive approach may be to adopt Justice O'Connor's opinion, which focused on whether the position is vacant.

How will this play at the U.S. Supreme Court? It really comes down to whether at some point the Court adopts the view of Justice O'Connor, no longer on the Court, or Justice Scalia, whom Justice Thomas joined. I long ago gave up predicting how the Court might rule on a matter involving the Americans with Disabilities Act. As a matter of preventive law and good employee relations, Justice O'Connor's approach bears serious consideration. That said, there is something intuitive about Justice Scalia's view, and considering the changes in the Court, his view could well prevail, though one never knows.

Notes

1. 42 U.S.C.A at § 12112(b)(5)(A).
2. 29 C.F.R. at § 1630.2(p)(2).
3. 29 C.F.R. at § 1630.2(p)(2)(ii),(iii); *but see* Olmstead v. L.C. by Zimring, 527 U.S. 581, 597 (1999), majority opinion of J. Ginsburg, holding in a Title II case that looking to the entire resources of a public entity to determine undue burden/fundamental alteration may not be appropriate.
4. 29 C.F.R. § 1630.15(d) (Westlaw, current through May 30, 2013; 78 Fed. Reg. 32,362).
5. *See* 74 Fed. Reg. 48,431–01, 48434–35 (WL Sept. 23, 2009).
6. *See* EEOC Appx. to Part 1630–Interpretive Guidance on Title I of the ADA at 1630.2 (July 1, 2011); *see also* Ransom v. State of Ariz. Board of Regents, 983 F. Supp. 895, 902 (D. Ariz. 1997).
7. *See* 29 C.F.R. § 1630.2(o)(3) and Interpretive Guidance regarding same.
8. *See, e.g.*, Johnson v. Lancaster-Lebanon, 757 F. Supp. 606, 617 (E.D. Pa., 1991). A case arising under IDEA.
9. 42 U.S.C.A. § 1981A(a)(3) (WL, current through Pub. L. 113-9 (excluding P.L. 113-4), approved May 1, 2013).
10. EEOC v. Sears, 417 F.3d 789 (7th Cir. 2005).
11. *Id.* at 793.
12. *Id.*
13. *Id.*
14. *Id.* at 794.
15. *Id.*
16. *Id.* at 792.
17. *Id.*
18. *Id.*
19. *Id.*
20. *Id.*
21. *Id.* at 797.
22. *See id.* at 802.
23. *Id.* at 793.

24. *Id.*
25. *Id.*
26. *Id.*
27. *Id.* at 794.
28. *Id.* at 793.
29. *Id.*
30. *Id.* at 794.
31. *Id.*
32. *Id.*
33. *Id.*
34. *Id.*
35. *Id.*
36. *Id.*
37. *Id.*
38. *Id.* at 797.
39. *Id.* at 803.
40. *Id.* at 804.
41. *Id.*
42. *Id.*
43. *Id.*
44. *Id.* at 805.
45. *Id.*
46. *Id.* at 806.
47. *Id.*
48. *Id.* at 806–07.
49. *Id.* at 806.
50. *Id.* at 807–08.
51. *Id.* at 808.
52. *See* Kelly v. Metallics West, Inc., 410 F.3d 670, 675 (10th Cir. 2005) and the cases cited therein.
53. *Id.*
54. D'Angelo v. Conagra Foods, Inc., 422 F.3d 1220 (11th Cir. 2005).
55. *See* 42 U.S.C.A. § 12201(h) (WL, current through Pub. L. 113-9 (excluding P.L. 113-4), approved May 1, 2013).
56. Office of the Architect of the Capitol v. Office of Compliance, 361 F.3d 633, 639 (Fed Cir. 2004).
57. Willis v. Conopco, Inc., 108 F.3d 282, 284–85 (11th Cir. 1997). Strangely enough, this case relies on the D.C. Cir. case cited in the very next endnote for its holding, but I don't read the holding of the D.C. Circuit case that way, as the D. C. Circuit case said that the burden of persuasion had wrongly been assigned to the plaintiff by the lower court. *See* Barth v. Gelb, 2 F.3d 1180, 1187 (D.C. Cir. 1993).
58. *Barth*, 2 F.3d at 1186–87.
59. *Borkowski,* 63 F.3d at 136–37.
60. Reed v. LePage Bakeries, Inc., 244 F.3d 254, 258–59 (1st Cir. 2001).

61. U.S. Airways, Inc. v. Barnett, 535 U.S. 391, 402 (2002).
62. EEOC v. United Airlines, Inc., 673 F.3d 543 (7th Cir. 2012), prior opinion vacated and lower court dec. rev'd and remanded at _F.3d_, 2012 WL 3871503 (7th Cir. Sept. 7, 2012).
63. EEOC v. Humiston-Keeling, Inc., 227 F.3d 1024, 1028 (7th Cir. 2000).
64. EEOC v. United Air Lines, Inc., 673 F.3d at 544.
65. *Id.*
66. *Id.*
67. *Id.*
68. *Id.* at 544–46.
69. *Id.* at 546–47.
70. EEOC v. United Air Lines, Inc., _F.3d_, 2012 WL 3871503, *1 (7th Cir. Sept. 7, 2012).
71. *Id.*
72. *Id.*
73. *Id.*
74. *Id.*
75. *Id.* at *4.
76. *Id.*
77. Shapiro v. Twp. of Lakewood, 292 F.3d 356 (3d Cir. 2002).
78. *Id.* at *3 n.1.
79. *Id.*
80. *Id.*
81. *Id.* at *4, *citing to* Smith v. Midland Brake, Inc., 180 F.3d 1154 (10th Cir. 1999 (en banc) and to Aka v. Washington Hosp. Ctr., 156 F.3d 1284 (D.C. Cir. 1998) (en banc).
82. US Airways, Inc. v. Barnett, 535 U.S. 391, 394, 403, 406 (2002).
83. *See* EEOC v. United Air Lines, Inc., _F.3d_, 2012 WL 3871503, at *4.
84. *US Airways, Inc.,* 535 U.S. at 409 (O'Connor, J., concurring).
85. *Id.* at 409–10.
86. *Id.* at 416 (Scalia, J., dissenting).
87. *Id.*
88. *Id.* (Justice Scalia actually cites with approval *EEOC v. Humiston-Keeling, Inc., supra.*)
89. *Id.* at 394, 403, 405–06.
90. *Id.* at 403.

Treatment of Alcoholics and Drug Addicts

4

THE TREATMENT OF ALCOHOLICS and drug addicts needs to be discussed separately, as they are governed by an entirely different set of rules. The ADA makes a distinction between recovering from drug abuse and actively using drugs.[1] Using drugs is not protected under the ADA. However, a person who has a record of drug use that substantially limits one or more of life's major activities is disabled for the purposes of the ADA.[2] Casual drug use in the past is not indicative of a disability, while substantial use is.[3] Determining whether the usage in the past was casual or substantial is not always easy. A person in a rehabilitation program or a person who has completed a rehabilitation program is disabled for purposes of the ADA.[4]

Furthermore, if an employer makes an erroneous assumption that a person is using drugs or alcohol, the person will be considered as being regarded as having a disability because he or she is *perceived* as having a mental or physical impairment.[5] The risk to an employer that erroneously perceives a disability, or perceives a disability without proof, is very real, as the case of *Miners v. Cargill Communications, Inc.* makes clear.[6]

In *Miners*, the plaintiff worked as a promotions director for a radio station, where part of her job involved going to bars to promote the radio station in a company van.[7] After a while, her supervisor, a recovering alcoholic, became suspicious that the plaintiff was drinking while at the bars.[8] A private investigator hired to follow the plaintiff observed her drinking and then called the supervisor.[9] The supervisor showed up at the bar and, when the plaintiff left, demanded the keys to the company van.[10]

The next day the president of the radio station informed the plaintiff that she faced termination unless she entered a chemical dependency program.[11] The plaintiff declined to enter the program and was terminated.[12] She brought suit alleging that she was terminated on the basis of a perceived disability—alcoholism—and not because she violated a company rule.[13] The court found that sufficient evidence existed that the plaintiff had been fired because of a perceived disability.[14]

In addition to the need for clear company policy, the lesson here is that the employer needs to examine all options before acting on a disability. It is entirely possible that the plaintiff was indeed an alcoholic. However, just observing the plaintiff drinking in a bar does not make her one. The employer would have been better off taking one of the following approaches. The employer could have requested a medical exam on the grounds that it was job-related and a business necessity (to be discussed in the next chapter). The exam could have helped determine how to proceed and, if necessary, justify the termination of the plaintiff. Alternatively, the employer could have focused on conduct and used a "no drinking" policy as the basis of some disciplinary action.

A person with an alcohol problem could well have a perceived disability ("regarded as" prong) under the ADA, as the *Miners* case makes clear. Prior to the ADAAA, it was also possible that an alcoholic might not have an actual disability under the ADA because there was no substantial limitation on a major life activity.[15] However, since the ADAAA now defines a major life activity under the ADA as including major bodily functions such as neurological and brain,[16] it is hard to believe that alcoholism would not be considered a disability. Also, a person who has been in alcohol rehabilitation is protected under the ADA. However, unlike with mental and physical disabilities, an employer can evaluate the alcoholic employee as if the disability didn't exist.[17] This is a critical distinction between alcohol and other disabilities. For example, if an alcoholic's job performance declines, he or she can be evaluated based on that performance. On the other hand, it would be a violation of the ADA to deny a person with a mental or physical disability a reasonable accommodation and then evaluate their performance without the accommodation.

While the preceding is very useful and important to know, there are two critical questions that the preceding discussion does not answer. First, how is a current user of drugs or alcohol defined? Second, from what point in time do you measure whether the person is a current user of alcohol or drugs? With respect to the first question, the ADA allows for a safe harbor for employers with respect to an employee who is using illegal drugs.[18] The question becomes how a current user is defined. That is, could a person be using drugs or alcohol one day, go into a rehabilitation program the next day, and then not be considered a current user so that they would be protected under the ADA? Several circuits have addressed this question.[19] While there are some differences among the circuits with respect to how to view whether a person is a current user of drugs or alcohol, the differences are subtle and may or may not create a conflict to the point where the U.S. Supreme Court would need to step in. There is, as we shall see below, a conflict in the circuits with respect to the point in time that is used to measure whether a person is a current user of drugs or alcohol.

The case that all the circuits consistently refer to in their decisions on this issue is *Teahan v. Metro-North Commuter Railroad Co.*,[20] a Rehabilitation Act case from 1991.[21] In that case, the plaintiff was employed as a telephone and telegraph maintainer from 1983 through 1988.[22] During that time, his alcohol and drug abuse led to his being excessively and repeatedly absent from work on numerous occasions.[23] On March 7, 1986, the plaintiff voluntarily enrolled in a 30-day rehabilitation program.[24] After he was discharged from that program, the plaintiff relapsed into further drug and alcohol use and continued to incur unauthorized absences from work.[25] Metro-North aggressively disciplined the plaintiff for the absences, including warning letters, three- and five-day suspensions, and 14- and 30-day actual suspensions.[26]

On December 10, 11, 17, and 18 of 1987, the plaintiff was absent without permission.[27] On December 28, 1987, Metro-North charged the plaintiff by letter that his failure on those dates to notify his work location of his inability to come to work, because of his previous record, constituted excessive absenteeism.[28] On December 28, before the plaintiff received a charge letter, the plaintiff had, in fact, voluntarily entered a substance abuse rehabilitation program.[29] He successfully completed that program and returned to work on January 28, 1988.[30] From that date until he was dismissed by Metro-North in April of 1988, he was not absent from work and appeared to have otherwise fully performed the requirements of the job.[31] His ability to return to work at all was due to the collective-bargaining agreement process needing to be exhausted.[32] Once that process was exhausted, the plaintiff was terminated.[33] He filed suit against Metro-North alleging discrimination in violation of § 504 of the Rehabilitation Act of 1973 based on his disability because of his being an alcoholic/drug addict.[34] Plaintiff argued on appeal that the district court had erred in the way it apportioned the burden of proof, since his excessive absenteeism was caused by his substance abuse problem.[35] The Second Circuit Court of Appeals agreed, and reversed and remanded for further proceedings.[36]

The first question the Second Circuit Court of Appeals had to deal with was whether the plaintiff was a current user. The Rehabilitation Act, like the ADA, contains a safe harbor for employers with respect to current users of drugs and alcohol.[37] Citing to legislative history, the Second Circuit said that the current-user safe harbor was not intended to be limited to a person using drugs or alcohol on the day of, or within a matter of days or weeks before, the adverse action in question. Rather, the safe harbor was intended to apply to a person whose illegal use of drugs or alcohol occurred recently enough to justify a reasonable belief that a person's drug use was current.[38] Therefore, the relevant inquiry is whether the employee's substance abuse problem was severe and recent enough so that the employer was justified in believing that the employee was unable to perform the essential duties of the job.[39] The Second Circuit believed that whether that person could do the essential duties of the job turned on several factors, such as the level of responsibility entrusted to the employee, the employer's applicable job and performance requirements, the level of confidence ordinarily required to adequately perform the task in question, and the employee's past performance record.[40]

In short, the *Teahan* court set up a two-step process for dealing with cases such as this. First, you have to determine whether the plaintiff was a current user.[41] Second, if the plaintiff was a current user, then it had to be assessed whether the plaintiff was otherwise qualified.[42] In determining whether such an individual could perform essential functions of the job, the *Teahan* court said that determining whether the individual was otherwise qualified required consideration not only of the conduct that is symptomatic of the disability, but also the work the employee performs and how the two interact.[43] Further, public safety concerns are an additional factor to consider.[44]

The second question is whether a current user is defined by when the employer notifies the employee of the problem or when the employee is actually fired. The answer to that question can make a difference, because it is quite conceivable that a person could enter into a rehabilitation program between the two time periods, as the plaintiff did in *Teahan*. The *Teahan* court said that it was their view that the time for assessment was the actual date of firing.[45] The court believed that such a rule best comported with the legislative purpose of ensuring that individuals going through rehabilitation were not discriminated against on the basis of past substance abuse.[46] It also, in their view, ensured that the integration of people with disabilities into the workforce was not an overly burdensome process for the employer.[47] Finally, the court believed that any burden on the employer did not outweigh the Rehabilitation Act's purpose—to afford substance abusers opportunities to overcome the disability and become fully integrated into the workforce as soon as possible.[48]

The *Teahan* case gets mentioned by other circuits that have addressed the "current user" issue and the time frame in which that is decided. It also gets mentioned with respect to "otherwise qualified." The circuits aren't all quite the same. For instance, the Fourth Circuit believes that the term "currently" refers to a periodic or ongoing activity in which a person engages, even if doing something else at that precise moment, which is not yet permanently ended.[49] From that, the Fourth Circuit said that current drug use refers to the illegal use of drugs that occurred recently enough to justify an employer's reasonable belief that involvement with drugs is an ongoing problem.[50]

The Ninth Circuit takes a slightly different approach. It has said that in order for the safe harbor not to apply to a current user, a significant length of time needs to transpire,[51] and that an employer was permitted to terminate an alcoholic employee for violating a rational rule of conduct even if aware that this conduct was related to the employee's alcoholism.[52]

The Fifth Circuit agrees with the Fourth and Second Circuits with respect to how a current user is defined,[53] and it also referenced the *Teahan* (Second Circuit) factors as well.[54] It disagreed with the Second Circuit with respect to the appropriate time that current user is measured against.[55] The Fifth Circuit believes that the notification date was the critical inquiry, that such a view was consistent with the prior precedent in its circuit, and that it also provided a fair remedy to both the employer and the employee.[56] To hold otherwise would penalize an employer that allows an employee to take a medical leave of absence rather than terminate him or her right away.[57]

In the Tenth Circuit, with respect to whether an individual was a current user, that circuit will look to whether the circumstances of the plaintiff's drug use *and recovery* (emphasis added) justify a reasonable belief that drug use is no longer a problem.[58] Since the Tenth Circuit also has the recovery piece in its test, another factor to consider in determining current use is the severity of the employee's addiction and relapse rates for whatever drugs were used.[59] The Tenth Circuit also agrees with the Ninth Circuit that nothing prevents an employer from terminating the employee for drug-related misconduct[60] (it is hard to believe that any of the circuits would be against terminating someone for drug-related misconduct).

So where does this leave us? With respect to when a current user is evaluated, the circuits are split between the time the individual was terminated and the time the individual is notified. With respect to current use, circuits are fairly consistent in terms of how that is defined, though the Tenth Circuit will also evaluate the circumstances of recovery.

As a preventive law measure, what is a company to do? Preventive law is great, and I am a firm believer in it. However, employers have businesses to run. Sometimes, too much preventive law can get in the way of running a business. It would seem much easier for business to run on the principle that the time for evaluating a current user would run from the time of notification and not from the time of firing. Second, adopting the approach of the circuits that do not focus on the circumstances of recovery (Second or Fourth Circuit) may be something that a business should consider. The circumstances of recovery, an additional piece of the Tenth Circuit and alluded to by the Fifth Circuit, runs the risk of allowing stereotypes about the potential for recovery to influence the termination decision, which could be problematic under the ADA.

Notes

1. 29 C.F.R. § 1630.3 (WL, current through May 30, 2013; 78 Fed. Reg. 32,362) and Interpretive Guidance regarding same.
2. 29 C.F.R. at § 1630.3(b)(1), (2).
3. Hartman v. City of Petaluma, 841 F. Supp. 946, 949 (N.D. Cal. 1994).
4. 29 C.F.R. at § 1630.3(b)(1).
5. 29 C.F.R. at § 1630.3(b)(3).
6. Miners v. Cargill Commc'ns, Inc., 113 F.3d 820 (8th Cir. 1997).
7. *Id.* at 821.
8. *Id.* at 821–22.
9. *Id.* at 822.
10. *Id.*
11. *Id.*
12. *Id.*
13. *Id.*
14. *Id.* at 824.
15. Maull v. Div. of State Police, 141 F. Supp. 2d 463, 473 (D. Del. 2001).
16. *See* 42 U.S.C.A. at § 12102(2)(B).
17. EEOC Interpretive Guidance on 29 C.F.R. § 1630.16(b).
18. 42 U.S.C.A. § 12114(a), (b) (WL, current through Pub. L. 113-9 (excluding Pub. L. 113-4), approved May 1, 2013).19. *See* Zenor v. El Paso Healthcare Sys. Ltd., 176 F.3d 847 (5th Cir. 1999); Teahan v. Metro-North Commuter RR. Co., 951 F. 2d 511 (2d Cir. 1991); Brown v. Lucky Stores, Inc., 246 F.3d 1182 (9th Cir. 2001); Mauerhan v. Wagner Corp., 649 F.3d 1180 (10th Cir. 2011); Shafer v. Preston Mem'l Hosp. Corp., 107 F.3d 274, 278 (4th Cir. 1997), *abrogated on other grounds* by Baird *ex rel.* Baird v. Rose, 192 F.3d 462 (4th Cir. 1999).
20. Teahan v. Metro-North Commuter RR. Co., 951 F. 2d 511 (2d Cir. 1991).
21. The Rehabilitation Act of 1973 applies to the federal government and to entities taking federal funds. The ADA took the principles of the Rehabilitation Act and extended them generally. The two laws are very similar substantively but they can differ in important respects.

22. *Teahan* at 513.
23. *Id.*
24. *Id.*
25. *Id.*
26. *Id.*
27. *Id.*
28. *Id.*
29. *Id.*
30. *Id.*
31. *Id.*
32. *Id.*
33. *Id.*
34. *Id.* at 514.
35. *Id.*
36. *Id.* at 514, 521.
37. *Id.* at 517 n.1.
38. *Id.* at 518.
39. *Id.* at 520.
40. *Id.*
41. *Id.*
42. *Id.*
43. *Id.* at 521.
44. *Id.*
45. *Id.* at 518.
46. *Id.*
47. *Id.*
48. *Id.* at 519.
49. *Shafer,* 107 F.3d at 278.
50. *Id.* at 279.
51. *Brown,* 246 F.3d at 1186.
52. *Id.*
53. *Zenor,* 176 F.3d at 854 n.3, 856.
54. *Id.* at 856–57.
55. *Id.* at 854 n.3, 855.
56. *Id.* at 854–55.
57. *Id.* at 855.
58. *Mauerhan,* 649 F.3d at 1188.
59. *Id.*
60. *Id.*

5

Pre-employment and Post-employment Medical Exams/Disability-Related Inquiries

WITH RESPECT TO PRE-EMPLOYMENT medical *exams*, a different issue from pre-employment medical *inquiries*, the EEOC has guidelines that bear discussing.[1] The EEOC defines a prohibited medical exam as any test or procedure seeking information about an individual's physical or mental impairment or physical or psychological health.[2] In assessing whether a test is a prohibited pre-employment medical exam, the EEOC will look to the following eight factors:

1. Whether the test is administered by a health-care professional or trainee;
2. Whether the results of the test are interpreted by a health-care provider or trainee;
3. Whether the test is designed to reveal an impairment or the state of an individual's physical or psychological health;
4. Whether the test is invasive;
5. Whether the test measures physiological or psychological responses as opposed to performance of tasks;

6. Whether the test is normally done in a medical setting; and
7. Whether medical equipment or devices are used for the test.[3]

Two critical points: First, one or more of the above factors may be enough for the EEOC to determine that a prohibited pre-employment medical exam is involved.[4] Second, even if a pre-employment medical exam is not involved, there still could be a pre-employment disability-related inquiry within that exam, and that inquiry would be in violation of the ADA.[5]

PERSONALITY TESTS

The issue of pre-employment disability-related inquiries within the context of nonmedical exams will arise frequently in the area of psychological pre-employment testing. Employers use such tests for many reasons, and they are not considered medical exams because they generally do not meet the EEOC criteria mentioned above. Nevertheless, most of these tests will contain pre-employment disability-related inquiries, and thus portions of the tests will violate the ADA. Unfortunately, when the ADA-violative portions of the tests are removed, it is conceivable, if not likely, that the validity of the whole test would be compromised. In short, expect to see more litigation in the area of pre-employment psychological testing. Employers would do well to have such tests reviewed to see if they are in fact medical exams issued pre-employment or if they contain impermissible pre-employment disability-related inquiries. An employer that fails to have these tests reviewed may wind up suffering the same fate as the defendant in *Karraker v. Rent-A-Center, Inc.*[6]

In *Karraker*, brothers desired to be promoted at the company they worked for, Rent-A-Center, Inc. In order to be promoted, the company required employees to take the ATP management training executive profile.[7] This battery of tests contained nine tests designed to measure math and language skills as well as interests and personality traits.[8] The tests they took included 502 questions from the Minnesota Multiphasic Personality Inventory tests (MMPI).[9] The defendant said they used the MMPI to measure personality traits.[10] However, as the court noted, the MMPI considers where an applicant falls on scales measuring traits such as depression, hypochondriasis, hysteria, paranoia, and mania.[11]

Further, the court noted that elevated scores on certain scales of the MMPI are used in the diagnosis of certain psychiatric disorders.[12] The way the defendant scored the battery of tests taken for promotion, it was possible for a person to be denied promotion based solely on his or her MMPI score.[13] The Karrakers, who were denied a promotion based on their MMPI results, sued on behalf of themselves and other employees of the 106 Illinois Rent-A-Center stores, claiming that using the MMPI as a basis for promotion violated the Americans with Disabilities Act.[14] The district court held that the MMPI did not violate the ADA, and the Karrakers appealed.[15]

The Seventh Circuit, in holding for the plaintiffs, reasoned as follows. First, the court noted that people with psychiatric disabilities frequently faced attitudinal barriers resulting from unfounded stereotypes and prejudice.[16] Second, the court referred to the EEOC definition of a medical examination as a procedure or test seeking information about an individual's physical or mental impairment or health.[17] The court referred to the EEOC's test (mentioned above), which appears in the EEOC's Enforcement Guidance on Pre-employment Disability-Related Questions and Medical Examinations,[18] for determining whether a medical examination occurred.[19]

The court noted that one of these factors may be enough to determine that a medical examination is involved.[20] The defendant offered various explanations as to why the MMPI was used as a means of promoting its employees, but the Seventh Circuit was not persuaded by any of these explanations.[21] The court said that either the MMPI was a very poor predictor of an applicant's potential as a manager (and posited that this might be the reason the MMPI was no longer used by the defendant for employees seeking promotions), or the tests were designed to measure more than just an applicant's mood on a given day.[22]

The court stated that the EEOC gives three examples of psychological tests that might or might not be considered medical exams.[23] The court noted that the first example—where an employer uses a psychological test to assess tastes and habits—bears a close resemblance to the test used in *Karraker*.[24] In that example, the EEOC notes that while the employer may be presumably testing for one thing, the same test is routinely used in a clinical setting to provide evidence leading to a diagnosis of a mental disorder or impairment.[25] The court concluded that the defendant's use of the MMPI was the same as the hypothetical defendant's use in the aforementioned EEOC example.[26] Thus, the Seventh Circuit held that the battery of tests used by the defendant were a medical exam having the likely effect of excluding employees with certain disorders from promotions.[27]

The moral for employers in light of this discussion is that "personality tests" should be checked thoroughly to see if some mental impairment may be revealed through their use. Such a check may call into question whether the test should be used at all, as taking out certain questions may compromise its validity. Nevertheless, keeping those questions may ensure the validity of the test but result in liability for the employer per *Karraker*.

The ADA allows medical exams of applicants *after* a conditional job offer by the employer. A medical exam or medical inquiry that tests for anything can be done after an offer of employment has been made and the offer is conditioned on the results of the medical exam,[28] though the employer still needs to worry about running afoul of the Genetic Information Nondiscrimination Act, which will be discussed later in this book. However, if employment is denied to an individual based on the medical exam, the basis of the denial must be job-related and consistent with business necessity, and it also must be the case that performance of the job cannot be accomplished with reasonable accommodations.[29] What is "job-related" must be determined by further litigation. However, considering the ADA's focus on the individual and on particular jobs, it could well be that "job-related" will refer to the specific job at issue and not to any broad definitions of jobs. Clearly, preventive lawyering demands that the specific job at issue be looked to rather than the broad class of jobs in assessing job-relatedness.

While pre-employment medical exams have broad latitude, after a conditional job offer the results of that exam can be used against an individual only where it is determined that the results are such that what was revealed by the test is job-related, does not allow the person to perform the essential job functions with reasonable accommodations, and is consistent with business necessity.[30] As mentioned earlier, a current employee can be requested to undergo a medical exam providing it is job-related and consistent with business necessity.[31]

Let's say an employee is struggling at work to the point where the employer demands that the person get psychological counseling. Is the employer in fact demanding that a person take a medical exam in possible violation of the ADA? A case that answers this question is *Kroll v. White Lake Ambulance Authority*.[32]

In this case, the plaintiff worked as an emergency medical technician specialist and was generally considered to be a good emergency medical technician and a good employee by her direct supervisor.[33] After the plaintiff became romantically involved with one of her co-workers, her direct supervisor and the office manager received reports of concerns from other employees about the plaintiff's well-being.[34] The plaintiff contended that those reports led to a request from the office manager that she receive psychological counseling.[35]

A few days after that, the person who had been her direct supervisor, and had been promoted to director, met with the plaintiff and the plaintiff's father following a dispute between the plaintiff and another employee.[36] At that meeting, the director informed the plaintiff and her father that he had received complaints regarding the plaintiff screaming at a male acquaintance while driving a vehicle containing a patient in emergency status, lights and sirens flashing.[37] The plaintiff was then told that, because of concerns as to whether she could perform her job safely, she must attend counseling in order to continue working.[38] Plaintiff told the director that she would not attend counseling, left the meeting, and did not return to work for the employer.[39]

While it was apparently not important to the decision, the plaintiff claimed at her deposition that because her employer told her she would have to pay for counseling out-of-pocket, she was not able to go to counseling because she did not have the funds, but she would have been willing to attend the counseling if it was provided to her free of charge.[40] She then filed a sex discrimination complaint with the Michigan Department of Civil Rights and the EEOC.[41] About a month later, she filed another complaint with the EEOC alleging ADA violations.[42] When she received the right-to-sue letter from the EEOC for both of her claims, she then filed a complaint in federal district court alleging that the employer violated the ADA by demanding that she attend counseling and then improperly fired her in retaliation for her refusal.[43] The district court granted the employer's motion for summary judgment and the plaintiff appealed.[44]

The question before the court was whether the demand for psychological counseling constituted a medical exam. In reaching the conclusion that the demand for psychological counseling constituted a medical exam, the Sixth Circuit reasoned as follows. First, they looked at legislative history as to what the term might mean, but the legislation had little to offer in that regard.[45]

Second, the Sixth Circuit said that the best interpretive aid for figuring out what a medical examination is would be to look at the EEOC's enforcement guidance on the subject.[46] While EEOC guidances to regulations can have a very mixed record with respect to how persuasive they are,[47] in the Sixth Circuit the guidelines have been held to be very persuasive authority with respect to statutory interpretation of the ADA.[48]

Third, the court referred to the EEOC's seven-factor test noted above for analyzing whether something is a medical examination.[49] They noted the guidance explains that tests designed to identify a mental disorder or impairment are medical examinations, while tests designed to measure personality traits, such as honesty, preferences, or habits, are not considered medical examinations.[50] In figuring this out, the EEOC guidance advises looking at the purpose of the test and the intent of the employer in giving the test, though the latter is not dispositive.[51]

Fourth, the court relied on the Seventh Circuit decision in *Karraker v. Rent-A-Center Inc.*, discussed above, saying it was the most analogous authority.[52]

Fifth, the employer attempted to say that while it insisted on counseling, it did not specify that the counseling be psychological in nature. The court was having none of it. More particularly, the court looked to both the *Oxford English* and a medical dictionary to say that the plain meaning of the request meant psychological counseling.[53]

Sixth, the court then explored each of the seven factors that the EEOC lists in its guidance to figure out whether a medical examination occurred. When doing that, the court found that factors one, two, and particularly three were such that the evidence clearly indicated a medical exam was at issue here.[54] The court said that the answer was so clear with respect to factors one, two, and particularly three that the scarcity of information for factors four through seven simply didn't matter.[55]

Finally, the court recognized that just because a medical exam was involved does not mean the employer could not still be entitled to summary judgment if the counseling request was job-related and consistent with business necessity.[56] However, since the district court did not even address that question in the first place and the parties did not brief it on appeal, the Sixth Circuit felt it proper to remand the case to the district court for the decision on that issue.[57]

Thus, we now know that a request for psychological counseling could well be considered a request for a medical exam. However, even though psychological counseling may be a medical exam, it is entirely possible that such a request could be job-related and consistent with business necessity. Also, it is not necessary for all seven factors of EEOC test to be satisfied for the court to find the medical exam.

Therefore, we still need to know how to define "job-related" and "consistent with business necessity." The Eighth Circuit refers to this as the employer having the burden of showing that the asserted business necessity is vital to the business and that the request for a medical examination or inquiry is neither broader nor more intrusive than necessary.[58] Finally, when it comes to determining whether the medical exam is job-related and consistent with business necessity and how that exam is evaluated, there may be considerably more leeway to the employer if it is engaged in public safety.[59]

POST-EMPLOYMENT TESTING: CAN IT BE DONE WITHOUT CAUSE?

In addition to business necessity, does an employer, with respect to a post-employment medical exam or inquiry, need some kind of cause before it can perform a medical exam? A case that explores both of these questions is *EEOC v. United States Steel Corporation*.[60] In that case, probationary employees (employees who had worked less than 1,040 hours) were subject to random drug testing.[61] The random drug testing was something agreed to by the corporation and the union that represented the workers in the factory and was enshrined in their basic labor agreement.[62] The new employees at the plant performed either of three functions (door cleaners, lidman, and coke oven laborer).[63] All three of those jobs are very close to or on the coke batteries, which contain molten coke and reach a temperature of up to 2100°F.[64] These employees deal with narrow work areas, dangerous heights, extremely large moving machinery, toxics and combustibles, superheated gases, and biosludge, as well as a number of mobile vehicles containing hot coke or bituminous coal.[65] As a result, these employees must wear layers of protective clothing, equipment, and masks.[66]

On January 29, 2008, the plaintiff was terminated after she failed both an initial and confirmatory breath alcohol test.[67] She filed a claim with the EEOC complaining that the test failed to account for her diabetes.[68] From there, the case becomes quite messy. It seems that the EEOC was quite anxious to investigate and pursue this, with the result that the defendant claimed that the procedural prerequisites were not met.[69] At any rate, the EEOC brought suit saying that this policy violated the ADA with respect to when a post-employment medical exam could be performed.[70] The EEOC's view was that medical testing is not permitted unless the employer has an individualized, reasonable suspicion of a safety concern.[71] Therefore, any random alcohol-testing policy must be per se invalid.[72]

Before moving on to the issue of what kind of cause is needed, if any, before conducting a medical exam, some of the other issues can be squared away first. First, before the EEOC can bring a case against someone, certain procedural formalities must be performed. United States Steel alleged that those formalities were not done in this case. The court, after detailing the sequence of events, said that it was a close call, but ultimately it was a question of fact as to whether the formalities had been observed.[73] Second, United States Steel also maintained that the random drug-testing provision was within the safe harbor contained in employee benefit plans, but the court was having none of it. The court said that this was a medical exam and not the type of thing that you would see in an employee benefit plan.[74] Furthermore, the random drug testing was part of the collective-bargaining agreement and was not voluntary.[75] Accordingly, that safe harbor exception did not apply.[76] Third, United States Steel argued that other federal laws allowed it to do the random drug testing and therefore the testing was permissible, but the court said the argument would not fly because the company had not shown that no other alternative measures existed that would ensure compliance.[77] Finally, the EEOC argued that its enforcement guidance, which required some kind of reasonable suspicion before doing a medical exam post-employment, was binding on the matter. However, the court rejected that argument because the guidance did not go through proper rulemaking, and therefore it was not binding on the courts and could be used or not at the court's own discretion.[78]

Turning to the merits of the case, the court first set forth the paradigm for figuring out how the job-related and business necessity defense works. First, it is the employer that has the burden of showing a medical examination is job-related and consistent with business necessity.[79] Second, whether a medical examination is consistent with business necessity is an objective test.[80] Third, the employee does not need to have a disability under the ADA to challenge a medical examination or inquiry.[81] Fourth, to determine whether an employer has shown that a medical examination or inquiry is job-related and consistent with business necessity, the employer has to show that a business necessity exists and that the policy at issue serves the asserted business necessity.[82] Fifth, any business necessity warranting a medical examination has to be vital to the business, such as ensuring that the workplace is safe and secure or reducing egregious absenteeism.[83] Sixth, in order to show that the policy serves the asserted business necessity, an employer must demonstrate the examination or inquiry genuinely serves the asserted business necessity and is no broader nor more intrusive than necessary.[84] Finally, if an employer argues that safety is the business necessity, then all the employer has to do is demonstrate that the medical test or inquiry makes *even a small* contribution to reducing the risk posed by unfit employees.[85]

With that in mind, the court was ready to take on the merits of the case and approached it in the following way. First, there is nothing in the text of 42 U.S.C. § 12112(d)(4)(A) specifically requiring employers to have suspicion, reasonable or otherwise, that an employee presents a safety hazard before they can conduct a random alcohol test on new employees.[86]

Second, the case law is all over the place on whether some form of reasonable suspicion or something else is required before such a test can be conducted.[87]

Third, the court looked to an analogous statute in the ADA, 42 U.S.C. § 12112(b)(6), dealing with qualifications that screen out people with disabilities, and said that nothing in that particular statutory provision would suggest that across-the-board medical screenings are per se violations of the ADA.[88]

Fourth, the fact that only new employees were subject to this random testing did mean that the employer has the burden of justifying the necessity of performing the medical examination only upon the new employees. The court believed that United States Steel more than met that burden in several ways. First, new employees work in very dangerous jobs that included molten hot coke, toxic waste products, and massive moving machinery, so no level of intoxication could be acceptable under those circumstances.[89] Second, the random drug-testing provision was negotiated between the union representing the workers and the corporation and was made part of the collective-bargaining agreement.[90] Third, many employers, federal and private, use random drug and alcohol testing for employees working in safety-sensitive or mission-critical positions, and their common theme is that random testing can and should be used by employees working in positions where even the smallest miscalculation could lead to dire consequences.[91] Finally, random testing deters other employees from bad behavior leading to bad consequences.[92]

Fifth, the court explored the viability of limiting the random drug testing to new employees. In essence, it said that there was a rational basis for limiting the testing to new employees only. That basis included the following elements:

Regular employees who have been on the job for a long period of time have proven they can follow appropriate safety standards and adequately perform their daily job, which is not the case with new employees.

New employees are less skilled at performing their jobs, less familiar with company rules, and have not fully internalized the importance of workplace safety.

Factory workers in training are inherently more dangerous to themselves and others because of their lack of training and familiarity with the job and are more likely to arrive at work in an unfit state.

New hires, until they fully can appreciate the risk in the workplace, are more likely to engage in risky behavior than regular employees, and there is no room for error when the dangers are as numerous as they are in this plant.

There is no way for the employer to tell who may be engaging in behavior demanding further investigation when everybody must be completely covered due to the hazardous conditions they work in.

Finally, even a four- to five-month differential (the policy applied to employees that had worked less than 1,040 hours—about four to five months full-time) can become critical given such high stakes.[93]

Therefore, probationary employees are not in the same place as regular employees and can be treated differently, and the random testing was warranted on new employees because they were less likely to comply with the alcohol policy.[94] Since the court reasoned this way with respect to new employees, it really had little choice but to say that to do it on non-probationary employees would result in a policy that would be broader and more intrusive than necessary (thereby running afoul of the ADA prohibition on post-employment medical exams).[95]

There are numerous things we can take away from this case. First, many practitioners probably assumed, based on an implied reading of the statute, which is certainly supported by the EEOC enforcement guidance, that some form of reasonable suspicion was necessary before a post-employment medical exam could be done. This case makes clear that we should no longer necessarily assume that.

Second, in the labor context, it really helps if a random drug- or alcohol-testing policy is part of the collective-bargaining agreement.

Third, the EEOC does have certain procedural formalities to go through before it is able to pursue a claim. It is certainly worth it for the defense to claim that the formalities were not observed, but such an argument may be a tough one to carry.

Fourth, enforcement guidances and the like are just persuasive authority, and an employer is free to argue that they should not apply. Such an argument, as was seen here, may indeed carry the day (such an argument was also successful in *Toyota Motor*, where the U,S. Supreme Court gave no deference to the EEOC's view on what constituted a substantial limitation on a major life activity).[96]

Fifth, this case does not really tell us what "job-related" means, but instead focuses on business necessity. From this case, if an employer has, for the lack of a better term, a "rational basis" for its policy, it may well prevail. Finally, if the employer has a "rational basis" for treating different kinds of employees differently, that may also carry the day as well. That said, this "rational basis" approach goes only so far. For example, this court, as noted above, said that a random drug-testing policy for employees who were no longer new would fail.

I would have expected the EEOC to have appealed this decision. However, the decision came down at the end of February 2013, and as of this writing, the end of May 2013, I could find no record in Westlaw that this case was appealed. I expect to see this issue litigated in the future and ultimately make its way to the U.S. Supreme Court.

CONFIDENTIALITY OF MEDICAL EXAMINATION OR MEDICAL INQUIRY RESULTS

The ADA requires that medical information obtained on an employee or prospective employee *as a result of a medical examination or a medical inquiry*[97] (emphasis added and see discussion below) be kept confidential.[98] To that end, medical information cannot be kept in regular personnel files,[99] and the confidentiality obligation of the employer extends even after employment has terminated.[100] An individual can voluntarily disclose his or her own medical information as long as the disclosure is truly voluntary—that is, the employee has not been requested, persuaded, coerced, or otherwise pressured to disclose the information. It should be noted that just because the individual self-discloses does not mean the employer is then free to disclose medical information at its whim.

The phrase, "as a result of a medical examination or medical inquiry" needs to be explored further. There is a case from the U.S. Court of Appeals for the Seventh Circuit holding that the obligation of the employer to keep medical information confidential extends to the employer only with respect to a medical inquiry or medical examination,[101] and it is worthwhile to explore that case further.[102]

In *EEOC v. Thrivent Financial for Lutherans*, the plaintiff was hired by a technology consulting agency to work as a temporary programmer for Thrivent Financial for Lutherans (Thrivent).[103] When the plaintiff started work for Thrivent, he was assigned as a business analyst in the Fraternal Support Service Department and worked for four months without incident.[104] During that time, the plaintiff was very good about notifying both the consulting agency and Thrivent when he planned to be absent from work.[105]

On November 1, 2006, the plaintiff failed to report to work.[106] Since the plaintiff had not notified anyone at Thrivent about his absence, his supervisor called the consulting agency to find out what was going on, but the consulting agency did not know either.[107] The supervisor at Thrivent then sent an e-mail to the plaintiff asking the plaintiff to call.[108] Shortly before 5 p.m., the plaintiff wrote a very long e-mail to his supervisor at Thrivent detailing why he had not been in contact sooner and going into elaborate detail about his preexisting medical conditions (severe migraines as a result of a 1984 accident).[109] His supervisor responded to the e-mail a few hours later urging the plaintiff to get better and to let him know if there was anything they could do.[110]

Despite the plaintiff's assurance that he was committed through the remainder of his contract, the plaintiff quit his job with Thrivent only a month later.[111] According to the plaintiff's supervisor, there was a very strong disagreement on expectations, and the plaintiff walked out on them.[112] After the plaintiff left Thrivent and the consulting agency, he had a difficult time finding a new job and began to believe that Thrivent was saying negative things about him to prospective employers for reference checks.[113] The plaintiff hired a firm that specializes in determining what is being said in references.[114] As a result of that firm's investigation, they found out that his migraines were being disclosed.[115] That led to the plaintiff filing a charge with the EEOC alleging disability discrimination, for which the EEOC found reasonable cause.[116] When the reasonable cause letter failed to achieve a settlement between the plaintiff and Thrivent, the EEOC filed suit, alleging that Thrivent had violated the ADA confidentiality provisions.[117]

The Seventh Circuit held that since the disclosure was not from a medical exam or medical inquiry, the confidentiality provisions did not apply,[118] and reasoned as follows. First, the court cited to *Merriam-Webster Dictionary* in saying that the phrase "medical examinations and inquiries" contained a coordinating conjunction, which is used to indicate connection or addition, especially of items within the same class or type.[119] The court found it very significant that the statute used the term "and" instead of the term "or" because that indicated the intent was to talk about things of the same type.[120] What the statute really says in essence is "medical exams and medical inquiries."[121] Second, the court reasoned that the use of the conjunction "and," indicated that the adjective "medical," modifies both "examination" and "inquiries."[122] Third, if one looks at the subject matter discussed in 42 U.S.C. § 12112(d), it becomes clear that the entire section is devoted to medical exams and medical inquiries and not to job-related inquiries in the broad sense.[123] Finally, the court distinguished cases cited by the EEOC on the grounds those cases involved an employer with preexisting knowledge that the employee was ill or physically incapacitated,[124] which was not the case with the plaintiff here. Instead, Thrivent was just checking up when an employee did not show up to work. As far as Thrivent knew, the plaintiff could have had transportation problems, marital problems, weather-related problems, etc.[125] Accordingly, for all these reasons, Thrivent was not required to treat the medical information the plaintiff sent in response to his supervisor's e-mail as a confidential medical record.[126]

When you extrapolate this case as to how it plays out in practice after this holding, things get very complicated. On the defense side, it seems to make sense, from a preventive law standpoint, to treat any medical information that you receive as confidential. After all, do you really need the litigation over whether the inquiry your client made was a medical exam or medical inquiry? On the other hand, this decision gives the employer wide latitude with respect to any information received that is not from a medical exam or medical inquiry in terms of how that information is kept internally or how it is disclosed to others. Before exercising such wide latitude, the employer would want to be certain that a medical exam or medical inquiry was not involved.

On the plaintiff's side, things are a lot more complicated. Under this case, to be protected, it would have to be a medical exam or a medical inquiry. Accordingly, a plaintiff would want to give only a very minimum amount of information to satisfy the employer. If the employer needs more information, then the plaintiff would want to have the employer make a specific request (i.e., make a medical inquiry). Any such communication by the plaintiff could be done explicitly or implicitly. That is, a plaintiff could simply say "I am not feeling well . . . and I'll be back soon." The employee could also say something like, "I am not feeling well and if you need more information, feel free to contact me, and I will have the appropriate information given to you." The permutations are many. The problem with this decision is that it puts the burden on the plaintiff, who wants to ensure that any disclosed medical information be kept confidential, to arrange any communication with the employer about why he or she is absent from work so as to ensure that the employer winds up making a medical inquiry—all of which adds a bit of manipulation, if not a bit of the adversarial process as well, to the employer/employee relationship.

It will be very interesting to see whether the other U.S. Court of Appeals follow the Seventh Circuit's reasoning. Certainly, in terms of how the statute is laid out, there is something to be said for the reasoning of the U.S. Court of Appeals for the Seventh Circuit. The problem lies in how this kind of decision will be applied by employers and employees in the future and whether Congress could have really intended for that to be the result.

There are also exceptions to the confidentiality provisions. They are as follows:

- Supervisors and managers may be told about necessary restrictions on the work or duties of the employee and about necessary accommodations.
- First aid and safety personnel may be told if the disability might require emergency treatment.
- Government officials investigating compliance with the ADA must be given relevant information on request.
- Employers may give information to state worker's compensation offices, state second injury funds, or worker's compensation insurance carriers in accordance with state worker's compensation laws.
- Employers may use the information for insurance purposes.[127]

Notes

1. EEOC Enforcement Guidance on Pre-employment Disability-Related Inquiries and Medical Examinations of Employees under the ADA *available* at http://www.eeoc.gov/policy/docs/guidance-inquiries.html.
2. *Id.*
3. *Id.*
4. *Id.*
5. *Id.*
6. Karraker v. Rent-A-Center, Inc., 411 F.3d 831 (7th Cir. 2005).
7. *Id.* at 833.
8. *Id.*
9. *Id.*
10. *Id.*
11. *Id.*
12. *Id.* at 834.
13. *Id.*
14. *Id.*
15. *Id.*
16. *Id.*
17. *Id.* at 835.
18. The EEOC's Enforcement Guidance on Disability-Related Inquiries and Medical Examinations under the ADA can be found at http://www.eeoc.gov/policy/docs/guidance-inquiries.html.

19. *Karraker,* 411 F.3d at 836, *citing to* the EEOC's 1995 enforcement guidance on preemployment disability-related questions and medical examinations.
20. *Id.* at 835.
21. *Id.* at 835–36.
22. *Id.* at 836.
23. *Id.*
24. *Id.*
25. *Id.* at 836–37.
26. *Id.* at 837.
27. *Id.*
28. 29 C.F.R. § 1630.14(b) (current through May 30, 2013; 78 Fed. Reg. 32,362).
29. 29 C.F.R. at § 1630.14(b)(3).
30. 29 C.F.R. at § 1630.14(b)(3).
31. 42 U.S.C.A. § 12112(d)(4)(A) (current through Pub. L. 113-9 (excluding Pub. L. 113-4), approved May 1, 2013).
32. Kroll v. White Lake Ambulance Auth., 691 F.3d 809 (6th Cir. 2012).
33. *Id.* at 811.
34. *Id.*
35. *Id.*
36. *Id.* at 812.
37. *Id.*
38. *Id.*
39. *Id.*
40. *Id.*
41. *Id.*
42. *Id.*
43. *Id.*
44. *Id.*
45. *Id.* at 815, n.8.
46. *Id.* at 815.
47. *See, e.g.,* Toyota Motor Mfg., Kentucky, Inc. v. Williams, 534 U.S. 184, 194 (2002) (referring back to *Sutton v. United Airlines* and noting that the persuasiveness of the EEOC regulations are far from clear).
48. *Kroll,* 691 F.3d at 815.
49. *Id.* at 815–16.
50. *Id.* at 816.
51. *Id.* at 816–17.
52. *Id.* at 817–18, n.10
53. *Id.* at 819.
54. *Id.*
55. *Id.* at 819–20.
56. *Id.* at 820.
57. *Id.*

58. Wisbey v. City of Lincoln, Neb., 612 F.3d 667, 673 (8th Cir. 2010). If the Sixth Circuit view will be the same as that of the Eighth Circuit with respect to job-related and business necessity, the litigation in the district court is likely to center on whether request for the medical exam was overly broad.
59. *Id.* at 674; *see also* McDonald v. Pa. State Police, 2012 WL 5381403, *12–13 (W.D. Oct. 31, 2012) (a Title II case discussing direct threat in a public safety context).
60. EEOC v. United States Steel Corp., 2013 WL 625315 (W.D. Pa., Feb. 20, 2013).
61. *Id.* at *1–*2.
62. *Id.*
63. *Id.* at *2.
64. *Id.*
65. *Id.*
66. *Id.*
67. *Id.* at *1.
68. *Id.* at *1, *3.
69. *Id.* at *3–6.
70. *See id.*
71. *Id.* at *20–*21.
72. *See id.* at *20–*22.
73. *Id.* at *11.
74. *Id.* at *23.
75. *Id.*
76. *Id.*
77. *Id.* at *25.
78. *Id.* at *20–*23.
79. *Id.* at *12.
80. *Id.*
81. *Id.*
82. *Id.*
83. *Id.*
84. *Id.* at *13.
85. *Id.* at *15.
86. *Id.* at *13.
87. *Id.*
88. *Id.* at *14.
89. *Id.* at *16.
90. *Id.*
91. *Id.*
92. *Id.*
93. *Id.* at *17.
94. *Id.*
95. *Id.* at *20.

96. *Toyota Motor,* 534 U.S. at 689.
97. *See* EEOC v. Thrivent Financial for Lutherans, _F.3d_, 2012 WL 5846208 (7th Cir. Nov. 20, 2012).
98. 42 U.S.C.A. at § 12112(d)(2)(B).
99. EEOC Guidance on Pre-employment Disability-Related Inquiries and Medical Examinations under the ADA.
100. *Id.*
101. *EEOC v. Thrivent*, _F.3d_, 2012 WL 5846208 (7th Cir. Nov. 20, 2012).
102. The discussion on *EEOC v. Thrivent Financial for Lutherans* is taken with some minor modifications from a blog entry of mine that I posted on Nov. 26, 2012.
103. *Id.* at *1.
104. *Id.*
105. *Id.*
106. *Id.*
107. *Id.*
108. *Id.*
109. *Id.* at *2.
110. *Id.*
111. *Id.*
112. *Id.*
113. *Id.*
114. *Id.*
115. *Id.*
116. *Id.* at *3.
117. *Id.*
118. *Id.* at *1, *7.
119. *Id.* at *5.
120. *Id.*
121. *See id.*
122. *Id.*
123. *Id.*
124. *Id.* at *6–*7.
125. *Id.* at *7.
126. *Id.*
127. *Id.*

The ADA, Health Insurance, and the Genetic Information Nondiscrimination Act

6

THE AMERICANS WITH DISABILITIES ACT (ADA) APPLIES TO ALL BENEFITS, conditions, and privileges of employment as well as employment decisions.[1] Therefore, how might the ADA apply to insurance benefits offered under a health insurance plan? Back in 1993, the EEOC issued Guidelines on the ADA and Health Insurance,[2] and considerable time was spent discussing these guidelines in the first edition of this book. However, those guidelines were not well received by the courts. There was one case that explicitly mentioned those guidelines,[3] but it did not fare well when Shepardized. In fact, when that case was Shepardized, another case was found that explicitly said the EEOC guidelines on disability distinctions in health insurance were entitled to no deference, and that was the nicest thing that court said about the guidelines.[4] What has happened over the years is that the courts are more likely to give the insurance company wide latitude in determining how their policy is to be configured.[5] That said, in the area of insurance and the ADA, there have been some developments that bear discussing in this new edition. In particular, wellness plans are now the rage. It makes sense for employers to ensure that their employees are healthy and, consequently, keep costs down for the employer. However, people in the disability community are rightfully concerned that information given as part of the wellness program may be used against them at a later time or that the information will not be kept confidential. In light of that concern, what happens if you have a wellness program that penalizes employee for not participating? Does such a program violate the ADA?[6]

A case that addresses this question is *Seff v. Broward County*.[7] In that case, Broward County had a group health insurance plan.[8] That plan contained two components, a biometric screening and an online health risk assessment questionnaire.[9] That information was used to identify employees who had asthma, hypertension, diabetes, congestive heart failure, or kidney disease.[10] Anybody found to be suffering from one of those diseases received the opportunity to participate in a disease management coaching program, after the completion of which they became eligible to receive co-pay waivers for certain medications.[11] To increase participation in the wellness program, Broward imposed a $20 charge beginning in April 2010 on each biweekly paycheck issued to employees who had enrolled in the group health insurance plan but refused to participate in the employee wellness program.[12] The plaintiff, who incurred the charges on his paycheck from June 2010 until January 2011, filed a class-action lawsuit alleging that the biometric screening in the online questionnaire violated the ADA's prohibition on non-voluntary medical examination and disability-related inquiries.[13] The district court found that the employee wellness program fell within the ADA's safe harbor provision and granted summary judgment for the employer, and the plaintiff appealed.[14]

In affirming the lower court's decision, the U.S. Court of Appeals for the Eleventh Circuit reasoned as follows. First, the court noted that the ADA contained a safe harbor. That is, the ADA itself says that it shall not be construed as prohibiting an entity subject to the ADA from establishing, sponsoring, observing, or administering the terms of a bona fide benefit plan that are based on underwriting risks, classifying risks for administering such risks in a way that is consistent with state law.[15] Second, the court said that there is no authority out there that suggests an employee wellness program had to be explicitly identified in a benefit plan's written documents to allow it to qualify for the safe harbor.[16] Third, the wellness program was part of the contract to provide county employees with a group health plan, and that program was only available to group plan enrollees.[17] Finally, Broward presented the program as part of this group plan in at least two employee handouts.[18] Therefore, the court found that all these factors indicated that the wellness plan fell within the safe harbor.[19]

While the preceding paragraph is certainly true, if the wellness plan is not careful, such a provision may well violate the Genetic Information Nondiscrimination Act.[20] That law makes it unlawful for an employer with 15 or more employees either: 1) to fail or refuse to hire, or to discharge, any employee, or otherwise discriminate against an employee with respect to the compensation, terms, conditions, or privileges of employment of the employee because of the employee's genetic information; 2) or to limit, segregate, or classify employees in such a way that it deprives or tends to deprive the employee of employment opportunities or otherwise adversely affect the status of the employee because of his or her genetic information.[21]

The Genetic Information Nondiscrimination Act also applies to employment agencies and training programs (unions). In addition to the above prohibitions, the Act also prohibits them from causing or attempting to cause an employer to discriminate against persons with a genetic history.[22] A private cause of action does exist, and administrative remedies must be exhausted first.[23] Violations can result in injunctive relief, damages, and attorneys' fees.[24] Finally, the Genetic Nondiscrimination Act specifically excludes a disparate impact cause of action, though the law does not rule out such a cause of action in the future, depending on what a commission devoted to that subject finds after studying the relevant data.[25]

With respect to inquiring about genetic information, including as part of a voluntary wellness program, an entity subject to the Genetic Information Nondiscrimination Act can neither require the individual to provide genetic information nor penalize that individual who chooses not to provide it.[26] Any such consent by the individual to provide that information must be knowing, voluntary, and in writing.[27] The authorization form for giving such consent must meet specific requirements.[28] Finally, with respect to a medical exam related to whether the person can perform the essential functions of the job, the employer is under an obligation to tell the health-care provider not to collect genetic information, including family medical history, as part of that medical examination.[29] The employer is also obligated to take additional reasonable measures within its control once it has been learned that genetic information is being requested or required.[30]

The Genetic Information Nondiscrimination Act is an important development because people with genetic conditions now have protections. Under the ADA as it existed prior to the amendments, it simply wasn't clear whether genetic conditions would be considered a disability because it is entirely possible that a genetic condition might not, at a given moment in time, substantially limit a major life activity. Are genetic conditions covered under the ADA as amended? They may be, for two reasons. First, the definition of a major life activity now includes major bodily functions, which is defined quite extensively.[31] Second, the ADAAA specifically states that an impairment that is episodic or in remission is a disability if it would substantially limit a major life activity when active.[32] Third, for the "regarded as" prong to apply, all the plaintiff now has to show under the amendments is that the employer perceived a physical or mental impairment; it is no longer necessary for the plaintiff to show that the employer also perceived a substantial limitation on a major life activity.[33] Taking these three provisions together, an argument can be made that genetic conditions are a disability under the ADA as amended[34] as well as under the Rehabilitation Act, since the two laws are to be construed in the same way.[35]

The fact that genetic discrimination may also lead to a cause of action under the Rehabilitation Act is very significant, particularly where the plaintiff is a federal employee. The Genetic Information Nondiscrimination Act does not apply to federal employees with respect to employment discrimination;[36, 37] rather, they are subject to Executive Order 13145, signed by Bill Clinton.[38] In July of 2000, the EEOC issued a policy guidance on Executive Order 13145.[39] The Executive Order does not create any new substantive rights;[40] therefore, being able to pursue a cause of action under the Rehabilitation Act would be a critical point for any plaintiff suffering genetic discrimination by the federal government.

Before leaving the Genetic Information Nondiscrimination Act, retaliation must be discussed. As with the ADA, the Genetic Information Nondiscrimination Act allows a cause of action for retaliation. As discussed elsewhere in this book, with respect to the ADA, it is far from clear whether legal remedies are allowed for a retaliation claim. Can the same be said for retaliation claim under the Genetic Information Nondiscrimination Act? The answer to that question is far from clear. *Kramer v. Banc of America Securities LLC* specifically zeroed in on 42 U.S.C.A. § 1981a(a)(2), which contains a separate remedy section for disability discrimination;[41] no separate section for the Genetic Nondiscrimination Act exists in 42 U.S.C.A. § 1981a, nor does the act reference the disability discrimination remedy section of 42 U.S.C.A. § 1981a(a)(2).[42] Thus, it is entirely possible that the courts will hold that retaliation under the Genetic Information Nondiscrimination Act includes legal remedies, while continuing to hold, in many cases, that the ADA does not include legal remedies for retaliation claims. Such a distinction could not possibly have been intended by Congress, but nevertheless is a possibility based on the way the statutes read.

Notes

1. 42 U.S.C.A. at § 12112(a).
2. EEOC Interim Policy Guidance on ADA and Health Insurance.
3. *See* Anderson v. Gus Mayer Boston Store, 924 F. Supp. 763 (E.D. Tex. 1996).
4. Weyer v. Twentieth-Century-Fox Film Corp., 198 F.3d 1104, 1117 (9th Cir. 1999).
5. *See* Doe v. Mutual of Omaha Ins. Co., 179 F.3d 557 (7th Cir. 1999).
6. In addition to the ADA, employers and the entities that design their insurance plans are also going to have to be aware of the Affordable Care Act. The Department of Labor in May 2013 issued final rules stating that a wellness program must be reasonably designed—i.e., that has a reasonable chance of improving the health of, or preventing disease of, participating individuals and is not overly burdensome, is not a substitute for discrimination based on a health factor, and is not highly suspect in the method chosen to promote health or prevent disease (http://www.dol.gov/ebsa/pdf/workplacewellnessstudyfinalrule.pdf at 18, 89–90 (to appear at 29 C.F.R. § 2590.702(3)(iii))). The specific provisions of those regulations are beyond the scope of this book, though I do not rule out covering it in future editions.
7. Seff v. Broward County, 691 F.3d 1221 (11th Cir. 2012).
8. *Id.* at 1222.
9. *Id.*
10. *Id.*
11. *Id.*
12. *Id.*

13. *Id.*
14. *Id.*
15. *Id.* at 1223.
16. *Id.* at 1224.
17. *Id.*
18. *Id.*
19. *Id.*
20. 42 U.S.C. § 2000ff (WL, current through Pub. L. 113-9 (excluding Pub. L. 113-4), approved May 1, 2013).As mentioned above, also needing to be considered are the final rules implementing the Affordable Care Act as well. Those rules can be found at http://www.dol.gov/ebsa/pdf/workplacewellnessstudyfinalrule.pdf (to appear at 29 C.F.R. § 2590).
21. 42 U.S.C.A. § 2000ff-1 (West, current through Pub. L. 113-9 (excluding Pub. L. 113-4), approved May 1, 2013).
22. 42 U.S.C.A. §§ 2000ff-2, 4 (WL, current through Pub. L. 113-9 (excluding Pub. L. 113-4), approved May 1, 2013).
23. Wright v. StoneMor Partners LLP, 2012 WL 4006120, *3 (W.D. N.C. Sept. 12, 2012).
24. 42 U.S.C.A. § 2000ff-6(a)(1), § 2000ff-6 (WL, current through Pub. L. 113-9 (excluding Pub. L. 113-4), approved May 1, 2013). 2000ff-6(a)(1) specifically references the EEOC and the Civil Rights Act of 1964, while 2000ff-6 specifically references 42 U.S.C.A. §§ 1981a and 1988, which are the statutes for allowing attorneys' fees and costs in civil rights actions.
25. 42 U.S.C.A. § 2000ff-7(a) (WL, current through Pub. L. 113-9 (excluding Pub. L. 113-4), approved May 1, 2013).
26. 29 C.F.R. § 1635.89(b)(2)(i)(A) (WL, current through May 30, 2013; 78 Fed. Reg. 32,362).
27. 29 C.F.R. § 1635.8(b)(2)(i)(B) (WL, current through May 30, 2013; 78 Fed. Reg. 32,362).
28. *Id.*
29. 29 C.F.R. § 1635.8(d) (WL, current through May 30, 2013; 78 Fed. Reg. 32,362).
30. *Id.*
31. *See* 42 U.S.C.A. at § 12102(2)(B).
32. 42 U.S.C.A. at § 12102(4)(D).
33. *See* 42 U.S.C.A. at § 12102(3)(A).
34. The Genetic Information Nondiscrimination Act itself seems to indicate that genetic conditions could well be a covered disability under the ADA when it references both the ADA and the Rehabilitation Act as laws that provide equal or greater protection to an individual who might be covered under the Genetic Information Nondiscrimination Act. *See* 42 U.S.C. § 2000ff-8(a)(1) (WL, current through Pub. L. 113-9 (excluding Pub. L. 113-4), approved May 1, 2013).

35. *See* 29 U.S.C.A. § 705(9)(B), (20)(B) (WL, current through Pub. L. 113-9 (excluding Pub. L. 113-4), approved May 1, 2013).
36. 42 U.S.C.A. § 2000ff(2)(B)(i) says that an employer is defined as under 42 U.S.C.A. § 2000e(b), which specifically excludes the federal government from the definition. *See* 42 U.S.C.A. §2000e(b) (WL, current through Pub. L. 113-9 (excluding Pub. L. 113-4), approved May 1, 2013).
37. Different rules apply with respect to the health insurance policy themselves. The Genetic Information Nondiscrimination Act does apply to the federal government in that way. *See* 42 U.S.C.A. § 300gg-1(e) (WL, current through Pub. L. 113-9 (excluding Pub. L. 113-4), approved May 1, 2013).
38. E.O. 13,145, 65 Fed. Reg. 6877 (Feb. 8, 2000).
39. Appx. F15, EEOC Policy Guidance on Executive Order 13145: To Prohibit Discrimination in Federal Employment Based on Genetic Information (EEOC Notice No. 915.002, July 26, 2000), *reprinted in* Charles Richey, 2 Manual on Employment Discrimination, Appx. F15 (database updated June 2009).
40. E.O. 13,145 at § 1-403, 65 Fed. Reg. 6877 (Feb. 8, 2000); *see also* Appx. F15, EEOC Policy Guidance on Executive Order 13145: To Prohibit Discrimination in Federal Employment Based on Genetic Information (EEOC Notice No. 915.002, July 26, 2000), *reprinted in* Charles Richey, 2 Manual on Employment Discrimination, Appx. F15 at VI (database updated June 2009).
41. *See* Kramer v. Banc of America Securities LLC, 355 F.3d 961, 965 (7th Cir. 2004); *see also* 42 U.S.C.A. § 1981a(a)(2) (WL current through Pub. L. 113-9 (excluding Pub. L. 113-4), approved May 1, 2013).
42. *See* 42 U.S.C.A. at § 1981a.

ADA and the Public Sector (Title II of the ADA)

7

EMPLOYMENT CONCERNS

TITLE II OF THE ADA applies to governmental entities, including employment, programs, activities, and benefits.[1] Title II is enforced not by the EEOC but by the Department of Justice (DOJ).[2] If a governmental entity has more than 15 employees and a discrimination suit is filed against it, is the governmental entity subject to Title I, Title II, or both? For example, if an agency has more than 15 employees, the EEOC regulations apply, although the DOJ has enforcement authority.[3] One lower court did hold that Title II applied to employment; however, that decision was reversed by the Eleventh Circuit on appeal.[4]

Title II of the ADA also imposes some additional requirements on the governmental employer. For example, if the public entity has more than 50 employees, it must have an internal grievance procedure for handling complaints of disability-based discrimination and a designated person to be the ADA coordinator.[5] Since many public entities already have a 504 coordinator because they receive federal funds, it is only natural to make that person the ADA coordinator as well.

While a grievance procedure is mandated for governmental entities of more than 50 employees, an entity with less than 50 employees may elect to have such a procedure in order to prevent problems. Having the procedure in place gives the entity a chance to resolve a dispute before it escalates into protracted litigation. It also gives the entity the chance to discover the concerns of the aggrieved employee and allows the plaintiff to vent his or her feelings. Finally, it may represent the only chance for the entity to head off a courtroom battle, because a person does have a private cause of action under Title II of the ADA,[6] and a plaintiff need not exhaust administrative remedies before filing suit.[7]

PROGRAM ACCESSIBILITY

A reading of the Title II regulations reveals that there is virtually nothing about employment contained in them. Instead, the focus of the regulations is on accessing governmental programs and activities. Thus, when dealing with the right of a person with a disability to access a governmental entity, these questions must be answered:

1) Does the person have a disability as defined by the ADA?
2) Is the person qualified?

If the answer to both is yes, one must determine whether the governmental program or activity is readily accessible to the individual with the particular disability.

Since the definition of a disability is the same under all Titles of the ADA, the second question can be considered first. Under Title II of the ADA, "qualified" has a different meaning than it does under Title I. In the context of Title II, a person with a disabling condition or disability is deemed to be qualified if he or she can, with or without reasonable modifications to rules, policies, or practices; the removal of architectural, communication, or transportation barriers; or the provision of auxiliary aids and services, meet the essential eligibility requirements for the receipt of services or the participation in programs or activities provided by a public entity.[8] This definition raises two more very significant questions: What is a reasonable modification, and what constitutes a program?

A reasonable modification to a program, benefit, or activity is whatever does not constitute an undue burden or a fundamental alteration in the program.[9] Proving an undue burden is very difficult,[10] and thus the governmental entity might be more successful arguing that the program would be fundamentally altered by the needed accommodation. The governmental entity is under a powerful disincentive to take the position that a modification would be an undue burden because where one exists, the CEO of the public entity must certify as such, and then all changes up to the point of undue burden must be paid for by the public entity.[11]

Program accessibility is a critical concept to Title II of the ADA. Title II analysis frequently depends on the definition of a *program* for two reasons. First, a Title II entity does not have to make an accommodation if it will fundamentally alter the program.[12] Second, under Title II of the ADA, existing facilities built before January 26, 1992, do not have to be accessible; only the program does.[13] For example, an English class is offered on the second floor of a building built before 1992 with no elevator. A mobility-impaired person wants to take that class. There is no reason why that class or an identical one taught by a different instructor could not be offered at an accessible location. That said, it pays to remember that facilities built after the effective date of the ADA must be readily accessible to persons with disabilities.[14] Thus, the question becomes what constitutes a program. As a preventive law measure, consider the following when trying to determine this issue:

1. Review the self-evaluation plan (a document that assesses all of a Title II entity's programs and reviews their accessibility) to see the governmental entity's view of what a program is.
2. Consider the commonalities in the delivery of the program's service, as programs are often built around a common set of services to a defined set of clientele.
3. Consider the common usage of the term *program* to the people in the governmental entity; what their particular program is may be fairly obvious to them. For example, in the mental health and intellectual disabilities field, it is common to have such programs as case management, cooperative living, client-support services, mental retardation residential care, etc., and everyone in the profession understands precisely what is being referred to.

4. Consult competent legal counsel to help determine what constitutes a program.

FOCUS ON HIGHER EDUCATION

If your college or university is a public entity, it is subject to Title II of the ADA. As mentioned earlier, with respect to Title II, a person is considered qualified if he or she can, with or without reasonable modifications to rules, policies, or practices; the removal of architectural, communication, or transportation barriers; or the provision of auxiliary aids and services, meet the essential eligibility requirements for receiving services for participating in programs or activities provided by the public entity.[15] It becomes terribly problematic trying to determine whether a person can meet the essential eligibility requirements of the program with or without reasonable accommodations if you do not know what the essential eligibility requirements are.

If your college is not a public entity, then it is subject to Title III of the ADA. Title III does not have the "otherwise qualified" concept, at least not explicitly. However, an entity subject to Title III of the ADA does not have to make an accommodation that would fundamentally alter the nature of the program or activity.[16] Therefore, while Title III may not have the "otherwise qualified," or "qualified" language, the analysis is the same, because how can you determine whether something is being fundamentally altered if you do not know what the essential nature of the business and its programs or activities are?

Also, when it comes to colleges and universities, almost all of them take federal funds. As such, their operations are subject to § 504 of the Rehabilitation Act, which requires that an entity receiving federal funds has their programs and activities be accessible to persons with disabilities.[17] Fortunately, the ADA is based in large part on § 504 of the Rehabilitation Act, and therefore, with some exceptions, the principles of compliance are the same for the ADA and for § 504 of the Rehabilitation Act.

Thus, how do you go about figuring out what your program is? Consider the following steps:

1. Set up a departmental committee to assess what are the essential eligibility requirements of the program. What are the fundamental things that the department wants the student to be able to do with respect to that course of study?
2. Consult with legal counsel to make sure that those essential eligibility requirements are fundamental and that they do not create a situation in which persons with disabilities are being screened out.
3. Have the committee, in conjunction with legal counsel, draw up the essential eligibility requirements and have them submitted to the department for a vote.
4. Once the department has signed off, make sure the university or college disability services department has a copy of those essential eligibility requirements. If, at that department vote, changes are made to the essential eligibility requirements, repeat steps 2 (legal counsel) and 3 (departmental vote), above.
5. Make sure those essential eligibility requirements are known to all stakeholders throughout the college and university system.

In doing this, everybody's role needs to be clear. That is, the department members are the subject matter experts and legal counsel is responsible for making sure the department is comfortable with what is fundamental and for ensuring that the language of the requirements does not screen out persons with disabilities. It is not for legal counsel to get involved as a subject matter expert.

It is quite conceivable that this process will involve a program designed to train people for professional fields. For example, nursing, pharmacy, and paralegal immediately come to mind. In such situations, a common mistake is to focus on whether that person will be able to get a job in their field, or whether they will be able to do the particular job they are training for, rather than on the program of study itself. Approaching it this way is a mistake for several reasons. It is entirely possible that a person with a disability is studying a subject just because he or she is interested in it, and has no intention of actually working in the field. While that may not happen often, it does happen.

Also, the focus of the university or college is giving students necessary training to be able to go into that profession. Whether they can actually perform in that profession beyond the academic environment is to be determined by others at a later time (many of those entities, as discussed in this book, would be subject to Title I of the ADA).

Finally, if the college or university makes the assumption that a person with a disability is not going to be able to participate in that profession and uses that as a reason to dismiss the student from the program, the college or university may be exposing itself to a claim of disability discrimination.[18]

THE CRITICAL NATURE OF ASSESSING THE PROGRAM AND ITS ESSENTIAL REQUIREMENTS

How a program is defined and its essential eligibility requirements can be critical to the outcome of a case. That was certainly true in *Concerned Parents to Save Dreher Park Center v. City of W. Palm Beach*[19] and in *Easley v. Snider*.[20]

In *Concerned Parents*, the city of West Palm Beach had established state-of-the-art recreational facilities, the Dreher Park Center, for persons with disabilities living in West Palm Beach and in the surrounding area.[21] Due to poor fiscal management, budget cuts became necessary, and the city elected to eliminate the recreational facilities.[22] A group of concerned parents banded together and sought a preliminary injunction under Title II of the ADA and under the Florida Constitution to prohibit the city from terminating the recreation programs.[23]

Two issues were before the court: What was the program at issue, and what were the essential eligibility requirements of that program? The court found that the program was the entire network of activities and services, and declined to adopt a more specific definition of programs that involved physical abilities.[24] The court also said the essential eligibility requirement for the program as defined above was simply the request for the benefits of the program.[25] With the program and the essential eligibility requirements thus determined, the court quite logically held that the city's action denied persons with disabilities access to the city's program and violated the ADA.[26]

Finally, the court in *Dreher* did not accept two defenses made by the city. First, the city claimed that it was important that the discrimination was not intentional.[27] The court dismissed that argument by saying intent was not the issue; the issue was whether the decision to terminate the programs for persons with disabilities had the effect of discriminating against them.[28] Second, the city said its decision was in keeping with the spirit of the ADA, as it would enable everyone to participate in an integrated setting.[29] The court dismissed that argument as well by noting that the ADA requires that the setting be the most appropriate for persons with disabilities and that the "ADA contemplates separate programming where necessary to provide qualified individuals with disabilities the aids and benefits of services that are as effective as those provided to others."[30]

The lesson from *Dreher* is that plaintiff lawyers need to define the program as broadly as possible, while defense lawyers need to define it as narrowly as possible.

Easley v. Snider is a bit different from *Dreher*. In *Easley*, the program was very clear, but the issues were the program's essential eligibility requirements and whether those requirements were a subterfuge for discrimination. In *Easley*, two persons with disabilities sought an injunction against the state of Pennsylvania for denying their inclusion in an attendant care program.[31] The rules of the program required that the participants be mentally alert.[32] Neither plaintiff met this requirement, and they brought suit challenging the requirement as being discriminatory in violation of the ADA.[33]

The plaintiffs won at the district court level, and the state of Pennsylvania appealed. The Third Circuit reversed.[34] In its ruling, the court noted that the rules for the program demanded that the person who participates in the program be able to do four things, two of which were critical: be capable of selecting, supervising and, if needed, firing an attendant, and be capable of managing their own financial and legal affairs.[35]

The court then turned to the policies of the program stated by the Pennsylvania General Assembly. Again, two of those findings are relevant in this discussion:

1. Priority recipients of attendant care services under this Act shall be those mentally alert but severely physically disabled who are at the greatest risk of being in an institutional setting; and
2. Recipients of attendant care have the right to make decisions about, direct the provision of, and control their attendant care services. This includes but is not limited to hiring, training, managing, paying, and firing of an attendant.[36]

Given the parameters of the program, the court went on to note that eliminating a mental alertness requirement would fundamentally alter the very nature of the program, which the ADA does not require.[37]

Finally, the court stated that it would consider, in determining if a program of a governmental entity discriminates, whether the plaintiff meets the program's requirements in spite of the disability and whether a reasonable accommodation could allow that person to receive the program's essential benefits.[38] Further, when determining whether an accommodation would allow the applicant to receive the benefit, the court is not to rely solely on the stated benefits, because programs may attempt to define the benefit in a way that effectively denies otherwise-qualified disabled individuals the access to which they are entitled.[39] The language revealing skepticism about relying on stated benefits is very significant, because in cases arising under the Rehabilitation Act of 1973, it was not unusual for courts to give deference to governmental entities in determining what the program was.[40]

ACTIVITY ACCESSIBILITY

High School Extracurricular Activity

Not all cases involving Title II concern access to a program. They may deal with access to an activity. Consider this scenario.

A public high school student has cerebral palsy. Her older sister is a cheerleader. Her sister is able to convince the school to allow the student with cerebral palsy to join the cheerleading squad as an honorary cheerleader. The student is made a part of the team and completes her duties. Fast-forward to the next year: The older sister has graduated and the younger girl wants to be a cheerleader again. The school says no, since she can't do the things that cheerleaders do—gymnastics, tumbling, etc. She brings suit under the ADA.[41]

As this is a public high school, the applicable section of the ADA is Title II, which applies to governmental entities, including employment, its programs, *activities,* and benefits.[42] In analyzing this situation, several questions must be asked. Does the cheerleader have a disability? Cerebral palsy is certainly a disability, because it is a physical impairment that substantially limits, even under *Toyota Motor*, various major life activities, including speech and walking. Also, due to the nature of the disability, mitigating measures are not an issue. Is cheerleading an activity? Certainly, it is common to think of cheerleading as one of the activities offered by the school. Is the cheerleader otherwise qualified? In light of the definition of *qualified*[43] under Title II of the ADA, one must determine the essential eligibility requirements of the activity. Is it tumbling? Cheering? Dancing?

The essential eligibility requirements of cheerleading at this school could only be determined through discovery. Not all cheerleading units have the same requirements. Some units focus on gymnastics, while others focus predominantly on cheering. A videotape of the cheerleading unit in action over the course of the prior season would be very helpful. Such a videotape probably exists, because most football teams tape their games. In assessing the essential eligibility requirements, it is instructive to first assess what is fundamental to carrying out that activity. In that way, determining essential eligibility requirements of an activity is analogous to determining the essential functions of a job.

Once the "essential functions"—essential eligibility requirements—of cheerleading have been determined, the next question is whether the cheerleader is able to meet those requirements with or without reasonable modification in the activity. If tumbling is essential to the cheering activity, there is probably no reasonable modification that can be put into place. But if cheering is essential to the cheering activity, there are probably any number of reasonable modifications that can be made.

Even if gymnastics is an essential eligibility requirement of cheering at this school, the matter is not necessarily resolved. It is entirely possible that the plaintiff might be able to do the essential activities with or without reasonable modifications if she were in a different section of the cheerleading unit—for example, a pom pom squad.

This case has an interesting postscript. The case settled, and the cheerleader was allowed to try out without performing the tumbling and gymnastics part. The settlement raises the issue of why the school district allowed the cheerleader to try out without completing the tumbling and gymnastic requirements, because if tumbling and gymnastics were an essential eligibility requirement of cheering at the school, the school district was under no obligation to modify the tryouts.[44] A different conclusion would be in order if tumbling were a marginal function of cheering at this school.[45] In the latter case, a waiver of these tryout requirements would have certainly been appropriate. Of course, it is entirely possible that other factors entered into the settlement, such as fear of losing at trial, the cost of litigation, and the like.

VOTING

Here's another scenario to consider. We don't normally think of voting as an activity, but it is. What if, due to a disability, you are unable to make it to the voting booth to vote? Would the voting authorities have to modify the system to enable you to vote? Of course, it would depend on what the modifications were, but it is important to note that the right to vote is a fundamental right. A case that discusses this is *Mooneyhand v. Husted*.[46] In this case, the plaintiff was a registered voter in Darke County, Ohio.[47] On October 30, 2012, she was hospitalized at the Northwest Ohio Psychiatric Hospital in Toledo, located in Lucas County, Ohio.[48] She wanted to vote but realized that she would not be able to leave the hospital to vote in person in the 2012 general election.[49] Accordingly, on October 31, 2012, with the assistance of the client rights advocate at the hospital, she made an application for an absentee ballot to the Darke County Board of Elections.[50]

When the ballot did not come in the mail by November 6, she contacted Disability Rights Ohio's voting hotline to explain her situation.[51] Disability Rights Ohio then contacted the director of the Darke County Board of Elections.[52] Disability Rights Ohio suggested that the Darke County Board of Elections fax or e-mail a ballot to the Lucas County Board of Elections, whereupon two officials from that board could then hand-deliver the ballot to the plaintiff at the hospital.[53] The Darke County Board of Elections then consulted with election counsel with the Ohio Secretary of State's office, who informed them that no provision in the Ohio election law allowed for the requested accommodation.[54] Disability Rights Ohio also contacted the Secretary of State's office directly, which informed Disability Rights that no accommodation would be made.[55] Disability Rights Ohio then filed a complaint and motion for a temporary restraining order (TRO) on the plaintiff's behalf, alleging that by refusing to make the reasonable modifications to policies and procedures to enable the plaintiff to vote in the general election, the Darke County Board of elections and the Ohio Secretary of State had discriminated against the plaintiff because of her disability in violation of the ADA and section 504 of the Rehabilitation Act of 1973.[56]

The plaintiff did receive her ballot in the mail on November 7. During a conference call the same day, the court directed the plaintiff to complete the absentee ballot and send it to the Darke County Board of Elections. and directed the board to accept it as a provisional ballot to be kept separate from the other absentee and provisional ballots pending a ruling on the motion for the TRO.[57]

In granting the motion for TRO, the southern district of Ohio reasoned as follows.

First, the court agreed that to carry out the modification to enable the plaintiff to vote required a slight accommodation to existing voting laws in the state of Ohio.[58] However, since the state must protect federally guaranteed civil rights as zealously as a federal court, the state law conflicted with federal law, in this case the ADA and the Rehabilitation Act, and under the Supremacy Clause, it is the state law that must be adjusted.[59]

Second, the modification proposed by the plaintiff would not have fundamentally altered the nature of the voting process.[60]

Third, the court, citing to federal regulations, said that the plaintiff's request for reasonable modification had to be granted unless that modification would fundamentally alter the nature of the service program or activity.[61]

Fourth, it could hardly be said that such a fundamental alteration would have occurred with the requested modification, since Ohio law already allows local boards of election to send absentee ballots by fax, e-mail, or Internet to members of the military and overseas voters.[62] Ohio law also permitted local board of elections members to hand-deliver absentee ballot to a person who is disabled or confined.[63]

Fifth, plaintiff's request that the Darke County Board of Election fax or e-mail or absentee ballot to the Lucas County Board of Elections, whereupon they would personally deliver it to her, watch her complete it, and return it to the Darke County Board of Elections via fax or e-mail, would be no more burdensome than already established procedures for personal delivery of an absentee ballot to a disabled or confined voter.[64]

Finally, the Secretary of State and the Darke County Board of Elections argued that allowing her to cast their vote a day late when she already knew the projected outcome of the election diluted the votes of people who already cast their ballots in a timely manner.[65] The court was having none of it, since it was the plaintiff who had her equal opportunity to exercise a right to vote denied because of her disability.[66]

In short, when it comes to accessing the programs and activities of governmental entities, the practitioner must keep in mind programs and how those programs are configured, and remember that activities of the governmental entity must be accessible as well.

ZONING

Consider the following:

> An entity runs a substance abuse program. It wants to move to a downtown location, which causes an uproar in the surrounding community. At the preliminary hearing, the application for the zoning variance is approved, but it is later appealed. The appellate level that hears the zoning request succumbs to political pressure and denies the variance. The entity sues, alleging that the action of denying the zoning variance violates Title II of the ADA.

This hypothetical scenario was the fact pattern in *Innovative Health System v. City of White Plains*, a case that came before the Second Circuit Court of Appeals.[67] The issues before the court were twofold: First, were decisions made pursuant to zoning regulations subject to suit under the ADA? Second, could an entity serving persons with disabilities, rather than just the persons with disabilities being served, bring suit for violations of Title II of the ADA?

Turning to the first issue, the Second Circuit noted, as discussed earlier, that the ADA does not define "services, programs, or activities."[68] However, the court looked for guidance to Section 508 of the Rehabilitation Act, which defined a program or activity of a governmental entity as all of the operations of the specific entities.[69] The court also looked to the dictionary definition of the term *activity*, which described it as a natural or normal function of operation.[70] Finally, the court looked to the *Department of Justice Technical Assistance Manual* and to the Preamble to the DOJ regulations on Title II of the ADA, which specifically mentioned zoning as one of the activities covered under Title II.[71]

With regard to the second issue, the Second Circuit held that Title II of the ADA specifically allows any person alleging discrimination on the basis of disability to bring suit, and that such language was consistent with congressional intent to allow private actions as broadly as possible under the U.S. Constitution.[72]

Having found that the service provider could bring the suit and that zoning is subject to Title II of the ADA, the court held that, based on the evidence of the public hearings, the denial of the zoning variance was nothing more than discrimination based on disability due to stereotypical attitudes.[73]

In such a situation, does a public entity have any defenses? It does indeed. If the public entity can show that the individuals possess a significant risk to the health or safety of the community and that no reasonable modification exists that would counteract the risk, then the people bringing the suit would not be protected by the ADA as they would no longer be qualified.[74] In essence, this is the same analysis as assessing whether a person is a direct threat under Title I of the ADA.[75] In deciding whether significant risks exist, one court looked to the nature, duration, and severity of the risks as well as the probability that potential injury would actually occur.[76] Legitimate safety concerns are okay, but not if those concerns are based on the perceived harm as a result of stereotypes and generalized fears.[77] That is, the risks must be serious in nature and more than hypothetical.[78]

What if a person with a disability wants to use property that he or she owns in a way that conflicts with the zoning ordinance? Does the public entity responsible for the zoning ordinance have to consider some kind of waiver or modification of that zoning ordinance to comply with the ADA? This was exactly the case in *Kulin v. Deschutes County*.[79]

In *Kulin*, the plaintiff was a severely disabled individual who supported himself and his family by operating a business on his residential property.[80] This business operated on a five-acre lot the plaintiff purchased in 1998.[81] The plaintiff had retinitis pigmentosa since birth and was legally blind.[82] He also had sustained permanent and disabling leg injuries in an automobile accident when he was 12.[83] Finally, he also suffered from low- and mid-back pain as well as neck pain as the result of the severe back injury that he sustained in that accident.[84]

Since owning the five-acre lot that he purchased in 1998, the plaintiff had made several improvements to the property, including the construction of a 900-square-foot residential garage in 2001; the construction of a 1,700-square-foot barn/shop in 2004; and the construction of a 4,940-square-foot warehouse in 2006.[85] The plaintiff completed each of these improvements only after obtaining planning and building permits from the county (the defendant).[86]

On December 14, 2006, after constructing the warehouse at the cost of $120,000, the plaintiff received a notice of violation from the county asserting that the warehouse violated the county's home occupation code.[87] After receiving notice of the violation, the plaintiff contacted the county and advised them that he was blind and running a business as a home occupation on his property and asked what he needed to do to bring his business into compliance.[88] The county invited him to comply with the requirements or propose a text amendment to allow an exception for persons with disabilities.[89]

The plaintiff's attorney submitted a proposed amendment to authorize an exception to the home occupation code to accommodate persons with disabilities.[90] The county planning commission recommended that the board of commissioners approve an amendment to the home occupation code, but without the provision addressing accommodation for persons with disabilities. The plaintiff then filed a variance application with the county requesting an accommodation under the ADA.[91]

The home occupation ordinance prohibited a participant from having more than two employees on the property, and the home occupation could not occupy more than 35% of the combined floor area of the participant's dwelling, including an attached garage and one accessory structure.[92] The plaintiff requested that he be allowed a total of five employees, and that he be allowed to use the warehouse on his property to store inventory on approximately six times the normal amount of permitted floor area.[93] The matter went to a hearing officer, who decided that the variance request for additional square footage in which to store inventory should be denied and also approved only two of the three additional employees that the plaintiff had requested.[94] The plaintiff then filed suit under the ADA, alleging that the county violated Title II by failing to implement consultation and request mechanism, notice of protections, and grievance procedures; by proceeding in the matter with deliberate indifference; and by failing to grant the plaintiff's requested accommodations in their entirety.[95]

With respect to the first allegation, the court (District Court of Oregon, Judge Coffin, Magistrate Judge) said that the zoning process was sufficient to satisfy any ADA requirements pertaining to consultation, notice of protections, and grievance procedures.[96] With respect to deliberate indifference, that didn't work either, because the county agreed to comply with whatever the federal court determined was the proper way to resolve the dispute.[97]

The most interesting part of this case is how the court dealt with allegation number three, the denial of requested accommodations. First, the court noted that Title II of the ADA requires that a public entity make reasonable modifications in policies, practices, or procedures when necessary in order to avoid discrimination on the basis of disability unless it can demonstrate that the modification imposes an undue financial or administrative burden or fundamentally alters the nature of the service, program, or activity.[98]

Second, the court cited to the district court decision[99] in what would eventually become *PGA Tour v. Martin,*[100] *in* which the court said that just because the requested accommodation alters a substantial rule or regulation does not render that accommodation unreasonable or unduly burdensome.[101]

Third, the court, citing to a Ninth Circuit case, said that neutral policies on their face may be in fact discriminatory if their effect is to keep persons with disabilities from enjoying the benefits of services that by law must be available to them.[102] Accordingly, the plaintiff did not have to show intentional discrimination in order to prevail.[103]

Fourth, with respect to the three additional employees, court found that permitting a third additional employee was necessary because the plaintiff could not employ two replacement employees if he could not cover the cost of doing so.[104] That is, hiring a third employee would not otherwise be a factor but for the plaintiff's disability.[105] Accordingly, the third employee was related to the plaintiff's disability and was necessary if the plaintiff was to be allowed to participate in the home occupation program.[106]

Fifth, with respect to the increased storage space, the plaintiff argued that he had to maintain his business on-site as a home occupation because, due to his disabilities, it was the only occupation that allowed him to take frequent rest breaks so that he could work a full day as well as feel safe and comfortable, and that because he must maintain his business on-site, the increased storage space was necessary for him to have an equal opportunity to earn a living on his property.[107]

The county argued that the purpose of the ADA was to place persons with disabilities on an equal footing rather than to give them an unfair advantage by providing them with greater rights than individuals without disabilities, and that the plaintiff was seeking an unfair advantage.[108] The court disagreed, for several reasons. First, the court noted that while the plaintiff attempted to operate other businesses on his property, his current business was the only one that happened to be feasible for him given his disability.[109] Second, the court said that while it was necessary to work from home, he would not be able to do so if he could not earn a profit to support himself and his family.[110] Third, the plaintiff had been entirely upfront with the county throughout the time he made the improvements on his property.[111] Fourth, the operating characteristics of the plaintiff's business were compatible with the surrounding land uses and did not, and would not in the future, have any adverse impact on resource values and other uses on the surrounding owners' land because customers did not come to the property.[112] Fifth, the plaintiff's requested accommodation of increased storage space would not cause an undue financial or administrative burden for the county, nor would it undermine the purpose of the code.[113]

In particular, the court said that the county had engaged in a series of actions, or inactions, over the course of time that would make it unreasonable to deny the plaintiff the use of the warehouse.[114] The court also said that over the course of approximately 14 years, the plaintiff had cultivated his business on his property that allowed him to accommodate his disability, to be self-reliant, and to support his family, and therefore denying the use of the warehouse would come at a high human cost.[115] The court also noted that the impact of the requested accommodation on the surrounding agricultural land-use would be inconsequential.[116] That is, while merchandise is delivered to the plaintiff's property by one large truck every 60 days and picked up daily by UPS, all other business activities occurred entirely within the business structures.[117] Further, the county community development director said that the plaintiff's business impact on the home occupation program would be negligible or very minor.[118]

The court also noted that the county had initially approved construction of the warehouse by granting the plaintiff a permit and questioned why such approval was given if the county believed that the warehouse would negatively impact the land zoned for agricultural uses.[119] Finally, the defendant argued that granting the plaintiff the accommodation would be a slippery slope, but the court dismissed that idea, since the ADA is an individually based law requiring case-by-case analysis.[120] Therefore whether a requested accommodation was necessary and reasonable as as well as whether it would fundamentally alter the nature of any program would depend on the specific circumstances of the case.[121] Accordingly, the slippery slope argument failed.[122]

What can we take from this case? First, if a person has severe disabilities and has found a way to be self-sufficient, a court may view that very favorably. Second, an attorney dealing with zoning, when faced with a waiver of those requirements by a person with a disability, needs to consider (certainly, as a matter of good preventive law), whether granting such a waiver would negatively impact the purpose of the zoning requirements and should not stop at its facially neutral language. Also, the attorney needs to keep in mind that the "slippery slope" is no defense.

Finally, I find extremely interesting the court's reliance on the district court case in what became *PGA Tour v. Martin*. In particular, the district court decision was cited for the proposition that the fact a requested accommodation alters a substantive rule or regulation does not render it unreasonable or unduly burdensome.[123] However, the U.S. Supreme Court did not say this in its decision. Rather, its focus was that walking was not a fundamental aspect of the game of golf. Therefore, since walking was a marginal rule, it was possible to insist consistent with the ADA, that the rule be waived depending upon the individual circumstances.[124] That most certainly is not the same thing as what the *Kulin* court was relying on. In short, due to *Kulin*'s emphasis on the plaintiff's ability to be self-reliant and its reliance on the district court opinion in what became *PGA Tour v. Martin* when in fact the U.S. Supreme Court said something quite different, it would not surprise me to see more governmental entities fight requests from persons with disabilities for waivers of zoning requirements.

SOVEREIGN IMMUNITY

In the first edition of this book, I talked about sovereign immunity and what might or might not happen *vis-á-vis* the ADA. In the first edition,

I set forth several reasons why I thought the Supreme Court would hold that Congress properly waived sovereign immunity of the states under the ADA. Among the reasons I gave were: 1) the ADA waives sovereign immunity;[125] 2) the Supreme Court at the time the first edition went to press had considered several ADA cases. While none dealt with sovereign immunity, the cases were written as if waiving sovereign immunity were a possibility; and 3) the preamble to the ADA, which was quite sweeping.[126] One possible effect of that preamble would be to put persons with disabilities in a higher equal protection class, thereby justifying Congress to enact a comprehensive law from which the states could be sued for private damages. Was I right? With respect to employment matters, it did not work out that way; i.e., Congress did not properly waive sovereign immunity.[127] With respect to non-employment matters, whether sovereign immunity was effectively waived is subject to a case-by-case analysis.[128]

Before proceeding further, it is necessary to briefly cover the standards of review in equal protection jurisprudence. Equal protection jurisprudence has three different levels of review—strict scrutiny, intermediate scrutiny, and rational basis.[129] The highest level of review is race-based classifications, "suspect class."[130] The second level of review is gender-based classifications, an "intermediate level" of review.[131] The last level of review is "rational basis," i.e., for everyone else.[132]

The way the system works is that classification is everything. That is, if a group of people fall into a "suspect class," it is virtually impossible for the government's discrimination against that class to stand (a notable exception being the case that set forth the "suspect class" classification).[133] If a group of people fall into the intermediate review classification, i.e., gender, then it is possible for the government discrimination to stand, but there would have to be very good reasons to allow it to proceed.[134]

The final level of review is "rational basis." If a group of people fall into this level of review, the government discrimination will in all probability stand, because the law merely has to be one that a rational legislator would make.[135] Hence, the *more* discrimination a group of people has suffered (the higher class of review they fall in), the *more comprehensive* Congress can get in redressing the discrimination faced by that group.

With respect to sovereign immunity in employment, the controlling case is *Board of Trustees of University of Alabama v. Garrett (Garrett).*[136] In *Garrett*, two separate plaintiffs who worked for the state of Alabama, one as a nurse at the University of Alabama–Birmingham Hospital and the other as a security officer at the department of youth services, sought money damages under the ADA as a result of alleged discrimination based on their disabilities.[137] The issue before the court was whether these plaintiffs had the right to sue the state via a private cause of action for money damages.[138] The U.S. Supreme Court, in an opinion written by Chief Justice Rehnquist, reasoned as follows.

First, the court noted that the Eleventh Amendment applied to the situation where citizens of one state sue that state for money damages.[139] The Court also noted that to hold a waiver of sovereign immunity valid, it had to find that Congress was carrying out the enforcement provisions of section 5 of the Fourteenth Amendment to the U.S. Constitution.[140] Whether the enforcement provisions of section 5 of the Fourteenth Amendment are satisfied *vis-à-vis* a statutory scheme entirely depends on what equal protection class a plaintiff at issue falls in.[141]

Second, the Court cited two cases, *Cleburne v. Cleburne Living Center, Inc.*[142] and *Heller v. Doe*,[143] for the proposition that persons with disabilities were in the "rational basis class."[144] At this point, the plaintiffs effectively lost their case, because being in the rational basis class meant that the ADA statutory scheme was an overly comprehensive way to redress the wrongs faced by persons who fell within that class.[145] It is unfortunate that the Court relied on these two cases for the proposition that individuals with disabilities were in the rational basis class because neither case actually held as such. In *Cleburne*, it is true that the Court said there was no rational basis for the government to discriminate against an independent living center that wanted to locate in a particular area of town.[146] However, *Cleburne* can hardly be said to be a typical "rational basis" review case. In *Cleburne*, the Court concluded that there was no rational basis for the governmental action only after a searching discussion of how government had been quite aggressive in trying to serve the needs of persons with mental retardation.[147] In fact, Justice Marshall, in an opinion joined by Justices Brennan and Blackmun, where he concurred and dissented, makes the point that the Court's reasoning does not resemble rational basis review at all because far too much attention is paid in the opinion to the rights of persons with mental retardation and to mental retardation in general.[148] Justice Marshall thought it would be more accurate to call the level of review of the majority in *Cleburne* "second order rational basis."[149] Turning to *Heller*, the Court specifically noted that they were not asked to decide what equal protection class persons with disabilities fit in; rather, the parties had already stipulated that persons with disabilities were in the rational basis class.[150]

Third, the Court found that the legislative record of the ADA failed to show that the states had discriminated against persons with disabilities in employment in an irrational manner over time.[151, 152]

Finally, two other points are worth noting. First, the Court said municipalities were not immune from liability for a private cause of action seeking money damages, as they were not a sovereign.[153] Second, the Court noted their decision applied only to money damages and not to a plaintiff seeking equitable relief against the state.[154]

The other case dealing with sovereign immunity is *Tennessee v. Lane*.[155] *Lane* is, in some ways, hard to reconcile with *Garret*. That the outcome was different is entirely due to Justice O'Connor, as she was the only justice in the majority in both cases.

In *Lane*, two paraplegics sued the state of Tennessee for their inability to access courthouses.[156] One of the plaintiffs could not access the courthouse where he had to make an appearance for a criminal case he was involved in.[157] The other plaintiff was a stenographer and simply could not go to certain job assignments because they were not accessible to mobility-impaired individuals.[158] They brought suit against the state of Tennessee for money damages and equitable relief, alleging violations of the ADA.[159] The issue before the court was the same as the issue in *Garrett*, except the question of whether Congress properly waived sovereign immunity involved Title II of the ADA rather than Title I.[160]

In an opinion by Justice Stevens, the Supreme Court held that Congress did properly waive sovereign immunity of the states with respect to Title II of the ADA, but such a waiver depended on the facts of each individual case.[161] The justices took great pains to distinguish *Garrett* from *Lane*. First, they noted that Title II of the ADA seeks to enforce a variety of basic constitutional guarantees, which are subject to a more searching level of judicial review.[162] They then proceeded to note some of those rights, including access to the courts, the right to be present at all stages of the trial where the defendant's absence might frustrate the fairness of the proceeding, the right to afford civil litigants a meaningful opportunity to be heard by removing barriers to their full participation in judicial proceedings, the right of a criminal defendant to a jury composed of a fair cross-section of the community, and the right of the public to access criminal proceedings.[163]

Second, the Court said that Title II of the ADA was enacted against a backdrop of pervasive discrimination against people with disabilities in the administration of state services and programs, which included the systematic deprivation of fundamental rights.[164] Some of the fundamental rights that states have limited for people with disabilities included the right to vote, the right to marry, and the right to serve as jurors.[165] The Court also noted the unconstitutional treatment of persons with disabilities by state agencies in many different settings, including unjustified commitment, abuse and neglect of persons with disabilities committed to state mental health hospitals, and irrational discrimination in zoning decisions.[166] Finally, the Court noted that the decisions of other courts document a pattern of unequal treatment in the administration of many kinds of public services, programs, and activities, such as the penal system, public education, and voting.[167]

Third, the Court mentioned it recently had decided *Nevada Department of Human Resources v. Hibbs*, 538 U.S. 721 (2003),[168] where it held that the Family and Medical Leave Act waived sovereign immunity of the states, and that the record of constitutional violations in *Lane* far exceeded the record in Hibbs.[169] This led the Court to conclude that where basic rights are involved, the standard of review should be at least as searching, if not more searching, than the review for sex-based classifications.[170] In short, the Court concluded that Title II of the ADA was not out of proportion to the harm meant to be redressed, and therefore sovereign immunity was properly waived.[171]

The next portion of *Lane* is unprecedented. The Court said there was nothing in the case law that required the Court to consider Title II of the ADA as a whole with respect to what equal protection class persons with disabilities fall in.[172] After making this statement, the Court holds that the ADA is proper legislation *vis-à-vis* the Enforcement Clause of the Fourteenth Amendment to the U.S. Constitution with respect to judicial services, noting a long history of unequal treatment in the administration of judicial services for those with disabilities, despite legislative efforts to remedy the problem.[173]

Finally, the very last paragraph of the majority opinion concludes that Title II of the ADA as it applies to the class of cases pertaining to the *fundamental right* (emphasis added) of access to the court is a valid exercise of the Enforcement Clause of the Fourteenth Amendment, and therefore, sovereign immunity was properly waived.[174]

So where does this leave us? The Supreme Court in *Lane* at various points in the majority opinion uses the terms "basic constitutional guarantees,"[175] "basic rights,"[176] "class of cases implicating judicial services,"[177] and "fundamental rights."[178] Clearly, the most narrow way to read *Lane* is to say that it applies only where a case involves judicial services. Yet a close reading of the decision suggests that *Lane* must cover other rights as well because of its reasoning, discussed above, and the broad rights terminology used in the case. In short, it would seem disability rights advocates have an opening under *Lane* to argue that sovereign immunity is waived regardless of whether a state consents whenever you have rights involving "basic constitutional guarantees," "basic rights," or "fundamental rights." In any event, to this author's knowledge, it is unprecedented for a class of people in equal protection jurisprudence to have their classification vary depending on the facts of the case.

It appeared that the U.S. Supreme Court would address the question of how far the waiver of sovereign immunity *vis-à-vis* Title II extended when it took the case of *United States v. Georgia*.[179] While it is true that the Supreme Court has already decided that states can be sued for violating Title II of the ADA with respect to prisons, it had not decided whether such suits could seek money damages.[180] The *United States v. Georgia* decision could have well turned on just how far the Court wanted to go in interpreting *Lane*. Would the justices stick to judicial services, or would they explore the case law pertaining to "basic constitutional guarantees," "basic rights," or "fundamental rights"? It turns out there were two surprises in the decision handed down by the Supreme Court in this case. First, it was unanimous.[181] Second, it sidestepped these issues entirely by holding that sovereign immunity was waived under Title II of the ADA where the alleged violation also rose to the level of a constitutional violation.[182] It reserved for a later date how the case-by-case analysis of Title II set forth in *Lane* might play itself out.[183]

As mentioned above, *Lane* leaves open as to how sovereign immunity might work with respect to other situations involving access to governmental entities. For example, would a public university or public college be able to claim sovereign immunity when sued for violation of Title II of the ADA?[184] A case that addressed this is *Doe v. Board of Regents of the University of Nebraska.*[185] In this case, a medical student who was granted a leave of absence to receive treatment for depression, insomnia, and anxiety was eventually removed from the medical school after he returned from that leave and things continued to not go well.[186] He brought suit alleging fraudulent concealment, disability discrimination, violation of his due process rights, and breach of contract.[187]

The court had several issues before it, but for our purposes the issue to focus on is whether the University of Nebraska could successfully claim immunity under the Eleventh Amendment to the plaintiff's suit for disability discrimination. There are essentially two questions involved. First, is education a fundamental right? Second, if not, does that mean that the state or an arm of the state automatically gets to claim sovereign immunity?

With respect to whether education is a fundamental right, the Nebraska Supreme Court said that it was not.[188] However, that does not answer the question as to whether the state still has the right to claim sovereign immunity. The Nebraska Supreme Court concluded that even though education is not a fundamental right, the University of Nebraska still could not claim sovereign immunity with respect to Title II of the ADA suit.[189] It reasoned as follows:

First, one of the things that U.S. Supreme Court did after deciding *Tennessee v. Lane* was to vacate several Title II decisions and remand them for reconsideration in light of that decision, including one from the Sixth Circuit concluding that sovereign immunity barred a student's Title II claim against the university.[190]

Second, the Nebraska Supreme Court relied on a case from the First Circuit in which they noted that there was a widespread pattern of a state's unconstitutionally excluding disabled children from public education and irrationally discriminating against disabled students within schools.[191]

Third, under the cases interpreting *Lane*, the judicial decisions, statutes, and personal antidotes collected by the congressional task force that indicated a general history of discrimination in public education were sufficient to support the Title II scheme.[192]

Fourth, the Title II scheme was a narrow remedy to redress discrimination in education because: Title II protects only qualified individuals with disabilities; a person must still meet the essential eligibility requirements of the program or activity regardless of disability; schools and universities are not required under Title II to undertake any measures imposing undue financial or administrative burden or threatened historic preservation interest; and a school or university is not required to fundamentally alter the nature of the program or activity.[193] Accordingly, the Title II scheme is a justified as a reasonably targeted system to prevent a persistent pattern of exclusion and irrational treatment of disabled students in public education especially when compared against the consequences of the harm from such discrimination.[194]

So, if you are dealing with a suit under Title II of the ADA and you know that sovereign immunity is something you going to have to deal with, then here are some things to be thinking about. First, if you are public entity, the very first thing you want to do is check to see whether the your state has explicitly waived its sovereign immunity with respect to Title II claims of the ADA. Illinois, for example, has waived sovereign immunity with respect to ADA suits but not in all cases.[195]

Second, if you are a public entity and find that the state has not waived its sovereign immunity with respect to Title II of the ADA lawsuits, feel free to argue that sovereign immunity prevents the lawsuit, since the Nebraska Supreme Court is definitely not the last word we are going to see on the subject. For example, see *Doe v. Board of Trustees of the University of Illinois*[196] for a contrary view.

Third, if you are student with a disability or are representing a student with a disability, it would be very helpful to compile an extensive dossier of any discrimination faced by students with disabilities in education by the states over time.[197] The more you can find as a plaintiff, the better your ability will be to argue that the Title II of the ADA scheme is a proportionate response to the discrimination meant to be redressed. Another thing a plaintiff would want to do would be to exhaust the school or university's administrative process.

Fourth, the plaintiff might want to consider filing a claim with the Department of Justice. On the public entity's side, *as discussed previously,* preventive systems are always best. Sure, you may win on sovereign immunity grounds, but winning on such a ground doesn't do anything for a university or college's image as being amenable to persons with disabilities. Sovereign immunity litigation is also no doubt expensive as the legal concepts are difficult and such litigation can necessitate a great deal of historical research. A grievance procedure/system that allows a full airing of the opinion with neutral and informed deciders is always recommended. If the public entity loses on sovereign immunity grounds, then a comprehensive and fair grievance system goes a long way toward ultimately winning the dispute, as courts are extremely hesitant to overturn academic decisions in general, and especially when they are the result of a comprehensive and fair airing of the grievance.

Fifth, if you are a plaintiff or a person representing one, you may also want to have a claim against the public educational institution alleging violation of § 504 of the Rehabilitation Act of 1973. Having such a claim would allow you to argue that sovereign immunity was waived, since the public entity in all probability receives federal funds, and Congress made it a condition of receiving federal funds that the states waive their sovereign immunity.[198] The Rehabilitation Act and the ADA are extremely similar, which makes sense, since the ADA was based on the Rehabilitation Act. However, § 504 of the Rehabilitation Act does contain "sole cause"[199] language, whereas Title II of the ADA contains "by reason of"[200] language. Accordingly, it is possible that causation under the two acts may be different, even though substantively they are otherwise the same.[201]

Sixth, keep in mind that sovereign immunity is not going to apply if you have a claim for prospective relief. Thus, a claim for injunctive relief could be very handy if you are a plaintiff or are representing one.[202]

Seventh, since you are seeing courts split on this, look for the question of whether Congress validly abrogated the state's sovereign immunity with respect to Title II of the ADA and the Rehabilitation Act of 1973 with respect to education to eventually wind up before the U.S. Supreme Court.

Before leaving the topic of sovereign immunity, how does sovereign immunity work in the context of a retaliation claim? On this, the rule is that a retaliation claim is barred if the underlying claim is barred by sovereign immunity.[203] That is, one would have to look at which title the underlying claim involves. If it is a Title I claim, then sovereign immunity would apply to the retaliation claim as well.[204] However, the same rule means that if a Title II claim is the underlying cause of action, then sovereign immunity could well be abrogated.[205]

REGULATIONS

Let's say you have a regulation that is having an impact on persons with disabilities as carried out by the regulated industry. Can you sue the regulator for violating the ADA? The answer is no, unless the regulated industry practice of discrimination results from the licensing requirements.[206] Therefore, the time to deal with regulations in terms of how they impact people with disabilities is when the regulations are being formulated. For administrative regulations to be binding, they must first be proposed, then commented upon, and then the comments are reviewed, whereupon the agency issues a final regulation. My experience in administrative rules review is that agencies are quite receptive to comments. The agencies want to make sure that the regulations are consistent with the law they are charged with implementing and that they do not impose overly burdensome requirements on the entities being regulated.

PUNITIVE DAMAGES

While a full range of remedies are available to the person aggrieved by a violation of Title II of the ADA,[207] the question arose as to whether punitive damages were available. The Supreme Court was presented with that very question in *Barnes v. Gorman.*[208]

In *Barnes*, a paraplegic confined to a wheelchair and lacking voluntary control over his lower torso, including the bladder, was arrested for fighting with a bouncer at a Kansas City, Missouri, nightclub.[209] While waiting for the police van to pick him up, he was denied permission to use the restroom to empty his urine bag.[210] The van that arrived was not equipped to take his wheelchair.[211] The officers removed him from his wheelchair and used a seat belt and his own belt to fasten him to a narrow bench in the rear of the van.[212] During the ride to the police station, he released his seat belt, fearing excessive pressure on his urine bag.[213] Consequently, the other belt came loose and he fell to the floor of the van, rupturing his urine bag and injuring his shoulder and back.[214] As he could not be lifted, the driver, the only officer in the van, fastened him to a support in the van for the remainder of the trip.[215] As a result of all this, he suffered serious medical problems, including a bladder infection, serious lower back pain, and uncontrollable spasms in his paralyzed areas, leaving him unable to work full-time.[216] He then brought suit against the Kansas City Board of Police Commissioners, the chief of police, and the officer who drove the van, claiming that he had been discriminated against in violation of Title II of the ADA because he was not reasonably accommodated in his transport.[217]

At trial, he won over $1 million in compensatory damages and $1.2 million in punitive damages.[218] However, the district court threw out the punitive damages award, holding punitive damages were not available under either Title II of the ADA or, for that matter, under section 504 of the Rehabilitation Act of 1973 (a law prohibiting discrimination against persons with disabilities by an entity receiving federal funds), which he also sued under.[219] The district court decision throwing out the punitive damages award was reversed by the Eighth Circuit, and appeal was taken to the U.S. Supreme Court.[220]

In holding that punitive damages were not allowed in a private cause of action brought under Title II of the ADA and section 504 of the Rehabilitation Act of 1973, the Court reasoned as follows. First, the Court noted that private causes of actions were available under Title II of the ADA and under the Rehabilitation Act of 1973 and that the remedies for both were the same based on how the statutes were set up.[221] Second, because the ADA and Rehabilitation Acts were tied to the spending power of Congress, the legitimacy of Congress's power to legislate rested on whether the recipient voluntarily and knowingly accepted the terms of the contract.[222] Third, since the acts did not mention punitive damages, the Court asked itself what would be the normal expectation for the recipient of a contract.[223] As causes of action for breach of contract do not allow for punitive damages, the Court found that it was not reasonable to expect the contracting party to believe that punitive damages could be imposed upon it for violating Title II of the ADA or section 504 of the Rehabilitation Act of 1973.[224] Because punitive damages could be a disaster for a public entity, the Court believed that the public entity would never have accepted federal funding if punitive damage liability were a possibility to that entity.[225]

Notes

1. 42 U.S.C. § 12132 (WL, current through Pub. L. 113-9 (excluding Pub. L. 113-4), approved May 1, 2013).
2. 42 U.S.C. § 12134(a) (WL, current through Pub. L. 113-9 (excluding Pub. L. 113-4), approved May 1, 2013).
3. 28 C.F.R. § 35.140(b)(1).
4. Bledsoe v. Palm Beach Soil and Water Conservation Dist., 942 F. Supp. 1439 (S.D. Fla. 1996), *rev'd on appeal* at 133 F.3d 816 (11th Cir. 1998); *see also* Elwell v. Okla. *ex rel.* Board of Regents of the Univ. of Okla., 693 F.3d 1303, 1306 (10th Cir. 2012). This is an excellent case for anyone wanting to read an in-depth discussion of the differences between Title I of the ADA and Title II of the ADA and why Title II does not apply to employment.
5. 28 C.F.R. § 35.107 (WL, current through May 30, 2013; 78 Fed. Reg. 32,362).
6. *See* 42 U.S.C. § 12133 (WL, current through Pub. L. 113-9 (excluding Pub. L. 113-4), approved May 1, 2013).
7. Peterson v. Univ. of Wis., 818 F. Supp. 1276, 1277 (W.D. Wis. 1993).
8. 28 C.F.R. at § 35.104.
9. 28 C.F.R. § 35.130(b)(7) (WL, current through May 30, 2013; 78 Fed. Reg. 32,362).
10. *See* Pa. Prot. and Advocacy Inc. v. Pa. Dep't of Public Welfare, 402 F.3d 374 (3d Cir. 2005).
11. 28 C.F.R. § 35.150(3) (WL, current through May 30, 2013; 78 Fed. Reg. 32,362).
12. 28 C.F.R. at § 35.130(b)(7).
13. 28 C.F.R. at § 35.130(a)(1).
14. 28 C.F.R. § 35.151(a) (WL, current through May 30, 2013; 78 Fed. Reg. 32,362).
15. 28 C.F.R. § 35.104 (WL, current through May 30, 2013; 78 Fed. Reg. 32362).
16. *See, e.g.*, PGA Tour v. Martin, 532 U.S. 661 (2001).
17. *See* 29 U.S.C.A. § 794(b)(2)(A) (WL, current through Pub. L. 113-9 (excluding Pub. L. 113-4), approved May 1, 2013).
18. *See* Peters v. Univ. of Cincinnati Coll. of Med., 2012 WL 3878601 (S.D. Ohio, Sept. 6, 2012).
19. Concerned Parents to Save Dreher Park Center v. City of West Palm Beach, 846 F. Supp. 986 (S.D. Fla. 1994), *consent decree entered* at 853 F. Supp. 424 (S.D. Fla. 1994), *final judgment entered* at 884 F. Supp. 487 (S.D. Fla. 1994).
20. Easley v. Snider, 36 F.3d 297 (3d Cir. 1994).
21. *Concerned Parents*, 846 F. Supp. at 988.
22. *Id.* at 989.
23. *Id.*

24. *Id.* at 990.
25. *Id.*
26. *Id.* at 989 n.8.
27. *Id.* at 991.
28. *Id.*
29. *Id.*
30. *Id.*
31. *Easley*, 36 F.3d at 299.
32. *Id.*
33. *Id.*
34. *Id.*
35. *Id.*
36. *Id.* at 300.
37. *Id.*at 302–04.
38. *Id.* at 302.
39. *Id.*
40. *E.g.*, Southeastern Cmty. Coll. v. Davis, 442 U.S. 397 (1979).
41. *See* William D. Goren, *On Gymnastics and Cheerleading: An Instructive ADA Case*, XV THE SPORTS LAWYER 3–4 (Spring 1997).
42. 42 U.S.C. at § 12132.
43. 28 C.F.R. § 35.104 (WL, current through May 30, 2013; 78 Fed. Reg. 32,362).
44. *Easley*, 36 F.3d at 302–04.
45. *Id.*
46. Mooneyhan v. Husted, 2012 WL 5834232 (S.D. Ohio, Nov. 6, 2012).
47. *Id.* at *1.
48. *Id.*
49. *Id.*
50. *Id.*
51. *Id.*
52. *Id.*
53. *Id.*
54. *Id.*
55. *Id.*
56. *Id.*
57. *Id.* at *2.
58. *Id.* at *3 n.2.
59. *Id.*
60. *Id.* at *4.
61. *Id.* at *5. The court may have gone too far here. In particular, when it says that the plaintiff requests had to be granted unless the defendant could demonstrate a fundamental alteration, that may have been overstating the point. A modification does have to be made absent a fundamental alteration, but it is quite a different thing to say that the particular modification requested must be made absent a fundamental alteration.

62. *Id.*
63. *Id.*
64. *Id.* at n.4.
65. *Id.* at *6.
66. *Id.*
67. Innovative Health Sys. v. City of White Plains, 117 F.3d 37 (2d Cir. 1997).
68. *Id.* at 44.
69. *Id.*
70. *Id.*
71. *Id.* at 45.
72. *Id.* at 47.
73. *Id.* at 48–49.
74. Bay Area Addiction Research and Treatment, Inc. v. City of Antioch, 179 F.3d 725, 735–36 (9th Cir. 1999).
75. *See* Chevron v. Echazabal, 536 U.S. 73 (2002). *Bay Area* was decided three years before *Chevron*. Considering how close the reasoning of *Chevron* is with this case, the practitioner would want to be very familiar with the *Chevron* case as well when dealing with these matters, even though *Chevron* was a Title I case and zoning questions are a Title II case. *See also* the similarity of *Bay Area* with the Department of Justice's definition of direct threat that appears in its regulations at 28 C.F.R. § 35.104.
76. *Bay Area,* 179 F.3d at 736.
77. *Id.*
78. *Id.*
79. Kulin v. Deschutes County, 872 F. Supp. 2d 1093 (D. Or. 2012).
80. *Id.* at 1096.
81. *Id.*
82. *Id.*
83. *Id.*
84. *Id.*
85. *Id.*
86. *Id.*
87. *Id.*
88. *Id.*
89. *Id.*
90. *Id.*
91. *Id.* at 1097.
92. *Id.* at 1096–97.
93. *Id.* at 1097.
94. *Id.*
95. *Id.* at 1098.
96. *Id.* at 1099.
97. *Id.*
98. *Id.* at 1099–1100.

99. Martin v. PGA Tour, 994 F. Supp. 1242 (D. Or. 1998).
100. PGA Tour Inc. v. Martin, 532 U.S. 661 (2001).
101. *Kulin,* 872 F. Supp. 2d at 1100, *citing to* Martin v. PGA Tour, 994 F. Supp. 1242, 1247 (D. Or. 1998).
102. *Kulin,* 872 F. Supp. 2d at 1100.
103. *Id.*
104. *Id.* at 1102.
105. *Id.*
106. *Id.*
107. *Id.*
108. *Id.*
109. *Id.* at 1103.
110. *Id.*
111. *Id.*
112. *Id.* at 1105.
113. *Id.*
114. *Id.*
115. *Id.*
116. *Id.*
117. *Id.*
118. *Id.*
119. *Id.* at 1106.
120. *Id.*
121. *Id.*
122. *Id.*
123. *Id.* at 1100, 1104.
124. *See PGA Tour Inc.,* 532 U.S. at 683–86.
125. 42 U.S.C.A. § 2000d-7 (WL, current through Pub. L. 113-9 (excluding Pub. L. 113-4), approved May 1, 2013).
126. *See* 42 U.S.C.A. at § 12101.
127. *See generally* Board of Trustees of Univ. of Ala. v. Garrett, 531 U.S. 356 (2001).
128. *See generally* Tenn. v. Lane, 541 U.S. 509 (2004).
129. *E.g.,* City of Cleburne v. Cleburne Living Center, 473 U.S. 432, 439–41 (1985).
130. *Id.* at 440.
131. *Id.*
132. *Id.* at 440–41.
133. *Id.* at 440.
134. *Id.* at 440–41.
135. *See id.* at 440–41.
136. Board of Trustees of Univ. of Ala. v. Garrett, 531 U.S. 356 (2001).
137. *Id.* at 362.
138. *Id.* at 360.
139. *Id.* at 364.

140. *Id.*
141. *See id.* at 364, 374.
142. Cleburne v. Cleburne Living Center, Inc., 473 U.S. 432 (1985).
143. Heller v. Doe, 509 U.S. 312 (1993).
144. *Garrett*, 531 U.S. at 366.
145. *Id.* at 372.
146. Cleburne, 473 U.S. at 446–50.
147. *Id.* at 443–47.
148. *Id.* at 456, 458 (Marshall, J., concurring and dissenting in part).
149. *Id.*
150. Heller v. Doe, 509 U.S. 312, 319 (1993). *See also* William D. Goren, *Counterpoint: Congress Did Properly Waive the States' Sovereign Immunity in Enacting the ADA?* DCBA BRIEF (Jan. 2001), *available at* http://www.dcbabrief,org/vol130101art1.html.
151. *Garrett*, 531 U.S. at 368.
152. The Office of Federal Contract Compliance in August of 2013 established a 7% hiring goal for federal contractors of 100 or more employees and a $50,000 or more contract. Critical to whether that 7% goal will survive a constitutional challenge will be answering the question whether the entities being regulated have discriminated against persons with disabilities in employment in an intentional manner over time.
153. *Id.* at 369.
154. *Id.* at 374 n.9.
155. Tenn. v. Lane, 541 U.S. 509 (2004).
156. *Id.* at 513.
157. *Id.* at 513–14.
158. *Id.* at 514.
159. *Id.*
160. *Id.* at 515.
161. *Id.* at 529–30.
162. *Id.* at 522–23.
163. *Id.*
164. *Id.* at 524.
165. *Id.*
166. *Id.* at 524–25.
167. *Id.* at 525.
168. Nev. Dep't of Human Resources v. Hibbs, 538 U.S. 721 (2003).
169. *Lane,* 541 U.S. at 527–28.
170. *Id.* at 529.
171. *Id.* at 533.
172. *Id.* at 530.
173. *Id.* at 531.
174. *Id.* at 534.
175. *Id.* at 522.

176. *Id.* at 529.
177. *Id.* at 531.
178. *Id.* at 524, 534.
179. United States v. Ga., 126 S. Ct. 877 (2006).
180. Pa. Dep't of Corr. v. Yeskey, 524 U.S. 206, 212–13 (1998).
181. United States v. Ga., 126 S. Ct. 877 (2006).
182. *Id.* at 882.
183. *Id.*
184. The discussion that follows is taken from an entry that I posted on my blog, http://www.williamgoren.com/blog/ on Dec. 11, 2012. What appears here is not exactly the same, since the medium is different. However, the resemblance is fairly close.
185. Doe v. Board of Regents of the Univ. of Neb., 280 Neb. 492, 788 N.W.2d 264 (2010).
186. *Id.* at 496–97.
187. *See id.* at 497.
188. *Id.* at 521.
189. *Id.*
190. *Id.* at 520.
191. *See id.* at 522.
192. *Id.*
193. Doe v. Board of Regents of the Univ. of Neb., 788 N.W.2d at 523–24, *citing to* Toledo v. Sanchez, 454 F.3d 24, 39 (1st Cir. 2006).
194. *See id.* at 524.
195. *See* 745 Ill. Comp. Stat. 5/1.5(d) (WL, current through P.A. 97-1132 of the 2012 Reg. Sess.).
196. Doe v. Board of Trustees of the Univ. of Ill., 429 F. Supp. 2d 930 (N.D. Ill. 2006).
197. *See Toledo,* 454 F.3d at 35.
198. *See Board of Trustees of the Univ. of Ill.,* 429 F. Supp. 2d at 940; Phiffer v. Columbia River Correctional Inst., 384 F.3d 791, 793 (9th Cir. 2004); *but see* Hurst v. Texas Dep't of Assistive and Rehabilitative Servs., 482 F.3d 809, 811–14 (5th Cir. 2007) (holding that the language of the Rehabilitation Act was too vague to support a waiver of Eleventh Amendment immunity).
199. 29 U.S.C. § 794 (WL, current through Pub. L. 112-197, approved Nov. 27, 2012).
200. 42 U.S.C. § 12132 (WL, current through Pub. L. 113-9 (excluding Pub. L. 113-4), approved May 1, 2013); *see also Toledo,* 454 F.3d at 30.
201. *See* K.M. v. Tustin Unified School Dist., _ F.3d _, 2012 WL 3988677, *8 (9th Cir. Aug. 6, 2013) (stating that due to the absence of "solely" from Title II of the ADA's causation language, motivating factor is the rule where more than one cause exists).
202. *See Board of Trustees of the Univ. of Ill.,* 429 F. Supp. 2d at 940–41.

203. Brooks v. Del. Dep't of Health and Social Servs., 2012 WL 113-4481, *4 (Dist. Del. March 30, 2012).
204. *Id.*
205. DeCotiis v. Whittemore, 842 F. Supp. 2d 354, 370 (D. Me. 2012).
206. *See* Noel v. New York City Taxi and Limousine Comm'n, 687 F.3d 63 (2d Cir. 2012), *rev'g* Noel v. New York City Taxi and Limousine Comm'n, 837 F. Supp. 2d 268 (S.D.N.Y. 2011).
207. Barnes v. Gorman, 536 U.S. 181, 184–85 (2002).
208. *See generally id.*
209. *Id.* at 183.
210. *Id.*
211. *Id.*
212. *Id.*
213. *Id.*
214. *Id.*
215. *Id.*
216. *Id.* at 184.
217. *Id.*
218. *Id.*
219. *Id.*
220. *Id.*
221. *Id.* at 185.
222. *Id.* at 186.
223. *Id.* at 187.
224. *Id.* at 187–88*.
225. *Id.* at 188.

Places of Public Accommodations and Commercial Facilities

8

UNLIKE TITLE II OF THE ADA, an entity covered by Title III of the ADA must have each of its facilities readily accessible to persons with disabilities. Program accessibility is not a concept found in Title III. If a building built before the advent of the ADA is involved, then the business has to make only structural changes that are readily achievable.[1] Where auxiliary aids and services are involved, changes must be made unless to do so would constitute an undue burden or a fundamental alteration in the nature of the goods, services, facilities, privileges, advantages, or accommodations being offered.[2] Finally, if there is an alteration in the facility or a new building is built (after the ADA went into effect), specific architectural accessibility guidelines must be satisfied.[3] These general principles give rise to several questions:

- What businesses are subject to Title III of the ADA, and are there any exemptions?
- What is meant by "readily achievable"?
- What is an auxiliary aid and service?
- What is meant by "undue burden"?
- What constitutes an alteration in a facility?

- Does Title III apply when a person with a disability wants to use a business that does not rely on a physical location (e.g., terms of an insurance policy, direct mail business, doctor's office for consultation, buying a product on the Internet, etc.)?

Title III of the ADA applies to all places of "public accommodations."[4] A place of public accommodation is a facility operated by a *private* entity that affects interstate commerce and falls into any of the following categories:

1. Places of lodging
2. Establishments serving food and drink
3. Places of exhibition and entertainment
4. Places of public gathering, such as a museum or library
5. Sales or rental establishments
6. Service establishments
7. Specified public transportation
   a. Terminals
   b. Depots
8. Public display or collection
9. Places of recreation (parks, etc.)
10. Places of education
11. Social service centers
12. Place of exercise or recreation (athletic in nature)[5]

Two other significant points regarding Title III bear mentioning. First, religious entities are exempt from Title III coverage.[6] For example, many private schools are religious in nature or run by religious organizations and therefore are exempt from Title III of the ADA, even though places of education are generally covered.[7] Second, it is entirely conceivable that a business not otherwise subject to the ADA could have a portion of its premises covered by the ADA. Apartment complexes are an example. Apartment complexes are not subject to Title III of the ADA as a place of public accommodation, but they are subject to the federal and state fair housing acts. Nevertheless, the area or office where the public goes to lease an apartment would be subject to Title III on the grounds that it is a service establishment or a sales and rental establishment.[8]

Consider the following scenario:

> A business is in an existing facility built before the ADA went into effect and is considered a place of public accommodation under Title III of the ADA. An architect reviews the facility and determines that there are numerous ADA compliance issues. What are the obligations of the business to make changes to comply with the ADA regulations on architectural barriers? What if the business leases the facility? Does the landlord have ADA obligations?

With respect to the existing facility question, the obligation exists to make whatever changes are readily achievable. The DOJ defines "readily achievable" as meaning without much difficulty or expense[9] and lists several factors to consider in making the determination. They are:

1. The nature and cost of the action needed.
2. The overall financial resources of the site or sites involved in the action.
3. The number of persons employed at the site.
4. The effect on expenses and resources.
5. Legitimate safety requirements that are necessary for safe operation, including crime prevention measures.
6. If applicable:
    a. The geographic separateness and the administrative or fiscal relationship of the site or sites in question to any parent corporation or entity.
    b. The overall financial resources of any parent corporation or entity.
    c. The overall size of the parent corporation or entity with respect to the number of employees.
    d. The number, type, and location of its facilities.
    e. The type of operation or operations of any parent corporation or entity, including the composition, structure, and functions of the work force of the parent corporation or entity.[10]

While these factors are vague, the DOJ gives some clarity in the regulations governing the removal of architectural barriers as to what may be readily achievable. Examples include:

- Installing ramps
- Making curb cuts in sidewalks and entrances
- Repositioning shelves
- Rearranging tables, chairs, vending machines, display racks, and other furniture
- Repositioning telephones
- Adding raised markings on elevator control buttons
- Installing flashing alarm lights
- Widening doors
- Eliminating a turnstile or providing an alternative accessible path
- Installing accessible door hardware
- Installing grab bars in toilet stalls
- Rearranging toilet partitions to increase maneuvering space
- Insulating lavatory pipes under sinks to prevent burns
- Installing a raised toilet seat
- Installing a full-length bathroom mirror
- Repositioning the paper towel dispenser in a bathroom
- Creating designated accessible parking spaces
- Installing an accessible paper cup dispenser at an existing inaccessible water fountain
- Removing high-pile, low-density carpeting
- Installing vehicle hand controls[11]

The DOJ also prioritizes the removal of architectural barriers as follows:

1. Provide access to a place of public accommodation from public sidewalks, parking, or public transportation.
2. Provide access to those areas of a place of public accommodation where goods and services are made available to the public.
3. Provide access to restroom facilities.
4. Take any other necessary measures to provide access to the goods, services, facilities, privileges, advantages, or accommodations of a place of public accommodation.[12]

"Undue burden" also plays a role in Title III analysis. A place of public accommodation must provide auxiliary aids and services unless to do so would constitute an undue burden or result in a fundamental alteration in the business.[13] To illustrate this principle, consider the following example:

> Every month the board of directors of a nonprofit social service agency meets. Persons with disabilities are very interested in attending, and they need various auxiliary aids and services in order to do so. What must the agency do?

Auxiliary aids and services include such varied items as:

1) qualified interpreters or other effective methods of making aurally delivered materials available to individuals with hearing impairments;
2) qualified readers, taped texts, or other effective methods of making visually delivered materials available to individuals with visual impairments;
3) acquisition or modification of equipment or devices; and
4) other similar services and actions.[14]

The same factors for determining whether the removal of barriers is readily achievable are also used by DOJ to determine the existence of an undue burden.[15] The entity must provide the auxiliary aid or service unless to do so would fundamentally alter the business or result in an undue burden (think financial) (*see also Olmstead v. L.C.*, discussed previously).

It's also possible that a person wanting to attend the board meeting may not need any auxiliary aid or service at all, but simply a change in the meeting time. This was precisely the case in *Dees v. Austin Travis County Mental Health and Mental Retardation*.[16] In *Dees*, a person with severe mental illness, who nevertheless was very active in the community as an advocate, brought suit on the grounds that the agency's 8:00 A.M. time for board meetings discriminated against her and others like her whose medication regimen did not permit them to be alert early in the morning.[17] The court was not persuaded that changing the time of the board meetings would be an undue burden or constitute a fundamental alteration in the nature of the agency's business.[18] While this was a Title II case, there is no reason to expect that the decision would not have equal applicability to the matter of board meetings of nonprofit entities subject to Title III of the ADA.

With respect to altering an existing facility, those alterations must be done in accordance with very specific architectural guidelines. The DOJ defines an alteration as any change to a business covered by Title III that affects or could affect the usability of the building or facility or any part of the building or facility—a very broad definition.[19] Further, if a portion of a facility containing a primary function is altered, then the path of travel to that portion of the facility must also be made readily accessible to persons with disabilities.[20] The DOJ defines primary function as a major activity for which the facility is intended, such as (but not limited to) customer services lobby, the dining area of a cafeteria, meeting rooms in a conference center, offices, and other work areas in which the activities of the entity are performed.[21] Finally, it is extremely important to note that many states have their own accessibility rules, and often they are stricter than the federal guidelines. Accordingly, it is extremely important to be knowledgeable about state laws and regulations in matters of architectural accessibility.

While all of this is very detailed and can be difficult to understand, many architects are already familiar with these requirements. However, do not rely solely on an architect's assurances that the ADA is being complied with, as architectural firms have been sued directly by persons with disabilities[22] as well as by the Department of Justice[23] for designing athletic facilities that were not in compliance with ADA architectural standards. Certainly, this hypothetical architectural firm would be liable for malpractice, as architects are expected to know that new facilities must be designed in accordance with strict ADA construction standards.

Another question is whether the tenant or the landlord has the responsibility for making needed modifications. The DOJ makes it quite clear that both are jointly liable when a place of public accommodation is not accessible.[24] Further, the terms of a lease do not matter *vis-à-vis* the person aggrieved, though they will govern how the costs will be apportioned.[25] Thus, preventive law demands the existence of language in the lease governing the responsibilities of the landlord and tenant for compliance with the ADA. Yes, it is good preventive law, but will it even work?

Can the obligation to comply with the myriad of requirements of the ADA be delegated to someone else? That is, acting on the advice noted above, let's say you are a major hotel and you are building out/renovating the hotel in a big way. You hire a firm with the idea that the build-out/renovations will be done in compliance with the ADA. That firm goes about its business in a way that is below the standard of reasonable due care. That is, the build-out does not comply with the ADA architectural guidelines. This causes you to suffer a tremendous amount of damages in fending off lawsuits from private plaintiffs as well as from the Department of Justice. Fortunately, since you took the advice above, you had a clause in your contract with the firm that did the build-out to indemnify you for any damages arising from any act, omission, or willful misconduct in the performance of its obligations. Relying on that clause, you seek indemnification from the company that did the build-out. Will that indemnification lawsuit succeed?

These were exactly the facts in *Rolf Jensen and Associates, Inc. v. Eighth Judicial District Court of the State of Nevada.*[26, 27] The facts of this case were that in 2002, Mandalay Corporation entered into a contract with Rolf Jensen and Associates Inc. to provide consulting services regarding construction of an expansion to the Mandalay Bay Resort and Casino in Las Vegas in compliance with the ADA.[28] The contract contained a provision providing Rolf Jensen would indemnify Mandalay for damages arising from any act, omission, or willful misconduct by Rolf Jensen in its performance of its obligations.[29] Once the expansion was constructed, the Department of Justice began an investigation of numerous violations of the ADA architectural guidelines.[30] That led to Mandalay entering into a comprehensive settlement agreement with the Department of Justice requiring them to bring the resort into compliance with the Americans with Disabilities Act.[31] To fix the problems, Mandalay estimated that the retrofit would cost more than $20 million.[32] Mandalay, per the clause in its contract, brought suit seeking indemnification.[33] Rolf Jensen maintained that the district court was required to grant its motion for summary judgment because Mandalay's claims were preempted by the ADA, and it sought a writ of mandamus from the Nevada Supreme Court to effectuate that.[34]

The Supreme Court of Nevada agreed with Rolf Jensen and reasoned as follows.

First, the court said that this was a situation involving conflict preemption. That is, there are two ways a federal law can impliedly preempt a state law. State laws can be preempted by field preemption, where congressional enactments so thoroughly occupy a legislative field or touch on a field in which the federal interest is so dominant that Congress effectively leaves no room for the state to regulate conduct in that field.[35] Alternatively, you could have conflict preemption. Conflict preemption concerns whether, in view of the federal law's purpose and effects, the state law claims contained in the suit (in this suit indemnification, breach of contract, breach of express warranty, and negligent misrepresentation) pose an obstacle to the accomplishment of Congress's objectives in enacting the federal law.[36]

Second, since this is a case of conflict preemption, the Nevada Supreme Court turned to what it saw as the goals of the ADA—not only to remedy discrimination against disabled individuals but to prevent it.[37] To ensure that, the ADA comprehensively covers discriminatory practices that persons with disabilities face in major areas of public life, including access to public accommodations.[38] The ADA also focuses on prevention as well. It provides that where a facility is not constructed to be readily accessible to individuals with disabilities, the owner, regardless of intent, is liable for unlawful discrimination.[39]

Third, with the exception of landlord-tenant relationships, no provisions exist within the ADA or its accompanying regulations permitting indemnification to reallocate liability between various entities subject to the ADA.[40]

Fourth, the Nevada Supreme Court agreed with Rolf Jensen that such claims of indemnification and the like were preempted because they diminish the owner's incentive to comply with the ADA and thereby frustrate Congress's goal of preventing disability discrimination.[41] In reaching this conclusion, the court relied heavily on a Fourth Circuit case, *Equal Rights Center v. Niles Bolton Associates*, which held that permitting an owner through an indemnification claim to recover its losses lessens the owner's incentive to ensure compliance with the ADA and the Fair Housing Act.[42] In other words, each entity subject to the ADA has a nondelegable duty to comply with that law.[43] To allow it to switch the obligation to comply onto someone else means that that individual who has the obligation to comply will not be accountable for discriminatory practices.[44] Or to put it another way, to allow such claims would let owners contractually maneuver themselves into a situation where they could ignore the nondelegable responsibilities under the ADA.[45]

Fifth, the remedial scheme set forth in the ADA does not provide for a right to indemnification.[46]

Sixth, Mandalay argued that permitting indemnification claims would have the overall effect of promoting ADA compliance by encouraging owners to seek advice from ADA consultants and therefore should be permitted.[47]

The Nevada Supreme Court disagreed, for several reasons. They said that owners are motivated to seek advice on ADA compliance in order to aid in their duty to construct facilities in compliance with the law.[48] To say that they contract with the consultants only to obtain indemnification should something go wrong simply diminishes to the extreme the role a qualified consultant plays in an owner's effort to meet ADA requirements.[49] Also, allowing such behavior has a debilitating effect on ADA compliance.[50] Therefore, the Nevada Supreme Court believed that the surest way to maximize ADA compliance would be to hold the owner's risk of noncompliance firmly in place, i.e., a nondelegable duty.[51] The owner of Mandalay, a highly sophisticated entity with ultimate authority over all construction decisions, is in the best position to prevent violations of the ADA.[52] Rolf Jensen still did have liability for its actions, but the liability extended to the individuals with disabilities rather than to Mandalay.[53]

Seventh, Mandalay claimed that its claims were not really indemnification claims at all, but rather it was seeking separate and distinct relief for Rolf Jensen's breach of its contractual and professional obligations.[54] The Nevada Supreme Court disagreed and said simply that such claims would be a subterfuge for indemnification and, for all the reasons discussed here, are preempted by the ADA.[55] Accordingly, it held that the lower court had no choice, quite literally, to grant Rolf Jensen's motion for summary judgment and issue the writ of mandamus (a writ that compels the performance of a governmental act).[56]

What does the Nevada Supreme Court decision mean for the preventive advice that says whenever you hire someone to deal with ADA compliance, make sure there is an indemnification clause in it? The decision does call into question whether such a clause would either be held to be preempted by the Americans with Disabilities Act or be held to be void against public policy.

If you are in Illinois, you might try to rely on two cases involving attorneys suing for wrongful discharge and claim that if indemnification was not allowed, then there would be no reason to hire such people to ensure ADA compliance (an argument specifically rejected by the Nevada Supreme Court, as we saw above). In those cases, the Illinois Supreme Court said that to allow an attorney to sue for wrongful discharge would jeopardize the attorney-client relationship.[57] In other words, why hire such a person at all if it would just come back to bite you?

That said, the states that have considered whether an attorney can sue for wrongful discharge have uniformly disagreed with the reasoning of the Illinois Supreme Court in both of those cases and have adopted, at least to some degree, the reasoning of *General Dynamics Corporation v. Superior Court*, which does not mince words with respect to how it believes that the Illinois cases, *Balla v. Gambro, Inc.* being one of them, were wrongfully decided.[58] In short, if you are in Illinois, the indemnification language may be worth a shot. If you are in another state, the indemnification language may run into the trouble it ran into in Nevada.

Assuming such an indemnification clause will fail, what is a company to do? A couple of possibilities are hiring a person to independently double-check the work of the contractor, or having your in-house counsel or other in-house personnel work with the contractor and any other consultants to ensure that the work/advice is done/given in the way it is supposed to be done/given. True, such a process increases the costs to the company. However, by doing so, it helps ensure that the company's nondelegable duty is satisfied and also increases the probability that the ADA will be fully complied with. You might also consider suing the architectural firm for malpractice using your state's negligence per se statute or principles of negligence. Whether such a suit would state a claim for indemnification and therefore be void may depend on the jurisdiction.

OTHER TITLE III ISSUES

Exhaustion of Administrative Remedies?[59]

Title I of the ADA requires that a person seeking to file a claim for employment discrimination must first file a claim with the EEOC or a substantially equivalent state agency and receive a right-to-sue letter before proceeding in court. If you wish to file a claim under Title III of the ADA, do you first have to exhaust administrative remedies? Title III does allow for administrative remedies. You could file a claim with the Department of Justice, but do you have to before being able to proceed in court? The answer to this question is no, unless your case is before a certain district court judge in Colorado.

The two opinions from the district court in Colorado, both written by the Honorable John Kane, albeit 16 years apart from each other, saying administrative remedies must be exhausted first are *Howard v. Cherry Hills Cutters, Inc.* and *Lillard v. Sunflower Farmers Market, Inc.*[60] In both cases, Judge Kane held that Title III of the ADA requires exhaustion of administrative remedies as a precondition to filing suit where the complaint contains allegations that are also prohibited by state or local law. In the first decision, Judge Kane seems to suggest that the reference to § 2000a-3(a) and 42 U.S.C. § 12188 necessarily includes a reference to 42 U.S.C. § 20000a-3(c).[61] In the second decision, he came to the same conclusion by saying that 42 U.S.C. § 12188 related back to 42 U.S.C. section 2000a-3(a), which in turn is limited by an exhaustion requirement in a separate section, 2000a-3(c), because 42 U.S.C. § 12188 refers to "remedies and procedures" of 42 U.S.C. § 2000a-3(a), and 42 U.S.C. § 2000a-3(c) would be a procedure.[62]

Judge Kane is alone in this view. Before the Ninth Circuit ruled on this same issue, there were decisions from other districts in the Ninth Circuit that agreed with Judge Kane, but those decisions would no longer be controlling, since we now will have a decision from the Ninth Circuit. The counter-argument to Judge Kane, as ably explained by the Ninth Circuit in *Botosan v. Paul McNally Realty,*[63] works like this: 42 U.S.C. § 12188 does say that the remedies and procedures set forth in section 42 U.S.C. § 2000a-3(a) are the remedies for violating Title III of the ADA, but there is absolutely no mention anywhere of 42 U.S.C. § 2000a-3(c). Therefore, since a principle of statutory construction is that what is not mentioned is excluded, it would not be proper to read 42 U.S.C. § 2000a-3(c) into the law.[64] *Botosan* also made mention of legislative history, the Code of Federal Regulations, and the DOJ's technical assistance manual as also supporting the conclusion that Title III actions do not require state notification.[65]

So what does this all mean? If you are representing a place of public accommodation, it might be worth it to argue that a person has not exhausted administrative remedies. I am skeptical as to whether such an argument would succeed, as the Ninth Circuit seems to be on solid ground with respect to its reasoning. Nevertheless, since one judge has adopted this position, making such a claim would not be a frivolous one, unless, of course, you are in the Ninth Circuit, the District Court of New Jersey,[66] or the Southern District of Ohio.[67] If you are a person with a disability or are representing one, it might make sense to file a claim with the Department of Justice anyway. After all, the DOJ is a deep pocket with a lot of resources, and it could bring those resources to bear to even obtain damages for an individual that typically would not otherwise be possible under Title III. Nevertheless, unless Judge Kane's view becomes widely accepted, the plaintiff is under no obligation to exhaust administrative remedies first.

Notes

1. 42 U.S.C.A. § 12182(b)(2)(A)(iv) (WL, current through Pub. L. 113-9 (excluding Pub. L. 113-4), approved May 1, 2013).
2. 28 C.F.R. § 36.303(a) (WL, current through May 30, 2013; 78 Fed. Reg. 32,362).
3. 28 C.F.R. § 36.401 (WL, current through May 30, 2013; 78 Fed. Reg. 32,362).
4. 42 U.S.C.A. § 12182(a) (WL, current through Pub. L. 113-9 (excluding Pub. L. 113-4), approved May 1, 2013).
5. 42 U.S.C.A. § 12181(7) (WL, current through Pub. L. 113-9 (excluding Pub. L. 113-4), approved May 1, 2013); 28 C.F.R. § 36.104 (WL, current through Nov. 13, 2009).
6. 42 U.S.C.A. at § 12187 .
7. 42 U.S.C.A. at § 12181(7)(J).
8. 42 U.S.C.A. at § 12181(7)(E).
9. 28 C.F.R. at § 36.104.
10. *Id.*
11. 28 C.F.R. § 36.304(b) (WL, current through May 30, 2013; 78 Fed. Reg. 32,362).
12. 28 C.F.R. at § 36.304(c).
13. 28 C.F.R. at § 36.303(a).
14. 42 U.S.C.A. § 12103 (WL, current through Pub. L. 113-9 (excluding Pub. L. 113-4), approved May 1, 2013). This definition resembles very closely the definition of auxiliary aids that was already present in the regulations. *See* 28 C.F.R. § 36.303.

15. 28 C.F.R. § 36.104 (WL, current through May 30, 2013; 78 Fed. Reg. 32,362).
16. Dees v. Austin Travis County Mental Health and Mental Retardation, 860 F. Supp. 1186 (W.D. Tex. 1994).
17. *Id.* at 1187.
18. *Id.* at 1190–91.
19. 28 C.F.R. § 36.402(b) (WL, current through May 30, 2013; 78 Fed. Reg. 32,362).
20. 28 C.F.R. § 36.403 (WL, current through May 30, 2013; 78 Fed. Reg. 32,362).
21. 28 C.F.R. at § 36.403(b).
22. *E.g.*, Johanson v. Huizenga Holdings, 963 F. Supp. 1175 (S.D. Fla. 1997).
23. *See* http://www.justice.gov/opa/pr/2013/May/13-crt-570.html (a settlement announced by the Department of Justice on May 16, 2013, with the architects and civil engineers involved in the design and construction of multifamily housing complexes located in Mississippi, Louisiana, and Tennessee).
24. 28 C.F.R. § 36.201(b) (WL, current through May 30, 2013; 78 Fed. Reg. 32,362).
25. *Id.*
26. Rolf Jensen & Assocs., Inc. v. Eighth Judicial Dist. Ct. of the State of Nev., 282 P.3d 743 (Nev. 2012).
27. The discussion that follows can also be found in my blog entry from Nov. 12, 2012, at http://www.williamgoren.com/blog/2012/11/12/ada-compliance-nondelegable-duty/. Due to the medium, there are some differences between the two, but those differences are minor.
28. *Id.* at 745.
29. *Id.*
30. *Id.*
31. *Id.*
32. *Id.*
33. *Id.*
34. *Id.*
35. *Id.* at 746. *See also* the discussion of the Air Carrier Access Act that appears in Chapter 10 of this book.
36. *Id.*
37. *Id.* at 747.
38. *Id.*
39. *Id.*
40. *Id.*
41. *Id.* at 748.
42. Equal Rights Center v. Niles Bolton Assocs., 602 F.3d 597, 602 (4th Cir. 2010).
43. *Id.*
44. *Rolf Jensen & Assocs.*, 282 P.3d at 748.

45. *Id.*
46. *Id.*
47. *Id.* at 749.
48. *Id.*
49. *Id.*
50. *Id.*
51. *Id.*
52. *Id.*
53. *Id.*
54. *Id.* at 750.
55. *Id.*
56. *Id.* at 751.
57. *See* Balla v. Gambro, Inc. 145 Ill. 2d 492 (1991); *see also* Jacobsen v. Knepper and Moga P.C., 185 Ill. 2d 372 (1998).
58. General Dynamics Corp. v. Super. Ct., 7 Cal. 4th 1164, 1183–88 (1994).
59. The discussion that follows can also be found in my blog entry from Dec. 3, 2012, at http://www.williamgoren.com/blog/2012/12/03/to-file-suit-under-Title-iii-of-the-ada-must-youfirst-exhaust-administrative-remedies/. Except for the medium, there will not be much difference between the two. I debated whether to put this in the remedy section. Ultimately, since it is a Title III issue, I elected to put it here.
60. Howard v. Cherry Hills Cutters, Inc., 935 F. Supp. 1148 (D. Colo. 1996); Lillard v. Sunflower Farmers Market, Inc., 2012 WL 5936543 (D. Colo. Nov. 27, 2012).
61. *Howard,* 935 F. Supp. at 1150.
62. *Lillard,* 2012 WL 5936543 at *1.
63. Botosan v. Paul McNally Realty, 216 F.3d 827 (9th Cir. 2000).
64. *See id.* at 832; *see also* Moyer v. Showboat Casino Hotel, 56 F. Supp. 2d 498, 501–02 (D.N.J. 1999); Love v. Omni Netherland Plaza Hotel, 2001 WL 1842450 (S.D. Ohio, May 10, 2001).
65. *Botosan, supra* note 63, at 832.
66. *Moyer, supra* note 64.
67. *Love, supra* note 64.

9 The ADA and the Health-Care Provider

THE AMERICANS WITH DISABILITIES ACT and the health-care provider needs a separate section of its own, as the jurisprudence in this area evolved in a completely different direction than any reading of the ADA and its regulations would have predicted. With regard to employment, the cases, particularly with respect to HIV, make a distinction between medical personnel who do invasive procedures and those who do not. When the individual with the disability is the patient, the cases are more typical of what one would expect from studying the ADA laws and regulations. While the courts are very pro-employer when cases involve medical personnel who are HIV-positive and engaged in invasive procedures, they are pro-plaintiff when it comes to personnel who will not do invasive procedures or when it comes to HIV-infected patients. To understand how this distinction evolved, one must look at the doctrine of informed consent.

The doctrine of informed consent is a legal doctrine mandating that health-care providers reveal all the material facts necessary for a reasonable patient to make the decision whether to undergo surgery.[1] It certainly can be argued that a reasonable patient would want to know the surgeon's HIV status. On the other hand, a person who is HIV-positive has a disability under the ADA,[2] and then there are the HIV confidentiality laws to consider as well.[3] To date, the courts are allowing broad latitude to the employer to deal with the HIV-positive health-care provider who performs or is involved in invasive surgery.[4] Virtually no latitude is being given to the health-care provider who refuses to care for a person with HIV.[5] Taking the doctrine of informed consent to its conclusion, some courts are imposing an obligation on the provider to disclose his or her HIV status,[6] even though HIV confidentiality laws would seem to suggest that the health-care provider would have some discretion in deciding whether to disclose his or her HIV status to others.

The other reason for the distinction is the ADA concept of direct threat—in particular, the factors that are used to determine when a direct threat exists. In *School Board of Nassau County, Florida v. Arline*, the U.S. Supreme Court held that whether a person is a direct threat and thereby not otherwise qualified depends upon evaluating:

- the nature of the risk (how the disease is transmitted);
- the duration of the risk (how long the carrier is infectious);
- the severity of the risk (the potential harm to third parties); and
- the probability that the disease will be transmitted and cause varying degrees of harm.[7]

With regard to the HIV-positive health-care provider performing invasive procedures, the courts have been concentrating on the latter two factors—the severity of the risk (extreme; death) and the uncertain, in their view, etiology of HIV. Of course, if a disease other than HIV were involved, those points might not be as significant.

A question also arises as to whether a physician with hospital staff privileges who suffers from discrimination based on a disability can sue that hospital for violating the ADA. There are two possible approaches. First, regardless of how the physician is classified, he or she may claim employee status because the hospital exercises sufficient control so he would be deemed an employee per *Clackamas*, discussed earlier in this book.[8] The other possibility is a Title III suit. A Title III suit would essentially borrow from *PGA Tour v. Martin* by claiming that the hospital cannot deny the privileges it offers by discriminating on the basis of disability. This approach has been successful in at least one case, *Menkowitz v. Pottstown Memorial Medical Center.*[9]

Will *Menkowitz* prevail? Great arguments for and against the holding in *Menkowitz* can be found in *Hetz v. Aurora Medical Center of Manitowoc County.*[10] In *Hetz,* the physician brought suit against the hospital and various insurance companies contending that his application for medical staff privileges at the hospital was denied because of his bipolar disorder and sleep apnea.[11] The court, discussing both the pros and cons of allowing a cause of action under Title III of the ADA under such a scenario, ultimately held that a Title III cause of action did exist.[12] In coming to that conclusion, the court went into extensive analysis of the arguments both in support and against such a holding.

The reasons arguing against allowing such a suit under Title III of the ADA are as follows and stem from Justice Scalia's dissent in *PGA Tour v. Martin.*[13] First, Justice Scalia believes that the traditional understanding of laws dealing with public accommodation is to provide rights for customers.[14] Second, he believes that traditional understanding of public accommodations law is supported by the text of Title III when it lists the type of entities qualifying as a place of public accommodation.[15]

Finally, Justice Scalia believes that extending Title III protection beyond clients and customers makes a muddle of the ADA as a whole.[16] That is, he believes that it is unreasonable to interpret the ADA to say that exemption for independent contractors under Title I does not exist under Title III.[17] Another way to put it is to say that Title III deals with the goods, services, and facilities offered to customers or patrons of the public accommodation and not to individuals who work at the facility, whether those workers be paid employees, independent contractors, or volunteers.[18]

On the other hand, excellent arguments exist for allowing such a suit, and the *Hetz* court explained those as well and ultimately decided that the arguments for allowing such a suit carried the day. First, the plain language of Title III does not limit its protection to only clients or customers.[19] Instead, the term used is "individual," the plain meaning of which would appear to cover a doctor applying for staff privileges.[20]

Second, while it is true that "clients" or "customers" is used to define an individual or class of individuals under Title III of the ADA, that phrase is a limitation only for the purposes of the clauses in those separate subparagraphs.[21] Such a drafting is indicative of supporting the argument that Congress did not intend the word "individual" to be synonymous with the phrase "client or customer."[22]

Third, the hospital is a place of public accommodation[23] (the court noted that the categories of places of public accommodations are to be construed liberally to afford people with disabilities equal access to the wide variety of establishments available to people without disabilities).[24]

Fourth, as a place of public accommodation, the hospital cannot discriminate against an individual based on his or her disability with respect to the full and equal enjoyment of its goods, services, facilities, privileges, advantages, or accommodations.[25]

Fifth, the ADA's use of the word "individual" rather than client or customer accurately represents the expansive purpose of the ADA, which is the remedy for widespread discrimination against disabled individuals.[26]

Sixth, in enacting the ADA, Congress noted that discrimination against persons with disabilities often takes the form of outright intentional exclusion.[27]

Seventh, Hetz was alleging outright intentional exclusion due to his disability and therefore, given the broad purpose of the ADA and its expansive definitions of what constitutes a place of public accommodation, the court felt it appropriate to insert limiting parameters that may exclude an individual from the ADA's protection who otherwise would qualify under the plain language of the statute.[28]

Eighth, the court noted that the Department of Justice's technical assistance manual explicitly lists the situation of the physician applying for staff privileges as being the type of situation covered by Title III of the ADA.[29]

Ninth, legislative history indicating that Congress primarily thought of Title III as applying to "customers or clients" doesn't mean that the statute should be narrowed because, rather than that demonstrating ambiguity, it demonstrates just how broad the law can be.[30]

Tenth, interpreting Title III to apply to individuals seeking staff privileges at the hospital did not, to the court's mind, run roughshod over Title I of the ADA because there was no overlap of protections, since the plaintiff was not an employee of the hospital entitled to protections of Title I of the ADA.[31] Nor did such an interpretation create absurd consequences, because the court was not concluding that all independent contractors would necessarily be covered by Title III of the ADA.[32] For that matter, neither is the plaintiff being allowed to circumvent the requirements of Title I by bringing suit under Title III, since the obligations of an employer under Title I of the ADA are different from the obligations of a place of public accommodation under Title III.[33]

Eleventh, the majority opinion in *PGA Tour v. Martin* was silent as to whether Title III of the ADA limited its protections to "clients or customers." The majority's silence on that question is a far cry from saying that they implicitly accepted Justice Scalia's reasoning with respect to "clients or customers."[34]

Twelfth, the court rejected the "slippery slope" argument. The court said that not all independent contractor relationships are going to be able to move forward under a Title III suit.[35] With respect to staff privileges, there are some unique factors at work. For example, in the situation before it, the hospital was simply offering a facility as a place of practice for an independent doctor.[36] That hospital does not pay the physician; rather, the physician owns the patients and collects fees from them directly.[37] Therefore, physicians in such a situation are working for themselves rather than for the hospital and are receiving the primary benefit from their use of the hospital's facilities.[38] Therefore, the relationship between the hospital and the physician seeking staff privileges is entirely within the language of Title III of the ADA because the physician is seeking the enjoyment of the hospital's facilities.[39] The court noted that it could well be a very different matter for an individual, such as a painter, who was hired and paid to perform services primarily for the benefit of the place of public accommodation.[40]

Finally, the court said that even if Title III were limited to clients or customers of the hospital, the plaintiff would nevertheless be someone who would be considered a client or customer of the hospital.[41] Just because the plaintiff was also providing medical services to the hospital's customer, that did not preclude him from being a "client or customer" seeking access to a separate privilege offered by the hospital.[42]

I look eventually for this question to head to the U.S. Supreme Court, as you are already seeing a split of decisions, and given the partisanship that currently exists, it is unlikely that Congress would clarify Title III on this issue one way or the other. With respect to what the Supreme Court will ultimately do, predictions are very dangerous.

I do feel comfortable in saying that a case involving this issue would likely be extremely close. Of course, that assumes that the current makeup of the Court stays what it is when this issue comes down.

Notes

1. The leading case on informed consent is *Canterbury v. Spence,* 464 F.2d 772 (D.C. Cir. 1972). Informed consent now exists in every state, though specific details of the doctrine may vary. Thus, the reader is encouraged to research his or her own applicable informed consent doctrine for specific answers. Nevertheless, the general principles of informed consent are the same in all jurisdictions.
2. *See* Bragdon v. Abbott, 524 U.S. 624 (1998).
3. Just about all states have laws protecting the confidentiality of HIV information. The specific laws vary in their provisions. Thus, the reader's particular state law should be consulted to see if and when the confidentiality provisions will be overridden in favor of a duty to warn per the doctrine of informed consent.
4. A hospital may reassign an HIV-positive surgical assistant without violating the Rehabilitation Act of 1973. *See* Bradley v. Univ. of Texas M.D. Anderson Cancer Center, 3 F.3d 922 (5th Cir. 1993); *see also* Bragdon v. Abbott, *supra* note 2.
5. *Bragdon, supra*; United States v. Morvant, 898 F. Supp. 1157 (E.D. La. 1995).
6. *E.g.,* Faya v. Almaraz, 620 A.2d 327 (Md. 1993). The states vary on the circumstances where such a cause of action would exist for failure to disclose HIV status. Thus, readers are advised to research their own state law before reaching any final conclusions. For example, Illinois and many other states require that there be actual exposure to HIV before such a claim would be allowed. *See* Doe v. Surgicare of Joliet, Inc., 268 Ill. App. 3d 793, 798 (3d Dist. 1994).
7. School Board of Nassau County, Fla. v. Arline, 480 U.S. 273, 288 (1987).
8. *See* Clackamas Gastroenterology Assocs., P.C. v. Wells, 538 U.S. 440 (2003).
9. Mentkowitz v. Pottstown Mem'l Med. Ctr., 154 F.3d 113 (3d Cir. 1998).
10. Hetz v. Aurora Med. Ctr. of Manitowoc County, 2007 WL 1753428 (E.D. Wis. June 18, 2007).
11. *Id.* at *1.
12. *Id.* at *15.
13. PGA Tour, Inc. v. Martin, 532 U.S. 661, 691 (Scalia, J., dissenting).
14. *Hetz,* 2007 WL 1753428 at *9, *citing to* PGA Tour at 692.
15. *Id.*
16. *Hetz, supra* note 14 at *9 *citing to* what should be *PGA Tour* at 693.
17. *Id.* at 693–94.

18. Bauer v. Muscular Dystrophy Ass'n, Inc., 268 F. Supp. 2d 1281, 1292 (D. Kan. 2003).
19. *Hetz,* 2007 WL 1753428 at *11.
20. *Id.*
21. *Id.*
22. *Id.*
23. *Id.*
24. *Id.*
25. *Id.*
26. *Id.*
27. *Id.*
28. *Id.*
29. *Id.* at *12.
30. *Id.* at *13.
31. *Id.*
32. *Id.*
33. *Id.*
34. *Id.* at *14.
35. *Id.* at *12.
36. *Id.*
37. *Id.*
38. *Id.*
39. *Id.*
40. *Id.* at n.2.
41. *Id.* at *14.
42. *Id.* at *15.

The Interrelationship between the ADA and Other Laws

10

ONE OF THE MOST DIFFICULT ASPECTS of dealing with the Americans with Disabilities Act is where it interrelates with other laws. This chapter will highlight some of the more common ways the ADA interacts with other laws and suggest ways in which such interactions may be effectively managed.

ADA AND COLLECTIVE BARGAINING

There are other ways in which the ADA can affect the collective bargaining context besides the reassignment context discussed earlier in this book, and several come to mind.

1. Whether an ADA claim must be arbitrated where there is a mandatory arbitration agreement.
2. Whether a mandatory arbitration agreement precludes an independent lawsuit by the EEOC.
3. Can the ADA be preempted by the law that governs collective bargaining, such as the Railway Labor Act?
4. If a public entity submits to a collective bargaining grievance procedure, does that mean it waived sovereign immunity?

5. Can the leave policy in a collective-bargaining agreement dictate what constitutes a reasonable accommodation?

With respect to the first question, in *Wright v. Universal Maritime Service Corporation,* the U.S. Supreme Court held that there was no presumption of arbitrability with respect to ADA claims.[1] Further, while the ADA could be waived under an arbitration clause, such a waiver must be clear and unmistakable.[2, 3]

With respect to the second question, the case of *EEOC v. Waffle House, Inc.*[4] is instructive. In *Waffle House*, Mr. Baker had signed a mandatory arbitration agreement with his employer, Waffle House.[5] After suffering a seizure at work, Waffle House terminated Mr. Baker.[6] Mr. Baker never activated the arbitration agreement, but he did file a timely claim with the EEOC.[7] When the EEOC's attempt to resolve the dispute failed, EEOC brought an enforcement action against Waffle House.[8] In holding that the EEOC had a full range of remedies available to it regardless of any arbitration agreement,[9] the U.S. Supreme Court reasoned as follows:

First, the Court said that the 1972 amendment to Title VII of the Civil Rights Act created a system whereby the EEOC had the primary burden of litigation.[10] Those same amendments authorized the courts to impose a full range of remedies, and nowhere do those amendments mention arbitration proceedings.[11]

Second, the Court noted that in 1991 Congress amended Title VII, which included amending the ADA accordingly, to allow the recovery of compensatory and punitive damages by a complaining party, which included the EEOC.[12]

Third, the 1991 amendments to Title VII contain no suggestion that an arbitration agreement between private parties changes in any way the EEOC's available options or remedies.[13]

Fourth, the Court drew on basic contract law when it stated that the EEOC was not a party to any arbitration agreement and therefore could not be bound by that agreement.[14]

Fifth, the Court noted that if the EEOC decides to file suit on behalf of a person, the EEOC is in complete control of that person's case.[15] In fact, the Court noted the EEOC has its own right to vindicate the public interest and does not stand in the shoes of the person upon whose behalf the suit is brought.[16]

Sixth, the Court reasoned that the statute granting power to the EEOC makes clear it has the authority to evaluate the strength of the public interest at stake.[17]

Finally, the pro-arbitration policies of the Federal Arbitration Act do not require an agency to relinquish its statutory authority if it has not agreed to do so.[18] In short, *Waffle House* stands for the proposition that while an employee may be bound by an arbitration agreement, the EEOC is certainly not.[19]

With respect to the third question, the Ninth Circuit, making an analogy between the ADA and Title VII of the Civil Rights Act, has held that the rights created by the ADA are independent of the collective-bargaining agreement, and therefore cannot be preempted by the law governing collective bargaining.[20]

With respect to the fourth question, an unpublished Michigan Court of Appeals decision from October 18, 2012, held that a governmental entity, by participating in the collective bargaining process with respect to a grievance, did not waive its sovereign immunity.[21] However, two notes of caution are in order. First, the decision is unpublished. Unpublished decisions come with restrictions, which the nature of depend on the jurisdiction. Whether they can be cited at all also depends on the jurisdiction. The precedential value of an unpublished decision is weak at best, again depending on the jurisdiction. That said, unpublished decisions can be useful to giving a client an idea of what the possibilities might be and where the law might be headed. Second, in this case you have a state court deciding a question of federal law. Accordingly, federal courts would not be bound in any way by this decision.

With respect to the fifth question, a collective-bargaining agreement and its terms can be used to help determine what might be a reasonable accommodation. For example, in *Shim v. United Air Lines, Inc.*,[22] the U.S. District Court for Hawaii held that United Air Lines' leave of absence policy, which allowed for a leave of up to three years, could be considered by the court to determine what is reasonable.[23] The court also noted that when an employee's request is consistent with documented employee leave policies, the courts are more likely to find the leave being allowed as a reasonable accommodation.[24]

WORKER'S COMPENSATION

Employers traditionally engaged in two worker's compensation practices that are now forbidden under the ADA. First, employers often asked a prospective employee what his worker's compensation history was prior to any conditional job offer. This practice is now illegal under the ADA, as it violates the ADA's ban on pre-employment medical inquiries.[25] Second, employers would—and many still do—insist on a full return to work after the employee suffered an on-the-job injury.[26] A full return to work policy says you cannot come back to work unless you are 100%.[27] I have written for years that this policy is very problematic under the ADA. But what do the cases say? A very instructive case from the Seventh Circuit on December 15, 2011, is *Powers v. USF Holland Inc.*[28]

In this case, the plaintiff was a long-haul truck driver who injured his back while driving his truck.[29] Following a worker's compensation leave, he successfully returned to work as a long-haul truck driver and worked without incident for two years.[30] As the birth of his child neared, he asked to switch to being a city driver.[31] After the switch, he began having problems with his back due to the physical requirements of the city driver position and asked to switch back.[32] However, the collective bargaining agreement did not allow for another change within the year, so the employer denied the request.[33] The plaintiff then took a medical leave of absence and later tried to return to work as a long-haul driver, presenting the employer with a medical release that limited him to road driver work and limited dock work.[34] The employer would not allow him to return, saying that it needed clarification on his medical restrictions and that he could not return to work as a truck driver unless the employer received a medical release without restrictions.[35] The plaintiff then sued, alleging violations of the ADA because of the "100% healed" policy.[36]

This is a case that turned on the rules that were in existence before the ADAAA went into effect and that fact resulted in the court finding that the plaintiff did not have a disability.[37] What is important for our purposes is that the court spent significant time talking about "100% healed" policies—how they play out under the Americans with Disabilities Act and how they might play out under the Americans with Disabilities Act as amended . The court noted that while 100% healed policies may be problematic under the ADA and under the ADAAA, the person who is making those allegations has to be a person with a disability first,[38] and Powers, as mentioned above, wasn't. However, the court noted that the risk of a 100% healed policy is greater, *if not absolute*, since the ADAAA changed the definition of "regarded as" disabled (emphasis added, but the emphasized words come directly from the opinion).[39] No doubt the court was referring to the fact that under the ADAAA, all the employer needs to do to suffer liability with respect to a "regarded as" claim is to regard a person as having a physical or mental impairment, since it is no longer necessary to show that the employer regarded the employee as having a substantial limitation on a major life activity.[40] Therefore, it logically follows that if an employer has a 100% return to work policy, it must be assuming that the employee has a physical or mental impairment or it would not be insisting on a release at all. Such an assumption would lead to the employee having the right to claim that the employer is regarding him or her as having a disability under the ADAAA.

In short, 100% return to work policies, which were never a good idea since the ADA went into effect, are certainly not to be recommended now. The only issue should be whether that particular person can perform, with or without reasonable accommodations, the essential functions of the job.

INDIVIDUALS WITH DISABILITIES IN EDUCATION ACT

The Individuals with Disabilities in Education Act (IDEA) governs the special education universe in public schools for grades kindergarten through 12 (K-12). The ADA and § 504 of the Rehabilitation Act of 1973 come into play because the definitions of disability under the ADA are far broader than those contained in the IDEA regulations, and especially so with the advent of the ADA Amendments Act. Hence, a school district needs to consider that when a student is not eligible for special education services under IDEA, the student may be protected under § 504 and the ADA. If the student does have a disability according to § 504 and the ADA, then the public school will have to modify its program to reasonably accommodate the student, even if that student is not eligible for special education services.[41]

It also works in reverse. That is, just because a person is covered under IDEA does not mean the individual is covered under § 504 of the Rehabilitation Act and/or the ADA.[42] Furthermore, a waiver or rejection of services under IDEA does not mean that there has been a waiver or rejection of services under § 504 and/or the ADA.[43] In fact, the school has a continuing obligation to offer services under § 504 and the ADA if that student is qualified to receive services that have not been otherwise rejected.[44] Finally, the school may have additional requirements imposed on it beyond IDEA as a result of the Rehabilitation Act and the Americans with Disabilities Act.[45]

FAMILY AND MEDICAL LEAVE ACT

It is impossible to practice in the area of the ADA without encountering the Family and Medical Leave Act (FMLA). The FMLA covers employers of 50 or more people[46] and permits an employee to take 12 weeks of leave (paid or unpaid, depending on whether the employer mandates the use of sick and vacation time first) to deal with his own or a family member's serious health condition.[47] Job protections are built into the legislation.[48] The scope of coverage of the FMLA and the ADA are very different. The ADA pertains to persons with disabilities, while the FMLA pertains to a serious health condition. The two are not the same. Nor does the term *serious health condition* mean what it appears to mean.[49] For example, one definition of a serious health condition is a period of incapacity of more than three days requiring continuing treatment from a physician.[50] That definition is extremely broad, much more so than any of the definitions of disability contained within the ADA.

The FMLA allows an employer to insist, providing there is a written policy, that an employee be certified as being eligible for leave or as being eligible to return to work from leave.[51] This creates a problem under the ADA, as the FMLA regulations stipulate that whether a person is eligible for FMLA or is allowed to return to work from the FMLA leave depends on whether the person can do the essential functions of the job.[52] Note that these regulations emphatically do not state that the certification must be based on whether the person can do the job *with or without reasonable accommodations*.[53] Thus, a trap for the unwary exists. For example, Person X is on FLMA leave and also has a disability. He desires to come back to work, so he is evaluated per written policy of his company. The doctor who examines X determines that he cannot do the essential functions of the job. The company denies the return to work. However, he can do the job with reasonable accommodations, perhaps with a short period of time off. In this scenario, the company has not violated the FMLA but has violated the ADA.[54] This problem can be solved by the company's evaluating the person based on whether he can perform the essential functions of the job with reasonable accommodations.

Forcing a person to take FMLA leave and not accommodating them under the ADA with reasonable accommodations may also be evidence of bad faith on the part of the employer as well as evidence of retaliation.[55] In *Mills v. Temple University*, a secretary and long-time employee was struck in the back by a coworker and flung forward.[56] She began experiencing severe pain within days of the incident. By the end of the following week, a worker's compensation incident report was completed and she was referred to a physician in Temple's occupational health unit.[57] She received treatment by the physician, which included a topical cream for pain, and the physician continued to see her continuously once a week until December 2008.[58] During that time, the plaintiff was released to return to work without any restrictions.[59] That physician referred her to an orthopedist before releasing her from worker's compensation medical care.[60] The orthopedist prescribed medication and physical therapy, and she continued to receive treatment by various physicians.[61] Even so, she continued to experience pain in the back while working and had difficulty lifting and filing patient charts.[62]

The plaintiff and the senior administrator for the cardiology department had discussions about this, with the result that student interns and permanent Temple staff took over filing for her toward the end of 2008, a fact that she shared with her direct supervisor as well.[63] While the plaintiff outside of work continued to engage in daily activities such as driving, caring for herself and her daughter, and shopping, she struggled with these activities, as she found them quite exhausting.[64]

What follows is an example of what can happen when competent personnel are not consulted in these kinds of things. After being released from worker's compensation medical care, she contacted the human resources department about how to pursue a worker's compensation claim, which ultimately proved unsuccessful.[65] The senior administrator for the cardiology department suggested that she apply for FMLA leave to protect the absences.[66] The first request for FMLA leave was denied because the physician asked to do the certification declined to provide a diagnosis or complete the certification, since that physician had only seen her once.[67] She then began seeing a pain management specialist who diagnosed kyphosis, degenerative discs, and bulging discs in her back.[68] He treated the plaintiff for six months, during which she received bimonthly epidural injection for back pain.[69] She applied for intermittent FMLA leave in May 2009 and had the doctor she was seeing fill out the certification.[70] This leave was approved.[71]

In June 2009, the student intern helping the plaintiff with filing left for the summer, leading to the filing piling up.[72] When her direct supervisor circulated an email asking several members of the staff, including the plaintiff, to assist with filing, the plaintiff responded the next day that she would not able to do filing since it would further injure her back and requesting whether further documentation about that was needed.[73] The direct supervisor said that she would need that documentation, and the plaintiff asked in response whether the FMLA certification would suffice.[74] The direct supervisor said no and asked for a doctor's note instead, which the plaintiff promptly furnished.[75] Once the letter was received, the senior administrator for the cardiology department said that filing was an essential function of the job and that she had to do it.[76]

After conferring with HR, they decided to send the plaintiff home and offer her continuous FMLA leave.[77] *Neither person consulted a doctor or Temple's Office of Labor and Employment before sending the plaintiff home.* (Emphasis added.)[78] The senior administrator for the cardiology department later that day sent an e-mail saying that the letter had been received, she was eligible for FMLA leave, and could return only if the doctor authorized that she could return to work fully and unrestricted.[79] The plaintiff called the senior administrator to discuss the matter and the call was not returned.[80] She then left the next day for vacation.[81] When she came back from vacation, she called her direct supervisor to discuss how to proceed and was referred to human resources, which told her that she could not return to work and was provided with an application for continuous FMLA leave.[82] Plaintiff then objected to taking unpaid leave for an injury that occurred on the job and did not understand why she had to complete another certification, since one had already been already approved.[83]

She never completed the application, and neither did she comply with Temple's procedure for absences, which eventually led to her being terminated from her employment for being absent without leave.[84]

While she was never able to find other employment once being terminated and lost her health insurance following her dismissal, the condition did improve so that she could treat it with Motrin or a prescription muscle relaxer.[85] She filed suit against Temple alleging discrimination and retaliation as well as interference under the FMLA and due process violations.[86]

In denying Temple's motion for summary judgment on the discrimination, retaliation, and FMLA claims (the plaintiff did not object to summary judgment being awarded to the defendant with respect to the due process violation), the court reasoned as follows. (While this case was brought up in the context of the intersection of the FMLA and the ADA, the court also had some very important things to say with regard to being substantially limited in a major life activity that bear noting here before we get to the FMLA and ADA discussion on good faith and retaliation.)

First, Temple argued that the plaintiff was not substantially limited in a major life activity because she experienced minimal pain that was being managed with pain medication and Motrin.[87] The court didn't buy the argument for three reasons. First, it referred to the ADAAA, which says that whether a plaintiff is substantially limited is a less searching analysis that it used to be and a question of fact.[88] It is interesting to note that "less searching analysis" really means that, as the court never even cited to the EEOC definition of substantial limitation under the ADAAA.

Second, whether a person is substantially limited is determined from the point in time at which the alleged discriminatory action occurred and not from the time of the decision on the case.[89] Finally, the court said that ample evidence existed to indicate that the plaintiff was substantially limited in her ability to lift.[90]

The plaintiff also argued that she was substantially limited in her ability to work as well.[91] The court's response to this is very interesting. Over the years, I have seen some courts focus on working as the end-all and be-all of a substantial major life activity. Of course, defense attorneys would prefer it that way as well, since it is very hard to show, pre-ADAAA as well as post-ADAAA, that a person is substantially limited in the major life activity of working. What is interesting here is that the court adopts the EEOC guidelines with respect to working by saying that if you can find a person substantially limited in any other major life activity, working as the major life activity never comes up.[92]

With respect to offering FMLA leave but never offering a reasonable accommodation option, the court held that such action was not in good faith.[93] Temple did not meet with the plaintiff regarding receipt of the letter, nor did it inquire from the plaintiff about what her limitations were or ask what accommodation she desired.[94] Instead, it immediately rejected the idea, after a short conversation among managers, of hiring a student intern to help with filing despite the fact that an intern had been doing that for over six months.[95] In short, this case puts an employer on notice that offering FMLA leave without exploring the accommodation process, especially if there are additional factors, is not a good-faith response (whether the employer acts in good faith is important, as discussed earlier in this book, since good faith is a defense to damages).

Last but certainly not least, the court held that ignoring a request for reasonable accommodation and offering FMLA leave instead could reasonably dissuade a person from requesting an accommodation because nobody wants to be sent home from work without pay.[96] In short, taking such an approach also opens up the employer to a retaliation claim.[97]

This case is very instructive for several reasons.

First, employers should realize that post ADAAA, showing a substantial limitation on a major life activity is going to be much easier than it used to be for a plaintiff to prove.

Second, plaintiff's attorneys and plaintiffs should take to heart that alleging working as the major life activity should be done only as a matter of last resort.

Third, offering FMLA leave without offering a reasonable accommodation process is both not a good-faith response, especially if other factors are present as well, but also possible evidence of retaliation. In short, the preventive law approach, discussed above, of offering the accommodation as an option to FMLA leave is not only good preventive law but now may be necessary in order to prevent liability.

Fourth, as if Temple did not have enough problems, it insisted on a full return to work. As discussed previously in the worker's compensation section of this book and the discussion of *Powers*, such a demand post-ADAAA is extremely problematic.

Fifth, it is curious how the termination happened without consulting counsel. An excellent preventive approach is to adopt a policy that nobody is terminated except for cause, and all such termination decisions are reviewed by counsel first. If my experience is any indication, such a policy significantly decreases outside legal fees.

Finally, since the last edition of the book, the Family and Medical Leave Act has been amended to allow for leave when a family member is called to active duty by the military, [98] and the Department of Labor issued final rules on February 6, 2013, implementing that statute.[99] However, those particular amendments do not affect the discussion with respect to how the FMLA relates to the ADA as amended.

ADA AND DISABILITY/ERISA BENEFITS

Consider the following scenario:

> Person X works for a company of more than 15 employees, develops a disability, and is terminated from her position because of that disability. She then files for Social Security benefits. Or perhaps she files for short-term or long-term disability benefits under the company's policy. She then brings suit under the ADA for failure of the employer to reasonably accommodate her disability.

The defense in this type of case is invariably based on the case of *Cleveland v. Policy Management Systems,*[100] where the person in some other proceeding has claimed total disability and is therefore estopped, or prevented, from claiming that he or she can do the job with or without reasonable accommodation. In *Cleveland*, the plaintiff filed for Social Security disability benefits and obtained them.[101] Subsequently, he filed an ADA suit and claimed that he was not reasonably accommodated.[102] To obtain SSDI, a person has to show that he is unable to perform any job in the economic marketplace.[103]

In holding that judicial estoppel might apply in such situations, Justice Breyer, writing for the U.S. Supreme Court, wasted no time in laying out the holding of the case. Justice Breyer said that the pursuit and receipt of SSDI benefits do not automatically estop the plaintiff from pursuing an ADA claim.[104] Nor does the law erect a strong presumption against the plaintiff's success in filing an ADA claim.[105] However, an ADA plaintiff cannot simply ignore her SSDI contention.[106] To survive a motion for summary judgment, the plaintiff must explain why the information in the SSDI filing is consistent with showing that the plaintiff is otherwise qualified for the position at issue.[107]

Justice Breyer took note of the apparent conflict between the ADA and SSDI, but proceeded to say the inherent conflict (ADA: "I can do the job if I am reasonably accommodated" v. SSDI: "I can't do any job in the economic marketplace") was not so severe that courts should apply a special negative presumption.[108]

The ADA and SSDI systems operate completely differently from each other. For example, the SSDI system does not factor reasonable accommodation into its calculus. Thus, an ADA suit claiming that the plaintiff can perform the job with reasonable accommodation may be consistent with claiming the inability to perform a job or jobs without it.[109] Justice Breyer noted that people receiving SSDI can work under certain parameters.[110]

Finally, even with all this said, an ADA plaintiff cannot ignore the SSDI and ADA apparent contradiction; a sufficient explanation must be forthcoming.[111] To defeat a summary judgment motion, the explanation must be sufficient to warrant a reasonable juror concluding that (assuming the truth of the claims made or the plaintiff's good-faith belief in the truth of those claims made in the SSDI filing) the plaintiff could perform the essential functions of the job with or without reasonable accommodation.[112]

Thus, the Supreme Court has clarified just how judicial estoppel will be treated in the future *vis-à-vis* the ADA. What it means for the practitioner is that when filing an SSDI claim or a long-term disability claim on behalf of the client, *form* will become very important. It will have to be made clear that the filing assumes that reasonable accommodations are a non-issue. Failure to take those precautions could well sink the client later if he or she pursues an ADA claim. Also, it is no longer SSDI that is the sole worry, as courts are now holding that representations made in a long-term disability application may also activate judicial estoppel.[113] Finally, ADA and SSDI practitioners must let the client know of the risks of judicial estoppel when taking on their ADA or SSDI matter. Failure to so advise the client invites the real risk of legal malpractice.[114]

The reason why failure to advise the client filing for an SSDI claim runs the real risk of legal malpractice can be traced to the elements of a legal malpractice claim in the transactional context. Legal malpractice is a state law claim, so the elements of a legal malpractice claim may be different from state to state. Therefore, readers are wise to check their own state law as to what the elements of a legal malpractice claim are. Legal malpractice can occur either in the litigation context or in the transactional context. The elements of both are the same. However, the elements of legal malpractice between a litigation case and a transactional matter may, depending on the state, be different when it comes to proving cause in fact.

To look at Illinois by way of example, the elements of a legal malpractice claim for both transactional and litigation matters are:

1) attorney owed the plaintiff a duty of due care arising from the attorney-client relationship;
2) attorney breached that duty; and
3) as a proximate result, the client suffered injury.[115]

The difference between transactional malpractice and litigation malpractice is (again, check your own state jurisdiction) in how cause in fact, often referred to as actual cause, is proven in the two types of cases. With respect to litigation cases, for a plaintiff to show actual causation, he or she would have to show that, but for the negligence of the attorney, he or she would have won the case.[116] However, with respect to a transactional matter, establishing cause in fact means showing that had the undisclosed risk been known, the plaintiff would not have accepted the risk and consented to the recommended course of action.[117] Therefore, since the *Cleveland Policy* case has been around since 1999, the risks of what can happen to a future ADA claim, depending on how the SSDI forms are filled out, has been known for some time. Accordingly, the SSDI attorney would do well to advise his or her client of the risks involved in filing for SSDI with respect to a future ADA claim and should, whenever possible, ensure that the SSDI forms are not filled out in such a way so that a future ADA claim is jeopardized. Also, the ADA attorney needs to advise his or her client of the impact an SSDI filing will have on his or her ADA claim.

AIR CARRIER ACCESS ACT

Private Cause of Action and Preemption of Federal Laws

If an airline discriminates against a person with a disability, the ADA is probably not the law involved; rather, it is the Air Carrier Access Act that applies. With respect to the Air Carrier Access Act, there are two questions. First, if an airline violates the Air Carrier Access Act, does a private cause of action exist? Second, if a private cause of action does not exist, could a person bring suit under a state disability discrimination law for the discrimination or does the Air Carrier Access Act preempt such a suit?

With respect to whether a private cause of action exists, a case that probably answered this question is *Lopez v. JetBlue Airways.*[118] In that case, a person with a disability alleged JetBlue discriminated against her by failing to provide timely wheelchair assistance during a roundtrip she took from JFK to Puerto Rico, with the result that she suffered pain and swelling in her foot as well as anguish, anxiety, and nightmares.[119] She filed a claim with the Department of Transportation (DOT) but the Department was unable to determine whether the airline had violated any regulations.[120] The DOT then took no further action against the airline with respect to the complaint.[121] The plaintiff then filed a complaint against the airline in U.S. District Court alleging violations of the Air Carrier Access Act and the ADA.[122] JetBlue filed a motion to dismiss, claiming that regardless of whether the claim fell under Air Carrier Access Act or the ADA, neither law allowed for a private lawsuit in this situation.[123]

The Second Circuit agreed with JetBlue's claims.[124] The Air Carrier Access Act is actually a single statute, 49 U.S.C.A. § 41705. The statute doesn't say much. The first section defines a person with a disability as under the ADA and says that an air carrier, including a foreign air carrier, may not discriminate against an otherwise qualified handicapped individual (for whatever reason, Congress has not amended the law to strike "handicapped" in favor of "person with a disability").[125] The second part of the statute goes on to say that a separate violation occurs for each individual act of discrimination.[126] The final section of the law says that the Department of Transportation is responsible for investigating such claims and for offering technical assistance.[127]

The Second Circuit was faced with two issues. First, is there a private cause of action under the Air Carrier Access Act? Second, does the ADA even apply to a situation involving airline transportation? With respect to the first issue, the Second Circuit said that the Air Carrier Access Act does not authorize a private cause of action.[128] The Second Circuit relied on a Supreme Court opinion holding that a statute must have a clear manifestation of congressional intent in order to create a private cause of action before the court can find that Congress implied a private cause of action.[129] In particular, the court noted that the Air Carrier Access Act does not expressly contain the right to sue the air carrier, and further, the statute provides an administrative enforcement scheme designed to vindicate fully the rights of passengers with disabilities.[130] That administrative scheme includes a mandate for the Department of Transportation (DOT) to investigate complaints that appear to be based on reasonable grounds; issue orders to compel compliance with statutory provisions after it has completed its investigation and given the air carrier an opportunity to be heard; review all complaints directed against air carriers of disability discrimination and publish disability-related complaint data; have the option to revoke an air carrier certificate; impose fines; or even request that the Attyorney General bring a civil enforcement action.[131] The Air Carrier Access Act also provides for the ability of an individual with a substantial interest in the administrative decision of the DOT to file a petition for review in the U.S. Court of Appeals.[132] Accordingly, while a person who suffered discrimination by the airlines cannot bring a private cause of action, he or she can file a complaint with the DOT.

What about the Americans with Disabilities Act? The court found that the ADA simply did not apply to the situation where a person is discriminated against by airlines in the course of air travel.[133] In particular, the court said that Title III of the ADA, which prohibits places of public accommodation from discriminating against persons with disabilities, was not in play at all because while the ADA does apply to terminals, depots, or other stations used for specified public transportation, that particular statute contains an exception for aircraft.[134] Therefore, the Second Circuit held that the terminal, depot, or other station reference contained in the public accommodation provisions of the ADA (Title III) was not meant to include a facility devoted primarily to air travel.[135] Keep in mind, if the airport is a public entity or takes federal funds, then Title II of the ADA and/or the Rehabilitation Act are in play with respect to the airport.[136]

But is that the end of the story? Not necessarily. In a footnote, the Second Circuit said that questions remain open. For example, could an air carrier be found to be an owner, lessor, lessee, or operator of a public accommodation?[137] Another question that remains open is whether a carrier could be held liable for disability discrimination if it was somehow involved in the provision of travel services other than by aircraft or located in a terminal, depot, or other station not primarily used for air travel.[138]

Finally, what about the regulations themselves? They are extremely comprehensive. The DOT requested comments on an update to the technical assistance manual that were due by October 3, 2012. It is the comprehensiveness of these regulations that leads us to the second question: whether a person wanting to sue under a state disability discrimination law with respect to the airlines would be preempted from doing so.

A case holding that the Air Carrier Access Act does preempt state law suits is *Segalman v. Southwest Airlines*.[139] In this case, the plaintiff flew Southwest Airlines several different times.[140] Southwest Airlines did not comply with the Air Carrier Access Act regulations with respect to stowing wheelchairs during any of those flights.[141] As a result, the plaintiff was not able to use his wheelchair upon arriving at his destinations.[142] The plaintiff had cerebral palsy and had to use a specific wheelchair.[143] Under the Air Carrier Access Act, there are very specific regulations dealing with how an airline is supposed to deal with a person's wheelchair.[144] Those regulations were not complied with. That caused him considerable distress, physical and mental anguish, and considerable inconvenience, as he had to get the wheelchair fixed in a variety of different locations.[145]

Instead of filing an administrative complaint with the Department of Transportation, which enforces the Air Carrier Access Act, the plaintiff filed suit against Southwest Airlines, alleging violations of the ADA, violation of the California Unruh Act, and violation of the California Disabled Persons Act.[146] Not surprisingly, in light of the above discussion, Southwest Airlines moved to dismiss the ADA claim. It also moved to dismiss the state law claims, arguing that the state law claims were preempted by federal law.

For the reasons mentioned earlier in our discussion of the Air Carrier Access Act, the Eastern District of California dismissed the ADA claim, saying act did not apply to discrimination against an individual by an airline; rather, the applicable law was the Air Carrier Access Act.[147] However, the court went even further when it said that since the federal government had issued extensive regulations implementing this particular statute, that meant the federal government intended to preempt the field with respect to other laws that might apply, certainly with respect to any laws under which the federal government had very specific applicable regulations (the Air Carrier Access Act has very specific regulations on how wheelchairs must be stowed).[148]

With respect to a private cause of action, *Segalman* has an interesting element to it. While the court said that no private cause of action exists under the Air Carrier Access Act, it also said that if somehow a private cause of action did exist, the statutory scheme was such that it required exhaustion of administrative remedies.[149] In this case, the plaintiff did not exhaust administrative remedies because he never filed a claim with the Department of Transportation.[150] This discussion of administrative remedies is very interesting, because there is nothing in this opinion that suggests that exhaustion of administrative remedies would change the equation with respect to whether a private cause of action existed in the first place.

So how do you deal with Air Carrier Access Act issues as a procedural matter? If you are a plaintiff, you definitely want to file with the DOT and go through that process. Once that process is complete, you could try filing in federal court. The problem with that approach is that the statute doesn't contain any indication you can go to federal court in the first place. That said, once that process is completed, the plaintiff may want to try to argue that the regulations themselves create a private cause of action, which for reasons discussed above would be a tough sell, but maybe it is worth trying. Also, if a state law deals with the situation and the Air Carrier Access Act regulations do not specifically pertain to the situation at issue, then a plaintiff might argue that violations of the state law occurred and were not preempted by the federal regulations. For reasons discussed below, a plaintiff may find it advantageous to ignore the discrimination and focus on a separate cause of action, such as personal injury, especially where new injuries arise or old ones are aggravated because of the discrimination.

On the defense side, the argument is pretty simple. The Air Carrier Access Act is the only law that applies with respect to air carriers, airports, and persons with disabilities. Further, the Air Carrier Access Act statute does not allow for a private cause of action. Also, the statutory scheme is such that a private cause of action (but see the discussion below for an avenue that a plaintiff could use to get around this problem) for violating the regulations should not be allowed either. For good measure, the defendant could argue that a plaintiff would need to exhaust administrative remedies first. With respect to administrative remedies exhaustion, I am not really sure I follow that argument because it simply would not come into play if no private cause of action existed in the first place. Also, by saying administrative remedies should be exhausted first, the implication is that a private cause of action exists after that.

Scope of Preemption

Certainly, as noted above, the defendant could argue that any state law claims are preempted by the regulations implementing the Air Carrier Access Act. However, that doesn't answer the question of whether, assuming preemption exists, the preemption applies to the standards or to the remedies or both.

A case from the Ninth Circuit, *Gilstrap v. United Airlines*,[151] addresses this very question. In this case, the plaintiff had difficulty walking due to a collapsed disc in her back, a knee replacement, another knee in need of replacing, and osteoarthritis.[152] In August 2008, she flew on United from Los Angeles to Calgary, from Calgary to Chicago, and from Milwaukee back to Los Angeles via Denver.[153] In December 2009, she flew from Burbank, California, to Madison, Wisconsin, by way of Denver.[154] When she booked both flights, she requested that United provide her with wheelchair assistance for moving through the airport.[155] During both trips, United failed to provide the plaintiff with the assistance that she requested.[156] At one airport she had to locate a wheelchair on her own; at another airport she obtained a wheelchair from United only after prolonged assistance and up to 45 minutes of waiting; and at other airports she was never able to locate a wheelchair at all and had to walk.[157] Further, she alleged that a United agent yelled at her, expressed skepticism that she actually needed a wheelchair, and on two occasions directed her to stand in line, which she was not able to do because of her disabilities.[158] At one point, a United agent unilaterally revoked her ticket and booked her for a later flight after telling her that is what she got for refusing to stand in line.[159]

She sued United in tort alleging several different causes of action under California law, including negligence, negligent misrepresentation, breach of duty of a common carrier, intentional infliction of emotional distress, and negligent infliction of emotional distress.[160] She also alleged that United violated Title III of the ADA as well.[161] She did not sue alleging violations of the Air Carrier Access Act; rather, the claim was that the Air Carrier Access Act was relevant to establishing negligence on the theory of negligence per se.[162]

Before proceeding further, a brief comment is in order about negligence per se. Negligence per se is a legal concept that basically says that violation of a statute can be used as a means of saying that the defendant was negligent. It is basic black-letter law that everybody learns in law school. Many states, such as California and Georgia, to name just two, have a statute that says violation of a statute, ordinance, or regulation can be used as a means of establishing negligence. The state statutes vary in their wording. They also vary in what happens once you show that the statute, ordinance, or regulation is violated. Basically, what can happen might vary from winning your case, if you can show that the statute was violated and the person alleging the violation of the statute, regulation, or ordinance was meant to be protected by that ordinance[163] to creating a rebuttable presumption of failure to exercise due care.[164]

The court had several potential issues before it. First, are the remedies under the Air Carrier Access Act exclusive—that is, do those remedies preclude other remedies? Second, if the remedies are not exclusive, what role does the extensive regulations implementing the Air Carrier Access Act play in any subsequent state law–based negligence suit? Third, does the Air Carrier Access Act provide for a private cause of action? Fourth, does the ADA apply to airline terminals?

With respect to the first issue, the Ninth Circuit found that the remedies in the Air Carrier Access Act are not exclusive. That is, the Air Carrier Access Act does not preclude other kinds of causes of action such as those lying in tort. The court found it extremely significant that the Federal Aviation Act, of which the Air Carrier Access Act is an amendment to, specifically says that any remedy under the Federal Aviation Act is in addition to any other remedies provided by law, and it also says that Department of Transportation certified air carriers have to maintain liability insurance sufficient to cover bodily injury, death, loss of property, or damage to property resulting from the operation or maintenance of the aircraft.[165] Therefore, the Federal Aviation Act on its face explicitly anticipated that other remedies besides those under the Federal Aviation Act may be utilized. Also, the court found that no conflict existed between federal and state liability standards in this case nor did allowing causes of action lying in tort frustrate the objective of the federal law.[166]

With respect to the second issue, the regulations are indeed extensive and pervasive. The court said in that kind of case, where the statute clearly says that the remedies are not exclusive, but you do have extensive and pervasive federal regulations, what happens is that those extensive and pervasive federal regulations establish the standard of care for the state law cause of action.[167]

With respect to the third issue, the court noted that there are opinions out there, as we have already seen, that say the Air Carrier Access Act, does not give rise to a private cause of action.[168] However, since the plaintiff did not sue under the Air Carrier Access Act, the court said that that was a question they did not have to reach.[169]

With respect to the final issue, as we have also seen above, the court found that the Americans with Disabilities Act was quite explicit that Title III does not apply to airport terminals.[170] However, in a footnote, the court said that the implementing regulations under Title II of the ADA do note that airports operated by public entities are covered by Title II of the ADA, but since the plaintiff did not make any claims under Title II it wasn't necessary to visit that question.[171]

So, what can we specifically take from this case? First, the Air Carrier Access Act does not preempt both standards and remedies because the Federal Aviation Act, of which the Air Carrier Access Act is a part of, allows for other remedies, and allowing for other remedies does not conflict with the purpose of the Federal Aviation Act. Second, while remedies under the Air Carrier Access Act are not exclusive, the standards contained in the regulations implementing the Air Carrier Access Act are the standards that will have to be used in any subsequent state law cause of action alleging injuries from violation of the Air Carrier Access Act regulations. Third, while this case doesn't address the question of whether a private cause of action exists for violation of the Air Carrier Access Act, for reasons mentioned earlier, it probably doesn't. Third, it is quite clear from the cases that Title III of the Americans with Disabilities Act does not apply to airport terminals, but Title II of the ADA could well apply to airport terminals.

So, how do you deal with Air Carrier Access Act issues especially since a person with a disability who is not properly accommodated during their time in an airport, is quite likely to have those disabilities aggravated in some way or have some new injury result. First, this case gives plaintiffs a real opportunity to redress violations of the federal regulation where the violation aggravated and/or caused plaintiff additional personal injuries. Second, airlines are going to have to make sure that their staff are fully trained on all the regulations and that steps are taken to minimize the risk of violations of any of the regulations. Third, if a client comes into a plaintiff personal injury law firm to talk about a situation where they were injured in an airport as a result of the Air Carrier Access Act regulations not being followed, the plaintiff's attorney would want to seriously think about filing state law tort claim lawsuits using the Air Carrier Access Act as the standards for liability. Fourth, since many airports are publicly owned, the plaintiff attorney may also want to consider bringing a cause of action under Title II of the Americans with Disabilities Act as well. Fifth, if the plaintiff alleges a violation of Title III, a likely successful argument by the defense is that Title III of the ADA does not apply to airport's terminals. Sixth, if the plaintiff brings suit under the Air Carrier Access Act, another likely successful argument is that a private cause of action does not exist under that act. Seventh, if a plaintiff brings suit under Title II of the ADA, the defense would want to argue that Title II applies to public entities and the airlines are not public entities, though the airport itself would be if publicly owned. Finally, if there is a personal injury suit based on state law claims, the defendant first would want to argue that the Air Carrier Access Act preempts state law remedies as well (but as we have seen in this case, that argument may not be successful). Finally, the defense needs to be prepared to deal with the Air Carrier Access Act regulations as the basis for liability in any state law tort-based claim.

To summarize: Whenever a U.S. Court of Appeals decides a case, a person losing would have two options. First, ask for a rehearing en banc. Considering that *Gilstrap* is the Ninth Circuit and considering the nature of this case, it is hard to say whether such a rehearing request would be granted (a majority of all Ninth Circuit judges would have to agree to do that). The other option, of course, is to appeal the case to the U.S. Supreme Court. In that situation, at least four justices would have to agree to hear the case. In that respect, it would help if a conflict existed between the circuits. There is a theoretical conflict between the circuits with respect to whether a private cause of action exists under the Air Carrier Access Act, but this particular case does not address that question because the plaintiff did not sue under that act. Also, since the Supreme Court decision in *Alexander v. Sandoval*, the circuits have not split on the question of whether the Air Carrier Access Act has a private cause of action component (they have all found that it does not). As for the other issues in *Gilstrap*, it would take further research, but this case does not seem to suggest that a conflict among the circuits exists concerning those other issues. Finally, even if the U.S. Supreme Court were to take this case, I wouldn't want to hazard a guess as to whether it would hold that the remedies under the Air Carrier Access Act were exclusive, especially considering the act's explicit discussion of other remedies in play and the insurance requirements. I do think it would probably be likely that the Court would decide that Title III of the ADA does not apply to airport terminals and, if the question were before it, would also decide, per *Alexander v. Sandoval,* that the Air Carrier Access Act does not have a private cause of action component to it.

Notes

1. Wright v. Universal Maritime Service Corp., 525 U.S. 70, 79 (1998).
2. *Id.* at 80.
3. There was some debate over whether a collective bargaining agreement, where a waiver was clear, could have its arbitration clause upheld. However, that question was answered in the affirmative by the U.S. Supreme Court in *14 Penn Plaza LLC v. Pyett*, _U.S._, 129 S. Ct. 1456 (2009).
4. EEOC v. Waffle House, Inc., 534 U.S. 279 (2002).
5. *Id.* at 282–83.
6. *Id.* at 283.
7. *Id.*
8. *Id.*
9. *Id.* at 298.
10. *Id.* at 286.
11. *Id.*
12. *Id.* at 287.
13. *Id.* at 288.
14. *Id.* at 289–90.
15. *Id.* at 291–92.

16. *Id.* at 297.
17. *Id.* at 291.
18. *Id.* at 294.
19. *Id.* at 297.
20. Saridakis v. United Airlines, 166 F.3d 1272, 1276–77.
21. Montgomery v. Dep't of Corr,, 2012 WL 5064823,*3 (Mich. App. Oct. 18, 2012).
22. Shim v. United Air Lines, Inc., 2012 WL 674 2529 (D. Haw. Dec. 13, 2012).
23. *Id.* at *9.
24. *Id.*
25. *See* EEOC Enforcement Guidance: Worker's Compensation and the ADA, September 1996.
26. The EEOC recently settled, to the tune of several million dollars, such a case with Sears. *See* http://www.law.com/jsp/article.jsp?id=1202434181647.
27. The discussion that follows would be very similar to my blog entry of Dec. 18, 2011. That blog entry can be found at http://www.williamgoren.com/blog/2011/12/18/full-return-to-work-r-i-p/.
28. Powers v. USF Holland, Inc. 667 F.3d 815 (7th Cir. 2011).
29. *Id.* at 817.
30. *Id.*
31. *Id.*
32. *Id.*
33. *Id.*
34. *Id.* at 818.
35. *Id.*
36. *Id.*
37. *Id.* at 822–23.
38. *Id.* at 824.
39. *Id.*
40. 42 U.S.C.A. at § 12102(3)(A).
41. *See* William D. Goren, *IDEA, Its Interrelationship to the ADA & Preventive Law*, 71 Fla. B. J. 76 (1997).
42. *See* Ellenberg v. N.M. Military Inst., 572 F.3d 815 (10th Cir. 2009). The reader is cautioned as to how far you might take this case. While the case does not explicitly say, it is quite clear that the 10th Circuit is relying on the ADA prior to the amendments that went into effect in January 2009. It is far from clear whether the 10th Circuit would be so convinced that a substantial limitation did not exist if it was relying on the amendments to the ADA. This is not to say that even if the case was brought under the ADA Amendments Act, the Military Institute would not have defenses available to it. Those defenses might include fundamental alteration or a claim that the applicant would not be otherwise qualified.

43. Kimble v. Douglas County School Dist. RE-1, _F. Supp. 2d_, 2013 WL 659109, *7 (D. Colo. Feb. 25, 2013).
44. *Id.* at *8.
45. *See* K.M. v. Tustin Unfiied School Dist., _F.3d. _, 2013 WL 3988677 (9th Cir. Aug. 6, 2013).
46. 29 U.S.C.A. § 2611(4)(A)(1) (WL, current through Pub. L. 113-9 (excluding Pub. L. 113-4), approved May 1, 2013).
47. 29 U.S.C.A. § 2612(a) (WL, current through Pub. L. 113-9 (excluding Pub. L. 113-4), approved May 1, 2013).
48. 29 U.S.C.A. § 2614 (WL, current through Pub. L. 113-9 (excluding Pub. L. 113-4), approved May 1, 2013); *see also* 29 C.F.R. § 825.214.
49. 29 C.F.R. § 825.113 (WL, current through May 30, 2013; 78 Fed. Reg. 32,362).
50. 29 C.F.R. § 825.114(a) (WL, current through May 30, 2013; 78 Fed. Reg. 32,362).
51. 29 U.S.C.A. § 2613 (WL, current through May 30, 2013; 78 Fed. Reg. 32,362); *see also* 29 C.F.R. § 825.305.
52. 29 C.F.R. § 825.123 (WL, current through Pub. L. 113-9 (excluding Pub. L. 113-4), approved May 1, 2013).
53. *Id.*
54. *See* EEOC Enforcement Guidance on Reasonable Accommodations and Undue Hardship under the Americans with Disabilities Act at #21 (October 2002).
55. *See* Mills v. Temple Univ., 869 F. Supp. 2d 609 (E.D. Pa. 2012). This case was discussed in my blog entry of December 17, 2012, and the discussion that follows is quite similar, though not exactly the same as the medium is different. That blog entry can be found at http://www.williamgoren.com/blog/2012/12/17/intersection-between-the-fmla-family-and-medical-leave-act-and-ada-americans-with-disabilities-act-as-amended-trouble-to-unaware-retaliation-claims-good-faith/.
56. *Id.* at 614.
57. *Id.*
58. *Id.*
59. *Id.*
60. *Id.*
61. *Id.* at 614–15.
62. *Id.* at 615.
63. *Id.*
64. *Id.*
65. *Id.*
66. *Id.*
67. *Id.* at 616.
68. *Id.*
69. *Id.*

70. *Id.*
71. *Id.* at 616–17.
72. *Id.* at 617.
73. *Id.*
74. *Id.*
75. *Id.*
76. *Id.*
77. *Id.*
78. *Id.*
79. *Id.*
80. *Id.*
81. *Id.*
82. *Id.* at 617–18.
83. *Id.* at 618.
84. *Id.*
85. *Id.*
86. *Id.*
87. *Id.* at 620–21.
88. *Id.*
89. *Id.* at 621.
90. *Id.* at 622.
91. *Id.* at n. 8.
92. *Id.*
93. *Id.* at 624.
94. *Id.* at 625.
95. *Id.*
96. *Id.* at 627.
97. *Id.* at 626–28.
98. *See* 29 U.S.C.A. § 2612(a)(3).
99. 78 Fed. Reg. 8834–8947 (Feb. 6, 2013).
100. *See, generally,* Cleveland v. Policy Mgmt. Sys. Corp., 526 U.S. 795 (1999).
101. *Id.* at 798–99.
102. *Id.* at 799.
103. *Id.* at 973–74.
104. *Id.* at 802–03.
105. *Id.* at 802.
106. *Id.* at 806.
107. *Id.* at 806–07.
108. *Id.* at 802–03.
109. *Id.* at 803.
110. *Id.* at 805.
111. *Id.* at 805–07.
112. *Id.* at 807.
113. *See* Opsteen v. Keller Structures, Inc., 408 F. 3d 390 (7th Cir. 2005).

114. *See generally* William D. Goren, *The Intersection of the ADA and SSDI and the Risks of Legal Malpractice*, DCBA Brief, http://www.dcba.org/brief/marissue/2006/art10306.htm.
115. Union Planters Bank, N. A. v. Thompson Coburn LLP, 402 Ill. App. 3d 317, 342 (5th Dist. 2010).
116. *See id.* at 343.
117. *Id.* at 344.
118. Lopez v. Jet Blue Airways, 662 F.3d 593 (2d Cir. 2011).
119. *Id.* at 595.
120. *Id.*
121. *Id.*
122. *Id.*
123. *Id.*
124. *Id.* at 596.
125. *See* 49 U.S.C.A. § 41705(a) (WL, current through Pub. L. 113-9 (excluding Pub. L. 113-4), approved May 1, 2013).
126. *Id.* at § 41705(b).
127. *Id.* at § 41705(c).
128. *Lopez,* 662 F.3d at 597.
129. *Id.* at 596, *citing to* Alexander v. Sandoval, 532 U.S. 275 (2001).
130. *Id.*
131. *Id.* at 597 and n.3.
132. *Id.* at 597.
133. *Id.* at 598.
134. *Id.* at 599. *See also* 42 U.S.C.A. § 12181(10) (WL, current through Pub. L. 113-9 (excluding Pub. L. 113-4), approved May 1, 2013).
135. *Id.* at 599.
136. Gilstrap v. United Airlines,_F.3d_, 2013 WL 930170, *14 n.11 (9th Cir. Mar. 12, 2013).
137. *Lopez,* 662 F.3d at 599 n.8.
138. *Id.*
139. Segalman v. Southwest Airlines, 2012 WL 5289308 (E.D. Cal. Oct. 24, 2012).
140. *Id.* at *1.
141. *Id.*
142. *Id.*
143. *Id.*
144. *Id.* at *6.
145. *Id.*
146. *Id.* at *2.
147. *Id.* at *3–5.
148. *Id.* at *5–7.
149. *Id.* at *5.
150. *Id.*

151. Gilstrap v. United Airlines, _F.3d_, 2013 WL 930170 (9th Cir. Mar. 12, 2013). The discussion that follows is very similar to my blog entry that appeared on March 18, 2013. The medium is different; the format is also a bit different. Also, the conclusion is different, as it combines the conclusions of two different blog entries dealing with preemption and the Air Carrier Access Act.
152. *Id.* at *1.
153. *Id.*
154. *Id.*
155. *Id.*
156. *Id.*
157. *Id.*
158. *Id.*
159. *Id.*
160. *Id.*
161. *Id.*
162. *Id.*
163. Val D'Aosta v. Cross, 526 S.E.2d 580, 585 (Ga. App. 1999).
164. *See Gilstrap* at *1.
165. *Id.* at *5.
166. *Id.* at *11.
167. *Id.* at **8–9.
168. *Id.* at *5.
169. *Id.*
170. *Id.* at *14.
171. *Id.* at n.11.

Procedural Issues and Remedies

11

STANDING

HOW DO YOU FASHION A COMPLAINT to convince the court that a plaintiff has standing to bring the suit? How do you fashion a complaint so that it survives a motion to dismiss? Or, on the defense side, what do you look for in trying to maximize your chances of winning on a motion to dismiss? What remedies are available with respect to violation of the various titles of the Americans with Disabilities Act? Can you still get a mixed-motive jury instruction after *Gross v. FBL Financial*? This chapter will address these questions and others.

In our system, the judiciary, in general, does not render advisory opinions.[1] There are a couple of exceptions. Some states, such as Massachusetts, have a system whereby a legislature can request an advisory opinion from their supreme court with respect to the constitutionality of proposed legislation. A couple of other instances look like advisory opinions but really aren't. For example, a federal court could ask a state court for its view of the state law with respect to a matter before the federal court. A party could also ask for a declaratory judgment, i.e., a declaration of rights, of the parties. However, in both of those cases an actual dispute is involved. Thus, in order to proceed with a lawsuit, a person must have a sufficient stake in the matter before being able to sue. Two recent cases address the issue of how you go about showing the court that standing exists so that a plaintiff can proceed with his or her claim in a Title II or Title III case where the plaintiff faced access barriers.

In *Hamlin v. North Wildwood City*, 2013 WL 1007297 (D. N.J. March 11, 2013), the plaintiff, Hamill, sued North Wildwood City for violations of the ADA and the Rehabilitation Act because its facilities were not accessible to persons with disabilities.[2] In particular, when he visited North Wildwood in December 2010, he did so for the purpose of checking out the streets to see if he would be able to access the beach, checking to see if he would be able to hand-cycle on the streets, and checking to see if he would be able to access the boardwalk.[3] In the process, he noticed that there was an area of sand between the ramp and the boardwalk so he would not have been able to make it to the ramp in any event.[4] He also noticed many curb-cuts that were problematic (for example, curb cuts led to grassy areas) and were also really dangerous as well.[5] Hamlin lived in Voorhees, New Jersey, and frequently visited the Jersey shore, including trips to North Wildwood.[6]

Another plaintiff, Lasky, visited North Wildwood in 2011, to see if he could find any places to rent.[7] He also experienced difficulty with curb cuts and had to use his wheelchair in the streets.[8] The open bathroom was also not accessible.[9] Lasky lived in Broward County, Florida, and had visited North Wildwood on numerous occasions.[10] Both plaintiffs were members of the Advocates for Disabled Americans, a group that held a yearly meeting at a restaurant in North Wildwood.[11] Lasky also intended to return to North Wildwood with his family for enjoyment, as it is a major tourist attraction.[12] Further, both plaintiffs intended to return in the capacity of testers.[13]

In order to have standing, a plaintiff must show an injury in fact that is: 1) concrete and particularized, and actual or imminent, not conjectural or hypothetical; 2) fairly traceable to a challenged action of the defendant; and 3) likely, as opposed to merely speculative, to be redressed by a favorable decision. The defendant tried to argue that the plaintiffs had not suffered any injury because they didn't actually try out the inaccessible places.[14] However, the court said that the ADA does not require a person with a disability to engage in futile gestures if he or she has actual notice of a facility's noncompliance with the ADA.[15] Rather, the person must prove knowledge of the barriers and that they would visit the facility in the imminent future but for those barriers.[16] The court said that the plaintiff had presented sufficient evidence showing that North Wildwood's facilities were inaccessible and that he had actual notice as a result of the visual inspections of the facilities.[17] The court said that the plaintiff did not need to engage in futile and possibly unsafe activities just to be able to establish that he suffered an injury in fact.[18] The court did not address explicitly whether the injury was fairly traceable to the challenged action of the defendant and whether it was likely that the injury would be redressed by a favorable decision; however, the decision clearly assumes that both of those elements were satisfied.

Thus, both plaintiffs were able to get to first base with respect to their Title II claim. However, it might perhaps be better to say that both plaintiffs were able to get halfway to first base because an injunction was at issue in this case. Whenever a person sues for an injunction, that person must demonstrate a real and immediate threat of future harm.[19] It is simply not sufficient for an ADA plaintiff seeking an injunction mandating removal of architectural barriers to manufacture standing by simply claiming that he or she intends to return to the defendant's establishment.[20] With respect to considering whether standing exists for obtaining injunctive relief, courts look to four factors: 1) the plaintiff's proximity to the defendant place of public accommodation; 2) the plaintiff's patronage; 3) definiteness of the plaintiff's plan to return; and 4) the plaintiff's frequency of nearby travel.[21]

The court held that both plaintiffs, Hamill and Lasky, were likely to return and therefore had standing to seek injunctive relief. With respect to Lasky, while he lived 1,206 miles away from North Wildwood, he did plead that North Wildwood was a major tourist attraction.[22] Second, Lasky had a history of making multiple visits to North Wildwood.[23] Third, he also alleged that he intended to return for the yearly meeting of the Advocates for Disabled Americans, which is held in North Wildwood every year at a local restaurant and of which he was president.[24] Fourth, he also intended to return to look for vacation rentals for his family.[25] Fifth, he intended to return to ask to assess accessibility problems (tester) in the North Wildwood area.[26] Interestingly enough, the fact that Lasky was a tester actually weighed in his favor with respect to standing because that meant he had real incentive and a higher likelihood of actually returning to North Wildwood.[27] Sixth, Lasky also planned to return to North Wildwood with his family for enjoyment.[28] The court also noted that Lasky visited New Jersey up to four times a year due to his role as president of the Advocates for Disabled Americans and in his role as a guardian ad litem for a disabled man in Camden New Jersey.[29] He also enjoyed attending Philadelphia sporting events, and his wife's best friend lived in New Jersey.[30]

With respect to plaintiff Hamill, he had attended the yearly meetings of the Advocate for Disabled Americans held in North Wildwood. He also alleged that he wanted to access the boardwalk for hand cycling but could not do so because of the barriers.[31] The court found it absurd to require Hamill to specify dates when he wanted to return to do hand-cycling when he could not do so because the barriers did not allow him to hand-cycle in the first place.[32] Finally, while he alleged that he frequently visited the Jersey shore, he did not provide details about these other trips.[33] However, since he lived in general proximity to North Wildwood, the court found that proximity indicated, albeit not strongly, that he intended to return.[34]

To summarize, the standing requirements with respect to Title II and Title III, especially when injunctive relief is involved in both cases, are essentially the same (for a Title III case dealing with standing, see *Harty v. Bull's Head Realty*).[35] With respect to establishing standing involving architectural accessibility issues under Title II or Title III, the biggest hurdle for the plaintiffs is going to be showing that they suffered an injury in fact that was concrete, particularized, and that was also actual or imminent. While the plaintiffs do not have to engage in a futile act, they are going to have to show knowledge of the barriers (not particularly difficult, especially for testers) and that they would visit the facility in the imminent future but for those barriers. The argument is going to be over whether they would visit the facility in the imminent future but for those barriers. On the plaintiff's side, that can be done by showing that the plaintiff has an ongoing connection to the community both in the past and in the future. Whether that ongoing connection is sufficient may vary from judge to judge. Certainly, the more specific the connection that can be alleged, the better off the plaintiff is going to be. On the defense side, boilerplate pleadings showing only general and tenuous connections are ripe for attack. Finally, if the person is only a tester, there may still be an argument as to whether a tester can have standing. However, in both of the cases discussed here, being a tester was actually favorable to the plaintiff because it indicated he had every intention of returning to the site.

THE COMPLAINT

A related issue, but one not exactly the same as what was just discussed, is that you not only have to show standing but you also have to plead your complaint in such a way that it gives the defendant notice as to what the dispute is about. In law school, I learned that the federal system is a notice pleading jurisdiction. The idea behind notice pleading is that you make a general statement about the case if you are a plaintiff and the rest is up to discovery. Once discovery is finished, the defense often files a motion for summary judgment. At the state level, the approach varies. Some states are much more fact-based, while others are much like the traditional federal system in their approach and leave it up to discovery. Some states, such as Illinois, fall in between. One of the things I am seeing quite a bit, particularly with prisoners but sometimes with individual plaintiffs as well, is that they are filing pro se complaints, which is generally not recommended. That said, even lawyers need to be aware of how the courts are deciding whether sufficient facts are pleaded in a complaint so that it survives a motion to dismiss, and that is the subject of this section.

To say that the federal system is a notice pleading situation is no longer entirely accurate thanks to two different cases, *Ashcroft v. Iqbal* and *Bell Atlantic Corporation v. Twombly*.[36] In those cases, the U.S. Supreme Court said that a simple recital of the elements of a cause of action supported by conclusory statements is not going to be sufficient to survive a motion to dismiss.[37] While legal conclusions can provide the framework of the complaint, they must be supported by factual allegations plausibly giving rise to an entitlement to relief.[38] Plausibility refers to a complainant pleading enough factual content to allow the court to draw a reasonable inference that the defendant is liable for the misconduct.[39]

So what does this all mean? It means that one should not take the notice pleading requirement of the federal court literally. That is, a better approach might be to adopt a hybrid system, such as the one in Illinois. Illinois uses a hybrid system. That is, it is not a notice pleading jurisdiction, but on the other hand it is not a pure factual pleading jurisdiction in its practice either. Rather, a complainant has to give enough facts to put the defendant on notice as to what the claim is. The language you might see in an Illinois case is that a plaintiff is required to allege facts stating the elements of the cause of action, and unsupported legal conclusions and factual conclusions are insufficient and will be disregarded.[40] There isn't much difference between a standard such as this and the standard called for by *Iqbal*, which requires a plaintiff's complaint to include sufficient facts of each element to support a reasonable inference that he or she is entitled to relief.[41]

What it all comes down to is that you want to take each element of the claim and then come up with specific facts to support them. For example, for a person to have an actual disability under the ADA, you would need a physical or mental impairment that substantially limits a major life activity. Therefore, you would want to allege facts showing a physical or mental impairment. You would also want to allege facts showing that a substantial limitation on a major life activity exists (recognizing that substantial limitation post-ADAAA is not the same as substantial limitation before the ADAAA). If it is a case involving reasonable accommodations, you're also going to have to allege facts to show that the person is a qualified person with a disability. That is, you would need to allege facts to show that the person can do the essential functions of the job with or without reasonable accommodations. In short, the methodology is pretty simple. As a plaintiff, you need to determine the elements of the cause of action and then allege the facts satisfying each element. Stay away from general conclusions and stick to specific facts. On the defense side, when you receive the complaint, figure out what are the elements of each of the causes of action that the plaintiff is alleging. If the plaintiff is not alleging specific facts to satisfy each element, then your chances for prevailing on a motion to dismiss increase substantially.

STATUTE OF LIMITATIONS

The whole idea of the statute of limitations is to prevent stale claims. Just about everything has a statute of limitations (the only two exceptions I can think of are claims arising under USERRA and capital murder claims). The ADA does have a statute of limitations to deal with, though it is not stated in the statute itself. Just what is the statute of limitations for an ADA claim? The answer depends on the title of the ADA involved as well as on an interpretation of a Supreme Court opinion. Let's look at how each of the titles break down.

Title I

With respect to a claim of employment discrimination (Title I), a person needs to file a charge within 180 calendar days from the date the discrimination took place.[42] The 180-calendar-day filing deadline is extended to 300 calendar days if a state or local agency enforces a law that prohibits employment discrimination on the same basis.[43] Once a Notice of Right to Sue from the EEOC is received, a plaintiff must file the lawsuit within 90 days.[44]

Titles II, III, and Retaliation

With respect to the statute of limitation for Title II and Title III claims as well as retaliation claims, the situation is a bit more complicated. With Title II and Title III claims, the applicable statute of limitations will be the state's personal injury statute of limitations.[45] The retaliation claim going to be derived from whatever Title is at issue.[46] Thus, if a person is alleging retaliation with respect to a Title II or Title III matter, the statute of limitation would be the state's personal injury statute of limitations.

However, it is never so simple. Might an argument be made that in some cases, as a result of the ADAAA, the statute of limitations would be a four-year federal statute of limitations rather than the personal injury statute of limitation of the respective state? 28 U.S.C. § 1658(a) sets forth a catchall four-year statute of limitations for actions arising under federal statutes enacted after December 1, 1990.[47] Obviously, since the ADA was signed by George H.W. Bush in July 1990, this catchall provision is not going to apply to the ADA. However, the ADAAA went into effect in January 2009 and thus arguably might be subject to this catchall provision. How do we know if a particular state's statute of limitations for personal injury is in play or whether the four-year federal catchall statute of limitations is in play? To answer that question, the U.S. Supreme Court decision in *Jones v. R.R. Donnelly & Sons Co.*[48] must be considered. In that case, the question was whether the amendment to the Civil Rights Act and a claim subsequently brought under the amendment to the Civil Rights Act was governed by the

Illinois personal injury statute of limitations or by the four-year federal catchall statute of limitations. In deciding that the particular claim before it was subject to the federal catchall limitation, the Court used a variety of terms as the standard for deciding when the catchall statute of limitations would apply, including: "creation of new rights of action and corresponding liabilities"; whether "the plaintiff's claim against the defendant was made possible by a post-1990 enactment"; and "whenever a post-1990 enactment creates a new right."[49]

Does the ADAAA create any new rights and corresponding liabilities or new claims? One court has suggested that it does not; rather, the ADAAA simply clarifies what was originally intended by the ADA.[50] Does that statement hold upon further analysis? After all, the Supreme Court in *Jones* recognized that the decision in a particular case as to whether new rights and corresponding liabilities for new claims were involved might be very complicated.[51] When you review the ADAAA, it certainly seems that the vast majority of it is really nothing more than clarifying the statute and letting the court know that prior interpretations of the ADA were not what Congress intended. However, there may be two situations where it might be possible to argue that new rights and corresponding liabilities for new claims were created by the ADAAA. The two areas that I believe may be subject to such an argument are "mitigating measures" and "regarded as."

With respect to mitigating measures, the ADA as originally enacted had no such language in it at all. Rather, the whole question of mitigating measures came up to the U.S. Supreme Court with *Sutton*.[52] Conversely, the ADAAA makes clear that mitigating measures are not to be considered in the analysis of whether a person has a disability unless the person is dealing with the situation of corrective lenses.[53] This can make a huge difference for a particular individual with a disability. For example, in past editions of this book I have discussed my own hearing loss (I am bilaterally congenitally deaf (65 db–90+db), and through the use of hearing aids and lipreading function entirely in the hearing world). Before the amendments act, the answer as to whether I had a disability could well have depended on the time of day (daytime or nighttime, depending on whether I was wearing my hearing aids). However, I most certainly would have a disability regardless of the time of day with the advent of the ADAAA. Did that create a new right for me? Arguably, yes.

The other area that may have created new claims and corresponding liabilities is in the area of "regarded as." Under *Sutton*, for a regarded-as claim to work, an employer has to perceive both a physical or mental impairment *and* a substantial limitation on a major life activity.[54] Now, under the ADAAA, the plaintiff has to show only that a physical or mental impairment was perceived and does not have to worry about whether an employer perceived a substantial limitation in a major life activity.[55] That change means that many more people will be able to show that they are protected under the regarded-as prong, which raises the argument that new rights and corresponding liabilities or claims were created for those individuals. However, you don't even have to reach this issue if the claim is filed within the statute of limitations for personal injury in your respective state's jurisdiction. Before leaving this topic, another thing to be aware of is that utilizing an internal grievance procedure does not toll the statute of limitations.[56]

To summarize, here is how the statute of limitations works with respect to the ADA. First, if it is a Title I case, then you have strict EEOC time lines to deal with. That is, a person has 180 days from the date of the alleged discrimination to file a claim with the EEOC, though it is possible, where an equivalent state agency (not every state may have an equivalent state agency) exists, that the deadline might extend to 300 days. With respect to Title II and Title III claims, you need to check the personal injury statute of limitations in your respective jurisdiction. If, for some reason, the claim is outside the personal injury statute of limitations, then you need to focus on whether the case involved mitigating measures or is a regarded-as claim. In either of those events, for the reasons mentioned earlier, it may be possible to argue that the claim would be subject to a four-year federal statute of limitations rather than the particular state's personal injury statute of limitations.[57]

SOME GENERAL THOUGHTS ON REMEDIES AND THE ADA

What are the remedies offered by the ADA? Each title offers different remedies, and they deserve separate treatment. Title I remedies are keyed into the Civil Rights Act of 1964, including the exhaustion of remedies requirement.[58] As mentioned above, prior to filing a lawsuit, a person alleging discrimination in employment based on disability must first exhaust the EEOC process and receive a right-to-sue letter. The EEOC has streamlined its procedures for processing complaints, and one should be able to procure a right-to-sue letter earlier than in the past. Once the EEOC process has been completed, a claim can be filed in court. If intentional discrimination can be proven, the remedies available under the Civil Rights Act of 1964, which include compensatory and punitive damages, can be obtained. However, if the issue of reasonable accommodations is involved, the employer can prevent an award of damages if it can show that it made a good-faith effort to accommodate the person with a disability.[59] The compensatory and punitive damages for violating the ADA can be very steep, and the maximum amount of damages available depends on how many employees an employer has in each of 20 or more calendar weeks in the current or preceding calendar year. The range is as follows:

- 15–100 workers: $50,000
- 101–200 workers: $100,000
- 201–500 workers: $200,000
- 501 or more workers: $300,000[60]

Attorneys' Fees

The ADA is one of those statutes that allow for recovery of attorney fees should the plaintiff prevail.[61] The question is, what does it mean to prevail? A case that addressed that issue is *Buckhannon Board and Care Home, Inc. v. West Virginia Department of Health and Human Resources*.[62] In *Buckhannon*, an operator of group homes for persons with disabilities failed an inspection by the fire marshal's office because the residents were not capable of self-preservation.[63] When it received orders to close the facility, it sued, alleging violations of the Fair Housing Act and the ADA.[64] Subsequent to the suit, the state legislature eliminated the self-preservation requirement.[65] Buckhannon then brought a claim for attorneys' fees, claiming that the lawsuit brought about a desired voluntary change in the defendant's conduct (commonly referred to as the catalyst theory).[66] Since not all of the U.S. Courts of Appeals agreed with the catalyst theory, the U.S. Supreme Court took the case to resolve the conflict.[67] In rejecting the catalyst theory, the U.S. Supreme Court reasoned as follows.

First, the Court, as it often does, referred to a dictionary, in this case the *Black's Law Dictionary* definition of the term "prevailing," which refers to a judgment or some relief being given by the court.[68]

Second, the Court looked to its prior case law to find it had declared that Congress had intended, with respect to other civil rights fee-shifting provisions, that the plaintiff receive at least some relief on the merits of the claim, even if the relief is nominal, before it can be said the plaintiff has prevailed.[69]

Third, the Court noted that it had previously said that private settlements enforced through a consent decree also result in a party being considered to have prevailed.[70]

Fourth, the Court noted that the legislative history of the Civil Rights Attorneys Fees Award Act was ambiguous as to whether Congress intended for the catalyst theory to apply, and, absent clear legislative intent to the contrary, the Court was unwilling to part with the American rule (which holds that each party to a suit is responsible for its own attorneys' fees).[71]

Finally, the Court was concerned that adopting the catalyst theory would lead to another set of full-blown litigation to determine why the defendant changed its conduct.[72]

What *Buckhannon* means for the practitioner is that he or she should probably avoid linking any fee to an award of attorneys' fees, if indeed the practitioner does this in the first place, and allow himself the flexibility of collecting under his other rate, oftentimes contingency on the plaintiff's side, should an attorneys' fees award not be in the cards. After all, most suits settle privately without any judicial oversight. Alternatively, the plaintiff's lawyer desirous of obtaining an attorneys' fee award should see if there is not some way to get the court involved in the settlement process and its oversight, such as a consent decree. Of course, on the defense side, the attorneys would want to settle privately without any future judicial oversight or any kind of decision on the merits.

Must it be a consent decree to get attorneys' fees or will a settlement with continuing oversight suffice? A case that answers this question is *Jankey v. Poop Deck*.[73] In *Jankey*, a mobility-impaired plaintiff entered a restaurant to have a snack.[74] However, when he needed to use the restroom, he was unable to do so because it was not accessible to a mobility-impaired person.[75] He then tried the restaurant next door, which was owned by the same person and part of the same building,[76] but the restaurant and bathroom there were not accessible to him either.[77] He brought suit, alleging violations of Title III of the ADA as well as California state law claims.[78] After aggressive litigation tactics on the part of his attorney, he entered into a settlement that required the defendant to make several architectural modifications in his restaurants.[79] The settlement agreement specifically provided that the district court retain jurisdiction to enforce the terms of the agreement.[80] Jankey's attorney then brought suit for attorneys' fees under Title III of the ADA, which the lower court denied, and Jankey appealed.[81] In reversing the denial of attorneys' fees, the Ninth Circuit noted the following.

For a litigant to be a prevailing party for purposes of awarding attorneys' fees, the litigant must achieve a material alteration of the legal relationship of the parties.[82] Here, the court reasoned that a material alteration of the parties occurred because the defendant agreed to make architectural modifications to his restaurants.[83] Also, the court noted that for a person to recover attorneys' fees as a prevailing party, the litigant must show, in addition to a material alteration of the legal relationship, that the alteration was judicially sanctioned.[84] With respect to this question, the Ninth Circuit held that the district court retention of jurisdiction to enforce the agreement satisfied this requirement.[85]

REMEDIES FOR RETALIATION

The ADA also protects against retaliation.[86] If a person claims retaliation, is that person entitled to the same remedies that he or she would otherwise be entitled to under Title I of the ADA? The answer is splitting the courts. In the Seventh Circuit, the answer is that the person would only be entitled to equitable remedies and not to compensatory and punitive damages.[87] In *Kramer v. Banc of America Securities, LLC*, the Seventh Circuit reasoned that a person was only entitled to equitable remedies because if you trace the ADA out in terms of the remedies that are described for retaliation in the statute, you can only reach the conclusion that punitive and compensatory damages (legal remedies) are not mentioned.[88] The fact that equitable remedies are the only remedy available for retaliation claims necessarily means that such a claim does not have a right to a jury trial unless the defendant consents and said consent is not withdrawn.[89]

Kramer is also the rule in the Ninth Circuit.[90] However, the Western District of Tennessee in *Baker v. Windsor Republic Doors*, disagreed with *Kramer*.[91] The district reasoned that legal remedies were available in retaliation cases, because retaliation is intentional discrimination and legal remedies are available for intentional discrimination.[92] The district did admit that if you follow out the remedies that are available for retaliation as listed in the ADA, you do reach the narrow conclusion that legal remedies are not explicitly allowed for a claim of retaliation.[93] However, the district said that was not dispositive, because such a narrow reading of the statute is not controlling if it produces a result that is absurd or contrary to other provisions of the ADA.[94]

As of this writing, we are not seeing a split among the circuits. Accordingly, it is difficult to say at this time whether such a split will occur and thereby increase the likelihood of the U.S. Supreme Court reviewing this issue. In the meantime, if you are a defense attorney and are sued for retaliation, you most certainly want to file motions to ensure that the retaliation claims are only subject to equitable remedies. If you are on the plaintiff's side, you are going to have to be prepared to argue that retaliation claims based on the ADA should include more than equitable remedies vis á vis the reasoning of the Western District of Tennessee in *Baker*.

Title II Remedies

Remedies under Title II of the ADA are linked to the Rehabilitation Act of 1973.[95] Accordingly, as mentioned earlier, courts, with the exception of a single judge,[96] have held that a person alleging violation of Title II does not have to exhaust administrative remedies prior to bringing suit.[97]

Title II of the ADA requires that governmental entities of 50 or more people have a grievance procedure for ADA complaints.[98] This requirement raises a legitimate question as to whether a person suing under Title II must first exhaust the public entity's internal ADA grievance procedure. While the Department of Justice says exhaustion of the internal grievance procedure would not be required,[99] one could present arguments in favor of it. Clearly, the court system is already clogged, and exhausting the grievance procedure offers an opportunity to communicate the problem to the employer and resolve it before a court fight. Undertaking the grievance procedure and handling it effectively would also allow the governmental entity to demonstrate good faith in trying to resolve the claim. Then, too, a person with a disability has an issue that needs to be respected, and airing the grievance internally often can resolve the entire dispute. Finally, equity would seem to demand that the governmental entity be given a chance to resolve the issue before becoming embroiled in litigation.

Regardless of any legal requirement to exhaust internal remedies first, good preventive lawyering would suggest that governmental entities, regardless of size, have an ADA grievance procedure, and that the plaintiff might want to consider exhausting that procedure first before filing suit under the ADA so as to avoid expensive litigation. If the plaintiff does choose to exhaust the internal grievance procedure, he or she needs to keep in mind that the statute of limitations is running during that process.[100]

Title III Remedies

Title III of the ADA operates quite differently from the other two titles. For instance, administrative remedies do not have to be exhausted,[101] and the only remedy available for a person who brings a private cause of action is injunctive relief and lawyers' fees.[102] The regulatory agency for Title III of the ADA—as well as Title II, for that matter—is the Department of Justice, and where the DOJ does bring a claim for violating Title III of the ADA, the court can fine violators up to $50,000 for a first violation and up to $100,000 for each subsequent violation.[103] No punitive damages are available.[104] With the remedies being so limited under Title III, there have nevertheless been some surprising developments. First, despite the limited remedies, many Title III suits get filed. Second, the DOJ has very actively pursued violations of Title III, and that has led to Title III violators paying fines and damages to the aggrieved plaintiff.

While it is true that the remedies for violations of Title III are limited to injunctive relief and attorneys' fees, what would happen if the facility did not meet the ADA architectural standards, and because of that a person visiting the facility was injured. Could a person use the architectural guidelines as a vehicle to argue for collecting damages under a particular state's statute that allows for the collection of damages where a statute is violated? On this, you would need to check your particular jurisdiction. In Georgia, for example, an argument can be made that such a suit would be allowed, since the plaintiff would be able to show in such a situation that the statute and regulations were intended to protect her or him, and that violation of the statute or regulation constituted a proximate cause of the injury and damages.[105]

CAUSATION, MIXED MOTIVE, AND THE ADA

In the last edition of the book, I did not spend a great deal time on the issue of causation and the ADA. However, since that time it has become quite an issue. That is, does a person alleging violation of the ADA have to show that the discrimination was the sole cause of the adverse action, or can causation be one of many necessary causes, or could it be a substantial factor?

A mixed-motive jury instruction says that liability can exist if the plaintiff can show that the adverse action was motivated by discrimination based on the protected characteristic—in this case, disability. If the defense can show that they would have taken the adverse action anyway despite being motivated by the disability, then the remedies that the plaintiff can receive are limited. Mixed motive comes from Title VII of the Civil Rights Act. The question is whether a mixed-motive jury instruction is possible under the ADA.

Until *Gross v. FBL Financial Services*,[106] mixed motive was certainly in play for ADA cases. However, the *Gross* decision said that because the Age Discrimination in Employment Act used the term "because of" for its causation standard and that the act did not explicitly link to mixed-motive provisions of the Civil Rights Act, then it has to be assumed that "but for" would be the standard for causation under the Age Discrimination in Employment Act.[107] This created the question as to whether the same logic would apply to the ADA. *Serwatka v. Rockwell Automation Inc.* says that the same logic does apply, at least with respect to claims arising prior to the amendments to the ADA.[108]

How mixed motive applies to the ADA, particularly post amendments, is a complicated question. In short, it would seem to break down this way. With respect to the Americans with Disabilities Act before the ADAAA, a strong argument can be made that a mixed-motive jury instruction is indeed dead but contrary authority, as just discussed and as will be discussed again, does exist. With respect to Title I of the Americans with Disabilities Act after the ADAAA, the answer is yes as a result of legislative history, the change in language from "because" to "on the basis of" and a U.S. Supreme Court decision on mixed-motive retaliation to be discussed shortly. That legislative history indicates that at least whenever the words "on the basis of" appear, mixed motive, whatever that may mean, is also still in play. In particular, the house report on the ADAAA says that the reason why "on the basis" was inserted into the ADA was to ensure that the "more direct language, structured like Title VII" placed the emphasis on the critical inquiry of whether a qualified person with a disability had been discriminated against on the basis of his or her disability and not whether a particular person was even a person with a disability and therefore subject to the protection of the act in the first place.[109] That same legislative history immediately after this makes clear that the indirect burden of proof, which presumes a motivating factor, is also in play, and that is why Congress purposely left in the term "qualified" when it amended the ADA with the ADAAA.[110]

With respect to Title III of the ADA, a mixed-motive jury instruction would most certainly be dead because despite the "on the basis of" language,[111] the remedies for violations of Title III in no way suggest that a mixed-motive jury instruction could be in play.[112] With respect to Title II of the ADA, that question is really complicated. As mentioned above, the remedies for Title II violations are tied into the Rehabilitation Act. The problem is that Title II uses the term "by reason of," while the Rehabilitation Act uses the term "solely by reason of."[113] One wonders why the word "solely" does not appear in Title II of the ADA, but does appear in the Rehabilitation Act, which creates the argument that Title II of the ADA and the Rehabilitation Act may indeed have two different causation standards.[114]

But is a mixed-motive jury instruction dead under the Americans with Disabilities Act prior to the ADAAA? *Lewis v. Humboldt Acquisition Corporation*[115] raises the question that a mixed-motive jury instruction may not be dead even under the ADA prior to the amendments act. In that case, the Sixth Circuit, sitting en banc, said that "sole cause" was not the standard for causation for ADA cases.[116] The majority opinion adopted the aforementioned *Serwatka* opinion, which held that "but for" was the proper standard.[117] However, there were multiple opinions where the judges concurred and dissented at the same time. In those opinions, they raised the question as to whether, for claims that came into existence before and after the ADAAA, a mixed-motive jury instruction (one of those opinions prefers substantial factor)[118] might still be possible. Those opinions based their conclusions on legislative history, the link of the ADA to the mixed-motive remedies section, and on the traditional interpretation of what "because" traditionally meant in civil rights cases.[119]

So what is a lawyer that represents either the plaintiff or the defendant to do? What is a corporation to do? From the plaintiff point of view, it might be better[120] if they had the ability to argue that a mixed-motive jury instruction was in play. Especially in employment, it can be very hard to show either "sole cause" or "but for." In light of *Lewis*, the defense or a corporation now has to consider that the *Gross* decision may not extend to ADA cases the way that *Serwatka* anticipates. In short, thanks to *Lewis*, an argument now exists that with respect to ADA cases, a mixed-motive jury instruction may be in play. Also, as we will see later when discussing retaliation, a recent U.S. Supreme Court opinion discussing causation with respect to retaliation will likely have a huge impact on this discussion.

The question goes beyond whether you can simply get a jury instruction for mixed motive. For example, can you allege more than one cause of action where one of the causes of action allows for a mixed-motive jury instruction but the other does not??

A case that answers this question is *Pearson v. Lawrence Medical Center*.[121] In this case, the plaintiff was a 59-year-old man with diabetes and high blood pressure.[122] The company hired an interim CEO who was promoted to CEO within two months and thereby became the plaintiff's direct supervisor.[123] Eventually, the plaintiff needed to visit his doctor more frequently because he was having difficulty with his insulin pump and also because he required a stress test to determine how well a stent implanted in his heart was working.[124]

Things went from bad to worse. The new CEO told the plaintiff that he needed someone 20 years younger to perform the duties of the job and that he did not like him missing work to attend doctor's appointments.[125] He placed the plaintiff on a performance improvement plan for three months, but instead of letting him finish out the performance improvement plan, terminated him within one week.[126] The plaintiff filed suit, alleging violations of the Family and Medical Leave Act, the Age Discrimination in Employment Act, and the Americans with Disabilities Act. The defendant's view was that *Gross* meant that the plaintiff had to elect the law he was going to proceed under, since motivating factor was not, in the defendant's view anyway, a possibility under the ADA.[127]

The court's (Northern District of Alabama) reasoning is very interesting. First, the court notes that there are cases that say you would have to elect the remedy, but it found such cases to be illogical.[128] The court noted that a sole-cause standard is not the same thing as a but-for standard.[129] The court said that a sole cause is a necessary cause, but a necessary cause does not have to be a sole cause.[130] That is, a particular result may have two or more necessary causes, and in the court's view, *Gross* is not to the contrary.[131] Therefore, if a plaintiff alleges causes of action involving different causation standards (motivating factor per Title VII or "but for" under the Age Discrimination in Employment Act or the ADA), it would still be possible for the plaintiff to prove motivating factor or substantial factor while also being able to show but-for causation with respect to the statutes requiring that linkage.[132]

So, what does the Alabama decision mean for the practitioner? First, a plaintiff faced with alleging causes of action with different causation standards (motivating factor and but for) will be able to file a claim alleging violations of laws with different causation standards. Second, the discussion of necessary cause and how it differs from sole cause allows for a plaintiff to file multiple causes of action even if both statutes (for example, the Age Discrimination in Employment and the ADA) use but-for causation.

What happens if you have more than one cause? Adverse employment decisions are frequently the result of more than one cause, such as performance issues as well as discrimination. What happens then, especially if "but for" is the standard? Perhaps we can analogize to tort law. Everybody who goes to law school learns in tort law (civil wrongs) that if you have one cause, the standard is "but for" causation. If you have more than one cause, the standard is "substantial factor." Might a similar system work with respect to employment discrimination?[133]

The California Supreme Court in *Harris v. City of Santa Monica*[134] was faced with this situation when a person sued under the state's antidiscrimination law, the Fair Employment and Housing Act, for pregnancy discrimination.[135] It was one of those situations where the employer clearly had dual motives. It terminated her for work performance issues, but it also discriminated against the plaintiff based on pregnancy.[136] In this case, it was the defense that asked for a particular form of a mixed-motive instruction; they wanted an instruction that said it was a complete defense to liability if it could show that it had a legitimate reason to make the same decision and that it would have made that decision regardless of the pregnancy discrimination.[137] The court rejected that instruction and instead gave an instruction saying that the plaintiff could prevail if it showed that the pregnancy discrimination was a motivating factor in the adverse action.[138]

The California Supreme Court begins the discussion by noting that the Fair Employment and housing Act contained the phrase "because of" with respect to causation.[139] However, the court said that when you investigated, three possible meanings of "because of" are possible: "but for," "substantial factor," or "motivating factor."[140] The court said that the legislative history of the Fair Employment and Housing Act was absent with respect to what "because of" might mean.[141] Accordingly, it looked to Title VII of the Civil Rights Act.[142]

The court referred to *Price Waterhouse v. Hopkins,*[143] 490 U.S. 228 (1989), where the U.S. Supreme Court held that a defendant may avoid a finding of liability only by proving by a preponderance of the evidence that it would have made the same decision even if it had not taken the plaintiff's prohibited characteristic into account.[144] The Court also held that the burden shifted to the defendant once the plaintiff was able to show a motivating factor, whereupon the defendant would have to show that it would have made the same decision at the time even without the discrimination in order to escape liability.[145] The California Supreme Court then noted that the Civil Rights Act of 1991 overturned *Price Waterhouse* with respect to the liability phase when it added language to the statute saying that while liability cannot be completely circumvented if an employer acted in motivation based on the prohibited characteristic, the remedy would be limited[146] (a conclusion backed up both by the legislative history of the civil rights amendments and by what *Gross* says with respect to how the Age Discrimination in Employment Act is not hooked into motivating factor while the Civil Rights Act is).[147]

The California Supreme Court goes on to mention particular sections of the Fair Employment Housing Act that talk about the purposes behind that act. In particular, the court says that it is a public policy of the state of California to ensure that discrimination in employment does not occur when it is based on various prohibited characteristics.[148] That Act also goes on to say that to be free of discrimination in employment on the basis of a prohibited characteristic is a civil right in California.[149] The California Supreme Court noted that in light of those purposes, it has held that the policy promoting the right to seek and hold employment free of prejudice is a fundamental one.[150]

The California Supreme Court then turned to how mixed motive was going to work. In particular, it noted that the Fair Employment and Housing Act has specific language talking about how the remedies need to be effective to deter and prevent unlawful employment practices[151] (with respect to remedies, the ADA does not contain as strong a statement; however, it does say that one of the purposes of the law is to "provide clear, strong, consistent, enforceable standards addressing discrimination by reinstating a broad scope of protection to be available under the ADA.").[152] On the other hand, the court was not looking to grant the plaintiff a windfall, either.[153] Therefore, to the California Supreme Court, "substantial factor" was the standard that made the most sense to strike the suitable balance between effective remedies and not providing a windfall to plaintiff.[154] In short, the way it will work in California with respect to the Fair Employment and Housing Act is that a plaintiff must first show by a preponderance of the evidence that discrimination was a substantial factor motivating his or her termination.[155] Once that happens, the employer gets to demonstrate that a legitimate, nondiscriminatory reason would have led it to make the same decision at the time.[156] If it can do that by a preponderance of the evidence, then the plaintiff can still prevail but, as with Title VII, the remedies are limited.[157]

What does this all mean for the Americans with Disabilities Act? First of all, substantial factor is a much easier concept to deal with than motivating factor, and therefore is consistent with the purpose of the ADA in desiring clear enforcement standards. Lawyers hate uncertainty unless it is to their advantage. It is becoming increasingly clear that "but for" does not mean sole cause. Further, as mentioned above, the legislative history is such that Congress had a very specific intent in mind when a change "because of," to "on the basis of" with respect to causation. Congress wanted that change to signify language more in tune with the Civil Rights Act.

On June 24, 2013, the U.S. Supreme Court issued its decision in *University of Texas Southwestern Medical Center v. Nassar*.[158] In that decision, the U.S. Supreme Court in a 5-4 ruling with Justice Kennedy being the swing vote, held that mixed motive is dead with respect to retaliation claims under Title VII of the Civil Rights Act.[159] The reasoning is such that this decision most certainly means mixed motive is dead with respect to retaliation claims under the ADA; thereby, giving a huge victory to ADA defense lawyers. On the other hand, the reasoning of the majority is such, that mixed motive is now very much alive under Title I of the ADA; thereby, giving a huge victory to ADA plaintiff employment lawyers. To understand how this could be is the question we explore here.

In this case, a physician of Middle Eastern heritage brought a claim against his employer alleging that he was discriminated against because of his heritage by his supervisor and also brought a retaliation claim alleging that he was retaliated against for complaining about the treatment he was receiving from his supervisor.[160] The jury found for him on both claims.[161] The U.S. Court of Appeals for the Fifth Circuit vacated the portion of the jury's verdict with respect to his constructive discharge claim but affirmed the jury's verdict with respect to his retaliation claim, adopting a mixed motive standard as the causation standard.[162] University of Texas Southwestern Medical Center appealed to the U.S. Supreme Court.[163] As mentioned above, in a 5 to 4 decision the U.S. Supreme Court held that with respect to alleging a claim for retaliation under Title VII of the Civil Rights Act, mixed motive is out and but for causation is in. However, the reasoning of their decision can only lead to the conclusion that mixed motive with respect to Title I claims of the ADA is now in and with respect to retaliation claims of the ADA is now out. Here's why.

First, Justice Kennedy and the majority make a distinction between status-based claims and retaliation claims.[164] Status-based claims are subject to a mixed motive analysis as a result of the *Price Waterhouse v. Hopkins* decision, which he discusses in some detail.[165] He also discusses how the Civil Rights Act was amended in 1991 so as to allow for limited recovery for mixed motive situations.[166]

Second, he spends some time talking about *Gross v. FBL Financial Services* and that but for causation is required for claims under the Age Discrimination in Employment Act.[167] He notes that Title VII is very comprehensive, and therefore, its specific structure needs to be taken as it is laid out.[168] In particular, the structure of Title VII of the Civil Rights Act makes clear that status discrimination gets treated in one way and that there is no indication that retaliation should be treated in the same way.[169] What is critical here for our purposes is that disability discrimination is status discrimination. That is, the plaintiff is alleging that an employer has discriminated against him based upon his or her status, i.e. having a disability.

Third, Justice Kennedy said that if Congress wanted mixed motive to apply to retaliation claims, "it could have inserted the motivating factor provision as part of the section applying to all such claims, *such as 42 U.S.C. § 2000e-5, which establishes the rules and remedies for all Title VII enforcement actions.*" (emphasis added)[170] With respect to the ADA, this language results in a virtual slam dunk that mixed motive is in play with respect to Title I claims because the ADA specifically references 42 U.S.C. § 2000e-5 as the remedies available to a plaintiff alleging discrimination under Title I of the ADA.[171]

Fourth, Justice Kennedy specifically cites to the ADA. In particular, he notes that the ADA is also a comprehensive statutory scheme and that Congress in the ADA clearly spoke to retaliation separate and apart from status-based claims.[172] This reasoning necessarily means that mixed motive with respect to retaliation claims under the ADA is dead (a huge victory for defense lawyers), but it also necessarily means that with respect to Title I claims of the ADA, mixed motive is very much alive.

Fifth, Justice Kennedy and the majority discuss that there are sound policy reasons for making retaliation claims difficult to prove. In particular, the number of retaliation claims filed with the EEOC has outstripped those for every type of status-based discrimination except for race.[173] Failing to hold otherwise, would contribute to the filing of frivolous claims. [174] It would also raise the costs, financial and reputational, on an employer whose actions were not in fact the result of any discriminatory retaliatory intent.[175] Finally, to hold otherwise would be inconsistent with the text and purpose of Title VII.[176]

Sixth, while the EEOC had a technical assistance manual saying that mixed motive applies to retaliation claims, Justice Kennedy was having none of it. In particular, he believed that the manual failed to address the specific provisions of the Title VII statutory scheme, the amendments to Title VII of the Civil Rights Act, and the *Gross* decision.[177]

This decision was one of those decisions with the 5-4 breakdown with the liberal justices and the conservative justices being evenly split and Justice Kennedy being the swing vote. Accordingly, there was a vigorous dissent by the liberal justices. Their reasoning was that the majority decision doesn't make any sense for a variety of reasons. First, retaliation for complaining about discrimination is tightly bonded to the core prohibition of discrimination based upon status and cannot be disassociated from it.[178]

Second, jurors are going to have a very difficult time figuring out why retaliation has one set of causation standards and status-based decisions has another set of causation standards.[179]

Third, until this decision, the Supreme Court had always held that a ban on discrimination encompasses retaliation.[180]

Fourth, the dissent found it strange that 42 U.S.C. § 2000e-2(m), the employment practices provision of the 1991 Civil Rights Act, which was designed to strengthen the act, was instead being used to actually limit the scope of remedies under that Act.[181]

Fifth, the dissent talks about how the statute the majority refers to in § 2000e-2 actually goes beyond just retaliation provisions.[182]

Finally, the dissent believed the EEOC technical assistance manual was entitled to deference.[183]

So what does this all mean for the practitioner and ADA plaintiffs and employers? It breaks down this way. Mixed motive is now available under Title I of the ADA. Mixed motive is not available for retaliation claims (Title V). What this means of course is that the possibilities for plaintiffs with respect to what they might be able to obtain in a Title I matter has just expanded as has the costs of litigation and its ultimate resolution to the defendant. On the other hand, the ability of the plaintiff to successfully prove a retaliation claim just got more difficult. All this said, this case still does not answer the question, which was discussed earlier in this chapter as to whether when dealing with but for causation you could still have more than one cause. On a practical level, this means an employer taking adverse action against an employee needs to make sure that they have good cause for that action independent of any possible discriminatory animus or run the risk of at least some liability per the remedies that exist if the plaintiff can show motivating factor under 42 U.S.C. § 2000e-5.

BURDENS OF PROOF

Disparate Impact

Turning to the area of the burdens of proof, it varies depending upon whether disparate impact or disparate treatment is involved. Both theories are available to a plaintiff alleging violation of the ADA.[184] However, the two theories differ. With disparate impact, you have a facially neutral policy that adversely impacts, in this case, persons with disabilities.[185] In a disparate impact case, it is possible for a facially neutral employment practice to be found discriminatory without evidence of the employer's subjective intent to discriminate against a class of people.[186] It does not even have to be an employment matter. For example, if a prospective law student has trouble getting accommodated by the LSAT, it stands to reason that his or her test scores may be lower than would otherwise be the case. Assuming such trouble in getting accommodated, could that person argue that the LSAT has a disparate impact on persons with disabilities? Let us say, for example, that a person with a disability challenges a law school's reliance on the LSAT on the ground that the inability to get accommodations results in a system that discriminates against persons with disabilities. Would the law school prevail in such a case? It most probably would, because the currency of the LSAT being what it is, the school would be able to show, with a strong basis in evidence per *Ricci v. DeStefano,* that the LSAT was job-related, so to speak, and consistent with business necessity.[187] This does not mean that the LSAT is free not to reasonably accommodate people who take the test or throw up obstacles that would discourage people with disabilities from taking the test.[188]

Disparate Treatment

A disparate treatment case is different. In a disparate treatment case, the employer treats some people less favorably than others because of their protected characteristic.[189] Whether an employer is liable for its disparate treatment depends upon whether the protected trait actually motivated the employer's decision.[190] In a disparate treatment case, absent direct evidence, the plaintiff must first make a prima facie case that they were discriminated against.[191] Once the plaintiff accomplishes this, it is up to the employer to offer a nondiscriminatory reason for the adverse employment action.[192] If the employer does so, then the plaintiff is given the opportunity to prove that it was more likely than not that the reasons given by the employer were really a pretext for discrimination.[193]

With respect to a disparate treatment case, sometimes you will see case law suggesting that a person needs to be replaced by someone outside of the protected class.[194] A case that shows the difficulties of requiring this is *Golembeski v. Moorestown Township Public Schools.*[195] In *Golembeski*, a culturally deaf teacher (a person who is deaf and used American Sign Language as his or her native language) alleged disability discrimination.[196] The defendant eventually wound up hiring a person that was not culturally deaf (cochlear implant) and then it claimed that the plaintiff could not show that she was replaced by someone outside of the protected class; therefore the defense argued that the plaintiff could not make her prima facie case.[197] The court didn't buy this argument for the following reasons.

First, the plaintiff noted that there was a critical distinction between a person who is deaf with a cochlear implant and a person, like the plaintiff, who is culturally deaf and relies on ASL; therefore, a resolution of the claim was particularly inappropriate on a motion for summary judgment.[198]

Second, the court noted that the Third Circuit specifically rejected the requirement that a person in a Title VII situation must be ultimately replaced by a person sufficiently outside the protected class, because such a requirement was particularly inappropriate when the classification of such individuals was categorical and not continuous.[199]

Third, the "replacement requirement" was not mandatory in the Third Circuit to begin with. To establish a prima facie case under the ADA for failure to hire, all the plaintiff had to show was that 1) she belonged to the protected category (person with a disability); 2) she applied for and was otherwise qualified for the job for which the employer was seeking applicants; 3) despite her qualification, she was rejected; and 4) after her rejection, the position remained open and the employer continue to seek applicants.[200] Filling the position with someone from outside the protected class was not mandatory to show but rather could be shown in the alternative if the person could not show that, after her rejection, the position remained open and the employer continued to seek applicants.[201]

The Third Circuit approach specifically rejecting a requirement that a person needs to be ultimately replaced by one sufficiently outside the protected class in order to make a prima facie case has very good policy reasons to support it with respect to ADA matters. First, the ADA has been amended so that many more people are included within the definition of a person with a disability. Second, and more important, no two disabilities, even the same ones, are handled the same by different people. For example, a person who is culturally deaf (born deaf, state schools for the deaf, and ASL) may have the same hearing loss as a person with a cochlear implant or even one who wears hearing aids, but the way they go about their business is dramatically different. Also, people with the same hearing loss may function entirely differently. In both of these situations, I am referring to people of the same type of disability, and still it would be very difficult to show true comparability, let alone what would happen if you try to compare different kinds of disabilities.

In short, I have never really understood how some opinions (not many) try to look for comparatives in ADA matters. As disabilities are very different, the full-on McDonnell Douglas paradigm, insisting that a person be replaced from someone outside of the protected class, fails. Furthermore, this case makes clear that such a paradigm is not required in the first place. What this case does is return the inquiry to whether the person with a disability is otherwise qualified and whether they were in fact discriminated against, rather than focusing on extraneous matters.

In a Title II case, a plaintiff to make a prima facie case must show proof similar to that shown in a Title I case. In order to recover, the plaintiff must show that (1) he or she is a qualified individual with a disability; (2) he or she was excluded from participation in or denied the benefits of some public entity's services, programs, or activities; and (3) the discrimination suffered was because of the disability.[202]

If a Title III case is involved, a plaintiff, to make a prima facie case, must show that (1) he or she is within the protected class of persons with disabilities; (2) the defendants are owners or operators of a place of public accommodation; and (3) the defendants discriminated against the plaintiff by denying him or her a full and equal opportunity to participate in or benefit from the defendants' program because of the disability.[203] Once a prima facie case is made, the plaintiff bears the burden of proving that a requested modification is reasonable.[204] Once that burden is met, the defendant must make the modification unless it can show that by doing so it would either alter the fundamental nature of its business or that the requested modification would pose a direct threat to the health or safety of others.[205]

Finally, in claims of retaliation,[206] plaintiffs must show that they engaged in statutorily protected activity, that they suffered an adverse action, and that there was a causal connection (see discussion earlier in this chapter of what casual connection means), between the two.[207]

VOIR DIRE

Does your state have a statute that allows the judge or judicial system to factor in a prospective juror's disability in deciding whether that juror can serve? Does that statute contain any reasonable accommodations/modifications language? In Illinois, the answer is yes to the first question and no to the second question. Illinois Supreme Court rule 434(c) provides that "if a prospective juror has a physical impairment, the court shall consider such a prospective juror's ability to perceive and appreciate the evidence when considering a challenge for cause."[208] There are also other Illinois statutes, one applying to civil trials, one to criminal trials, and one to juvenile proceedings with identical language.[209] In light of the discussion we've had in this book so far with respect to Titles I, II, and II of the ADA as amended, are such statutes even valid? For the reasons that follow, this author believes that statutes such as these, which lack language pertaining to reasonable accommodations or reasonable modifications with respect to prospective jurors with disabilities, violate both the Supremacy and Equal Protection Clauses of the U.S. Constitution. Furthermore, since such statutes, to this author's mind, violate the equal protection rights of persons with disabilities under the U.S. Constitution, it necessarily follows that *Batson v. Kentucky*[210] applies to persons with disabilities.

Some states specifically address the fact that some prospective jurors will need reasonable accommodations for their disabilities as part of the discussion when deciding whether that person can serve as a juror. For example, North Dakota,[211] Indiana,[212] Rhode Island,[213] Colorado,[214] and Utah[215] all have statutes that facially allow for reasonable accommodations in jury selection. Those states will not run into problems with the Equal Protection Clause or the Supremacy Clause. On the other hand, there are states that have no such reasonable accommodation language in their statutes. Alaska (a person may be excused from jury service for a physical or mental disability);[216] Delaware (a person with a physical or mental disability that renders him or her incapable of satisfactory jury service is not qualified);[217] Minnesota (challenges for cause are in order if the person has a physical or sensory disability that will impair that juror's ability to try a particular case);[218] and New Jersey (a person cannot have a mental or physical disability that prevents him or her from properly serving as a juror)[219] all facially lack reasonable accommodation language (the list is meant to be illustrative and not exhaustive), and could well run into trouble with respect to the Equal Protection Clause and the Supremacy Clause of the U.S. Constitution.

With respect to the Supremacy Clause, it is axiomatic that whenever a federal law conflicts with a state law, the state law must give way.[220] The harder question is, when does a federal law actually conflict with a state law? After all, federal and state laws often cover the same subject.

There are two ways a federal law can conflict with state law. First, a federal statute might implicitly override a state statute either when the scope of the statute indicates that federal law is intended to occupy the field exclusively or when state law is in actual conflict with federal law (field preemtption).[221] Second, there can be implied conflict preemption, which occurs when it is either impossible for a private party to comply with both state and federal requirements or where state law stands as an obstacle to the accomplishment and execution of the full purposes and objectives of the federal law.[222] There is nothing in the ADA of 1990 even as amended that suggests it is intended to occupy the field exclusively. However, there is both an actual conflict with the ADA *vis-à-vis* the Illinois Supreme Court rule and the similar statutes of other states, and a conflict with the accomplishments and execution of the purposes and objectives of the ADA (implied conflict preemption).

As previously mentioned, Title II of the ADA prohibits a public entity from discriminating against an otherwise qualified individual with a disability with respect to their programs, services, and activities of that public entity.[223] Under Title II, a qualified individual with a disability is an individual who, with or without reasonable modifications to the rules, policies, practices; removal of architectural, communication, or transportation barriers; or the provision of auxiliary aids and services, meets the essential eligibility requirements for services with respect to the programs or activities provided by that public entity.[224] Certainly, the opportunity to serve on a jury is an activity offered by a public entity, and perhaps part of a larger program, the administration of justice, as well.[225] The actual conflict occurs because the ADA mandates that reasonable modifications be made for an otherwise qualified individual, and, as we have seen, there are rules and statutes that contain no such provisions.[226] Of course, it is possible that courts, despite what the statute might say, engage in a reasonable accommodation analysis, but the Illinois Supreme Court rule and the various other state statutes discussed here on their face do not mandate that any such analysis occur, whereas the ADA does.

The Illinois Supreme Court rule and the various state statutes lacking reasonable accommodation language are also a victim of implied preemption as well, because there is a conflict with the accomplishments and execution of the purposes and objectives of the ADA. The purposes and objectives of the ADA were discussed in great detail in the case of *Tennessee v. Lane*.[227] In *Lane*, two mobility-impaired individuals brought suit against the state of Tennessee under Title II of the ADA, alleging that they were entitled to damages because certain Tennessee courthouses were not accessible.[228] One person could not access a courthouse to make court appearances on his own behalf, while the other person could not access the courthouse to do her job.[229] In holding that Congress properly forced the states to waive their sovereign immunity with respect to Title II of the ADA, the U.S. Supreme Court spent a great deal time of talking about the purposes and the objectives of the ADA.

First, the Court noted that Congress enacted Title II of the ADA against the background of pervasive unequal treatment of persons with disabilities with respect to the administration of state services and programs, of which many of those statutes are still on the books.[230]

Second, the Court also noted that it, as along with many other courts, had previously identified a history of unconstitutional treatment of disabled persons by state agencies in a variety of public programs and services.[231]

Third, the Court noted that its decisions demonstrated a pattern of unconstitutional treatment in the administration of justice.[232]

Fourth, the Court noted a prior decision had said that the exclusion of a segment of society that plays a major role in the community cannot be squared with the constitutional concept of a jury trial.[233]

In short, Title II of the ADA, is aimed at the enforcement of a variety of basic rights, such as the right of access to the courts.[234] Thus, it is hard to see how *Lane* would allow for a Supreme Court rule or a state statute that allows discrimination against persons with disabilities, regardless of whether those disabilities could be accommodated, when the purpose of a supervening federal law is to fully integrate persons with disabilities into all aspects of society to the greatest extent possible.[235]

With respect to the Equal Protection Clause, an argument can also be made that the Illinois Supreme Court rule at issue here and the various state statutes lacking reasonable accommodation language also violate the equal protection rights of persons with disabilities. Equal protection jurisprudence invariably turns upon which class the affected person falls into. The three classes of equal protection jurisprudence are strict scrutiny (race), intermediate scrutiny (gender), and rational basis (everyone else).[236] Until *Lane*, the class that a person fit into for equal protection purposes depended entirely on that person's characteristics and not on the facts of the case. However, *Lane* makes very clear that where a person with a disability fits with respect to the equal protection jurisprudence depends entirely on the facts.[237] As far as this author knows, the disabled are the only group of people whose equal protection tier depends on the facts of the case. Thus, the question becomes which equal protection tier persons with disabilities would fit into with respect to an Illinois Supreme Court rule, corresponding Illinois state statutes, and the statutes of other states that allow for discrimination based on disability with respect to serving on juries.

In *Lane*, as mentioned earlier in this book, the U.S. Supreme Court held that Congress rightfully waived the state's sovereign immunity because Title II of the ADA was a law consistent with enforcing the Equal Protection Clause of the Fourteenth Amendment with respect to the fundamental right of accessing the courts.[238] The Court also said, with respect to the fundamental right of accessing the courts, that persons with disabilities were at least in the intermediate scrutiny class, if not higher.[239] But which class? If a person with a disability is in the strict scrutiny class, then clearly the rule and corresponding statutes being talked about here must fail, because the government is going to be a hard-pressed to find a compelling reason[240] why persons with physical disabilities should be discriminated against in jury selection without factoring in reasonable accommodations, particularly when a federal law demands that they do so. However, if the person with a disability falls in the intermediate scrutiny class, then there is a possibility that the law might withstand an Equal Protection Clause challenge.[241] Finally, if the person with a disability with respect to jury selection falls in the rational basis class, then the Illinois Supreme Court rule and the various state statutes lacking reasonable accommodation language at issue here would probably stand.[242]

Are there any explanations as to why particular groups of people fall into different tiers? An excellent case with respect to the strict scrutiny class of equal protection jurisprudence is the California case *Sail'er Inn Inc. v. Kirby*.[243] In Sail'er, the California Supreme Court threw out a California law prohibiting a bar from hiring women bartenders.[244] In throwing out that law, the court talked about the cases that have found a plaintiff in a suspect class, the strict scrutiny class, of equal protection jurisprudence. They noted that suspect classes tended to have certain characteristics. First, class members are locked into the class by accident of birth.[245] Also, the characteristic frequently bears no relation to the ability to perform or contribute to society.[246]

With respect to persons with disabilities, there are two problems here.

First, people can become disabled after they are born—though, unless a disability is temporary, they are certainly locked into the class.

Second, whether persons are disabled frequently bears no relation to their ability to perform or contribute to society, especially if they are reasonably accommodated as required by the ADA.[247] However, there are certainly some disabilities that in some contexts cannot be reasonably accommodated.

Third, another characteristic underlying suspect classifications is the stigma of inferiority and second-class citizenship associated with them.[248] *Lane* makes clear that there is a long history by governmental entities of treating people with disabilities as inferior and as second-class citizens.[249]

Finally, it simply may not matter whether these particular characteristics of a suspect class are met, because if the discrimination touches upon a fundamental right, strict scrutiny may be activated.[250]

Since *Lane* makes it clear that accessing the courts is one such fundamental right,[251] it is not a stretch to say that serving on a jury, which certainly is part of accessing the courts, touches upon a fundamental right, and therefore the Illinois Supreme Court rule and the various statutes at issue here are subject to strict scrutiny.

While it is quite possible that serving on a jury would be subject to a strict scrutiny analysis, it's also possible that it might not be. Could the Illinois Supreme Court rule and others state laws lacking reasonable accommodation language be subject to an intermediate scrutiny analysis? If so, would they survive? For a law to survive intermediate scrutiny, the law must serve important governmental objectives and must be substantially related to achievement of those objectives.[252] It's hard to say what the important governmental objective is with respect to the Illinois Supreme Court rule and the various other state statutes lacking reasonable modification language. If the objective is to ensure that only people who can be jurors with or without reasonable accommodation can serve, then one wonders why the laws do not say as such. It is hard to see how allowing discrimination based on disabilities (in Illinois, the focus is entirely on physical disabilities; curiously, mental disabilities are not mentioned by the Illinois Supreme Court rule and its corresponding state statutes), without facially factoring in reasonable accommodations, is substantially related to the achievement of ensuring that only people who are competent to serve as jurors may serve. After all, if persons with a disability can be reasonably accommodated, there should be no reason why they can't serve as jurors.

Finally, this author does not see how it is possible that, with respect to serving on a jury, persons with disabilities could be in the rational basis class. However, in terms of employment, as mentioned earlier, persons with disabilities are in such a class.[253] Even so, as already mentioned, the language of *Lane* strongly suggests that rational basis would not be the classification of a person with a disability with respect to serving on a jury, and therefore the constitutionality of the Illinois Supreme Court rule and the other state statutes lacking reasonable accommodation language discussed here is questionable.

BATSON CHALLENGES

Few cases today actually go to trial. However, the ones that do go to trial involve picking a jury first. Jurors aren't so much picked as they are eliminated. In jury selection, there are three kinds of jury challenges. First, there is a peremptory challenge. Peremptory challenges can be made by an attorney for any reason whatsoever. Depending upon the jurisdiction and type of case, attorneys have a certain number of challenges they can use and no explanation is necessary. For example, if an attorney did not like the color of a prospective juror's shirt, it is theoretically possible that he or she could use a peremptory challenge to eliminate that person from the jury pool.

The second kind of challenge is a challenge for cause, whereby an attorney can exercise a challenge if he or she can convince the court that the prospective juror is hopelessly biased. For example, a prospective juror who is totally opposed to the death penalty would be able to have a challenge for cause exercised against him or her if that prospective juror would be serving on a capital murder case.

Finally, there is something called a *Batson* challenge, which comes from the case of *Batson v. Kentucky*, which has its civil equivalent in *Edmondson v. Leesville Concrete Company, Inc.*[254] In a *Batson* challenge, an attorney who is using peremptory challenges to exclude jurors based on a prohibited characteristic, such as race or gender, can be challenged by the other attorney to show cause to the court as to why the peremptory challenges are being used in that way.[255] If the explanation the attorney gives is not sufficient for the court, then the court can impose penalties upon the attorney for using the peremptory challenges in a discriminatory fashion.[256]

Batson challenges can only be used on behalf of a person who falls into the equal protection class of intermediate scrutiny or strict scrutiny.[257] As discussed elsewhere, the equal protection class that persons with disabilities fit into depends on the facts of the case.

What are the courts saying in decisions with respect to *Batson* challenges on behalf of persons with disabilities after *Tennessee v. Lane*? The issue has simply not come up much. However, it did arise in 2007 in the D.C. Circuit Court of Appeals. In that case, *United States v. Watson*,[258] Watson, in a protest against the treatment of tobacco farmers by the government, drove a tractor along with a Jeep and a trailer holding a metal box into a pond and remained there for two days.[259] He also drove a tractor onto an island in the middle of the pond that he had driven into causing a 3½-foot wave.[260] Finally, when a Park Service employee caught up with him and noted a metal box, he implied that the chemicals in the metal box were explosive and that he was willing to die for his cause.[261] He was then indicted for threatening and conveying false information concerning the use of an explosive and for destruction of government property.[262] During jury selection, the prosecutor used peremptory challenges to eliminate from the jury pool two visually impaired prospective jurors.[263] Watson's attorney essentially exercised a *Batson* challenge.[264] However, the district court overruled the *Batson* challenge, saying there was a substantial amount of visual evidence in the prosecution's case.[265]

On appeal, Watson argued that the *Batson* challenge should have been granted. Rejecting that claim, the U.S. Court of Appeals for the District of Columbia Circuit argued as follows. First, the court said that disability has never been given strict scrutiny by the Supreme Court.[266] Is this true? Not really, for several reasons. First, the court immediately cites to *City of Cleburne,* a case we have talked about in another context and where the U.S. Supreme Court claimed that it was using rational basis to find that a group home for persons with mental retardation had a right to be located wherever it wanted to be. However, unlike most cases involving rational basis, the Court engaged in a very extensive discussion of the discrimination faced by those with mental retardation and then threw the restriction out.[267] It is probably more accurate to say that this decision is about a "rational basis plus" case rather than just regular rational basis.[268]

Second, *Lane* specifically says that there will be situations where persons with disabilities will fall into at least intermediate scrutiny classification if not higher. More specifically, U.S. Supreme Court said: "Title II is aimed at the enforcement of a variety of basic rights, including the right of access to the court at issue in this case, *that call for standard of judicial review at least as searching, and in some cases more searching, then the standard that applies to sex-based classification.*" [Italics added][269]

Third, the *Watson* court cited to language from the *Cleburne* decision where the court referred to the mentally retarded and how singling them out for special treatment reflected the real and undeniable differences between the retarded and others.[270] Accordingly, the Supreme Court declined to presume that any classification drawn on the basis of disability was the result of unconstitutional discrimination.[271] However, the citation to this language of *Cleburne is* not without its own problems.

First, the language of that opinion is quite jarring to persons with disabilities and to those who are familiar with the terminology *vis-á vis* persons with disabilities. For example, the *Cleburne* court uses the phrase "mentally retarded." That is a phrase that has not been used for some time. For quite a while, the phrase used was "a "person with mental retardation." Now, even that phrase is passé. Rather, the phrase now being used is a "person with intellectual disabilities."

Second, the *Cleburne* decision came down in 1985, five years before the ADA was even signed by the first George Bush and seven years before it went into effect.

Third, the original Americans with Disabilities Act contained language within it, as mentioned in the first edition of this book, that suggested Congress intended for persons with disabilities to fall into an equal protection class higher than rational basis.[272]

Fourth, the *Watson* court said that the U.S. Supreme Court has declined to treat disabled as a suspect class because it recognized the reality that states may have legitimate reason for treating differently persons with reduced ability to perform certain functions.[273] However, this ignores the reality that Title II of the ADA and the Rehabilitation Act of 1973 both demand that governmental entities make reasonable modifications to their programs and activities so that persons with disabilities can reach the same starting line as people without disabilities.

Fifth, the court went on to say that it would follow *United States v. Harris,*[274] which held that persons with disabilities were in the rational basis class, and therefore a litigant who was otherwise able to exercise a *Batson* challenge could not do so.[275] Of course, the problem with following this particular case is that *Harris* predates the Supreme Court's analysis of the equal protection class that persons with disabilities fall into with respect to employment and accessing governmental entities.[276]

Finally, even if *Watson* is correct, which I don't think it is, the *Watson* court did give a ray of hope, so to speak, to jurors with disabilities. Specifically, they said that the attorney challenging the peremptory exclusion of the blind jurors did not offer any expert opinion, even in secondary form, that a blind juror would be able to fully assess the strengths and weaknesses of the government's visual evidence.[277] For that matter, the attorney challenging the peremptory challenges did not suggest any means of accommodating blind jurors, much less request that the government provide an accommodation by presenting, say, descriptive oral testimony of the scenes and events depicted in the videotapes.[278]

In short, can a person use *Batson* to challenge the exclusion of prospective jurors with disabilities? I still remain convinced that it can and that *Watson* has difficulty withstanding in-depth analysis. Regardless, *Watson* creates an opening for attorneys to successfully use *Batson* challenges on behalf of persons with disabilities if they are willing to make the effort to put an expert on the stand to explain how persons of various disabilities would be able to do their jobs as jurors effectively, and by showing that all the prospective juror with a disability needs is certain specified reasonable accommodations/modifications. In other words, if you are an attorney and the opposing attorney is using peremptory challenges to eliminate persons with disabilities from the jury pool, a two-step process is suggested. First, argue that *Batson* challenges are permissible. Second, in conjunction with or in addition to that argument, have an expert ready to be called who can discuss how people of various disabilities process information and what specific accommodations they need in order to do so. Finally, if the court refuses to allow the accommodations, argue violation of Title II of ADA and, since the court no doubt accepts federal funds, also argue violation of the Rehabilitation Act of 1973.

CLASS ACTIONS

Here's a fact, also mentioned elsewhere in this book, no two disabilities, even the same ones, are the same. Accordingly, it makes perfect sense that the ADA requires individual analysis throughout. Further, as mentioned earlier, under both Title I and Title II of the ADA, in addition to having a disability, the person must be qualified—that is, capable of performing the essential functions of the job with or without reasonable accommodations with respect to Title I or, with respect to Title II, capable of meeting the essential eligibility requirements with or without reasonable modifications. Title III does not have any such "qualified" language, but a similar analysis has to occur because you have to assess whether the nature of the business is being fundamentally altered. It is for all these reasons that class actions involving persons with disabilities are going to be extremely difficult, if not almost impossible, to pull off. Let's take a look at the case law to see why.

Class actions are governed by Federal Rule of Civil Procedure 23. Under that rule, the party seeking certification as a class has to demonstrate that 1) the class is so numerous that joinder of all members is impracticable; 2) there are questions of law or fact common to the class; 3) the claims or defenses of the representative parties are typical of the claims or defenses of the class; and 4) the representative parties will fairly and adequately protect the interests of the class.[279]

Once that is done, the proposed class has to satisfy at least one of three requirements in Federal Rule 23(b). Those requirements allow the class to be maintained in any of three different circumstances: 1) where prosecuting separate actions by or against individual class members creates a risk of either inconsistent or varying adjudications or adjudications that, as a practical matter, would be dispositive of the interests of the other members who are not parties to the individual adjudications, or which would substantially impair or impede their ability protect their interests; 2) where the party opposing the class has acted or refused to act on grounds applicable generally to the class so that final injunctive relief or corresponding declaratory relief is appropriate respecting the class as a whole; 3) where questions of law or fact common to class members predominate over any questions affecting only individual members, and a class action is superior to other available methods for fairly and efficiently adjudicating the controversy.[280]

Before moving further, when the EEOC brings enforcement action, it is not subject to Rule 23.[281] Before bringing suit, the EEOC must conciliate (give the opposing party a chance to resolve the claims).[282] There is a conflict among the circuits as to how far the EEOC must go in conciliating the claim prior to bringing suit. In the Sixth Circuit, all the EEOC has to show is that it made a good-faith effort to conciliate the claim it is asserting, thereby providing the employer with ample notice of the prospect of suit.[283] However, in the Eighth Circuit the law is quite a bit different. The Eighth Circuit found a clear and very significant distinction between facts that are gathered during the scope of an investigation and facts that are gathered during the discovery phase of an already filed lawsuit.[284] Therefore, the Eighth Circuit said that the EEOC cannot use discovery and a resulting lawsuit as a fishing expedition to uncover more violations.[285] In short, the Eighth Circuit said that the EEOC had the responsibility to make a reasonable investigation of the charge.[286] Thus, in the Eighth Circuit, an argument can be made that the claim of each class member must be reasonably investigated before that claim can become part of a subsequent suit.[287]

The difference between the two approaches is rather stark and presents a conflict among the circuits. Will the Supreme Court be asked to step in? It is not clear. Also, considering the hostility that the U.S. Supreme Court can display toward the EEOC, the EEOC may not feel it is in its interest to appeal to the Court. Finally, in the spring of 2013, I attended the national convention of the EEO section of the labor and employment action of the American Bar Association recently. At that conference, EEOC commissioners indicated that the message of the Eighth Circuit was being heard and that they were going to work hard to improve the investigation process. Thus, I am not sure you will see this go to the Supreme Court. Do expect to see developments with respect to the EEOC investigation process.

However, if you are not the government carrying out an enforcement action, you have to deal with Rule 23 of the Federal Rules of Civil Procedure. The class-action world changed in June 2011 with the decision of the U.S. Supreme Court in *Wal-Mart Stores, Inc. v. Dukes*.[288] In particular, focusing on the commonality requirement of class-action litigation, the Court made several statements that are very problematic with respect to persons with disabilities being able to prosecute class actions.

First, they said that commonality requires a plaintiff to demonstrate that the class members have the same injury.[289]

Second, there must be a common contention, and that common contention must be capable of classwide resolution, which means that a determination of the truth or falsity resolves an issue central to the validity of all of the claims in one stroke.[290]

Finally, what matters to class certification is not the raising of common questions, but rather the capacity of the classwide proceeding to generate common answers apt to drive the resolution of litigation.[291]

With respect to the same injury, I suppose you could have a class of people that were not hired, or a class that were wrongfully fired. The common contention is a lot more problematic for people with disabilities because, as mentioned above, a person must have a disability and also must be qualified as well.[292] Finally, that individual analysis required by the ADA (whether it be under the qualified language of Title I or Title II or trying to determine a fundamental alteration under Title III), necessarily means that you will not have common answers.

Typicality is also going to present problems in most ADA cases. The typicality requirement is met if the class representative's claims are generally the same as those of other class members with respect to both the legal theory advanced and the factual circumstances underlying the theory.[293] Typicality is usually measured through a three-part test that looks at whether the representative's claims are generally the same as the class members' claims in both the legal theory at issue and the underlying facts; whether the class representative is subject to a defense that may not be alleged against many other class members and that may become a major issue in the litigation; and whether the class member representative's interests are sufficiently aligned with other class members.[294]

Again, the nature of the ADA is such that it's going to be extremely difficult to meet the typicality requirement for several reasons.

First, each ADA inquiry is, by its very definition, highly individualized, and the facts involving one person may be different in key particulars from the facts involving other class members.[295]

Second, it is quite possible that class members may be subjected to different defenses. For example, judicial estoppel per *Cleveland v. Policy Management Systems*, statute of limitations,[296] and whether an accommodation is reasonable may all differ depending on the class member and the particular facts base by that class member.[297]

Third, what class members want may vary from situation to situation. Some may want to return to work, others may want specific accommodation, and yet others may want to transfer.[298] All of those are very fact-specific inquiries.

Finally, the individual inquiries necessitated by the ADA also make satisfying Rule 23(b) of the Federal Rules of Civil Procedure extremely difficult, even if somehow the person with a disability could have his or her class get by Federal Rule of Civil Procedure 23(a). After all, since everything is so individualized, it would be hard to argue that the adjudication would be inconsistent, as it is all turning on its own facts. Also, it would be hard to argue that an individualized decision would also be dispositive of the interest of other members who are not parties, again because of the individualized factual determination necessary in ADA litigation. It would also be hard to argue, again because of the individualized determinations required, that questions of law or fact common to class members predominate over any questions affecting only individual members.

So is a class certification even possible anymore? It may be possible if people have a common disability or a common requested accommodation,[299] though I am skeptical about the common disability even making the cut, since people with the same disabilities can be very different. It also may be possible if there are systemic violations, such as where a state has a system that encourages sheltered workshops rather than integrated employment.[300]

What about a pattern or practice claim, such as a "100% return to work healed" policy? Even that may be problematic because, according to the Third Circuit, you still would have to figure out whether the individual claiming discrimination had a disability and was able to perform the essential functions of the job with or without reasonable accommodations—an individualized fact inquiry.[301] The only out may be a "regarded as" claim.[302] You would have to argue that if an employer regards a person as having a disability, the "otherwise qualified" analysis does not apply, because a person who is regarded as having a disability is not entitled to a reasonable accommodation.[303] Further, to show that someone has been regarded as having a disability, that person only has to show a physical or mental impairment and not whether the impairment is substantially limiting;[304] therefore, the "otherwise qualified" argument does not apply and a class action could proceed, because the individualized determinations would not be critical when the class is limited to those who have been regarded as having a disability since substantial limitation on a major life activity never comes into play. Finally, while this argument has a certain logic to it, it's far from clear whether it would be successful,[305] though it could be worth trying in certain circumstances.

In summary, the EEOC, since it does not have to deal with Federal Rule of Civil Procedure 23, is going to have a better shot with respect to class-action litigation. Even so, it still, per the above, may have to investigate in a reasonable way each of the claims that it uses as part of the class action. With respect to individuals with disabilities, it is going to be extraordinarily tough to maintain class actions. Even if an individual alleges a "pattern or practice," he or she is still going to have to deal with the "qualified" problem.[306]

Notes

1. The information that follows with respect to standing is taken from my blog entry from March 2013. Since the medium is different, it appears slightly different here. That blog entry can be found at http://www.williamgoren.com/blog/.
2. Hamill v. North Wildwood City, 2013 WL 1007297, *1 (D.N.J. Mar. 11, 2013).
3. *Id.*
4. *Id.*
5. *Id.*
6. *Id.*
7. *Id.* at *2.
8. *Id.*
9. *Id.*
10. *Id.* at *2.
11. *Id.*
12. *Id.*
13. *Id.*
14. *Id.* at *4.
15. *Id.*
16. *Id.*
17. *Id.* at *5.
18. *Id.*
19. *Id.*
20. *Id.*
21. *Id.*
22. *Id.* at *6.
23. *Id.*
24. *Id.*
25. *Id.* at *7.
26. *Id.*
27. *Id.*
28. *Id.*
29. *Id.*
30. *Id.*
31. *Id.* at *8.
32. *Id.*
33. *Id.*
34. *Id.*
35. Harty v. Bull's Head Realty, 2013 WL 1131625 (D. Conn. Mar. 18, 2013).
36. Ashcroft v. Iqbal, 129 S. Ct. 1937 (2009); Bell Atl. Corp. v. Twombly, 550 U.S. 544 (2007).
37. Ashcroft v. Iqbal, 129 S. Ct. 1937, 194950 (2009). The information that follows is taken from my blog entry from March 2013. Since the medium

is different, it appears slightly different here. That blog entry can be found at http://www.williamgoren.com/blog/.

38. *Id.* at 1950.
39. *Id.* at 1949.
40. People *ex rel.* Madigan v. Tang, 346 Ill. App. 3d 277, 283 (1st Dist. 2004).
41. *Compare id.* with Wells v. West Ga. Tech. Coll., 2012 WL 3150819, *3 (N.D. Ga. Aug. 2, 2012).
42. *See* http://www.eeoc.gov/employees/timeliness.cfm . The discussion that follows regarding the statute of limitations is very similar to my blog entry from April 15, 2013. There is a difference between the two due to the medium. Also, because of the difference in mediums, you will find more citations here than you will in the blog entry.
43. *Id.*
44. *Id.* Note: Not all states would have an agency that would qualify for a 300-day period and the practitioner needs to be cognizant of that.
45. *See* Cordova v. Univ. of Notre Dame du Lac, _ F. Supp. 2d_, 2013 WL 1332268, *3 (N.D. Ind. Mar. 29, 2013).
46. *See* Stamm v. New York City Transit Auth., 2013 WL 244793,*9 (E.D.N.Y. Jan. 22, 2013).
47. 28 U.S.C.A. § 1658(a) (WL, current through Pub. L. 113-9 (excluding Pub. L. 113-4) approved May 1, 2013).
48. Jones v. R.R. Donnelly & Sons Co., 541 U.S. 369 (2004).
49. *Id.* at 381–82.
50. *Cordova*, 2013 WL 1332268, at *5.
51. *Jones*, 541 U.S. at 384–85, n.18.
52. Sutton v. United Airlines, 527 U.S. 471, 482 (1999).
53. 42 U.S.C.A. § 12102(4)(E)(i), (ii), (iii) (WL, current through Pub. L. 113-9 (excluding Pub. L. 113-4), approved May 1, 2013).
54. *Sutton*, 527 U.S. at 489.
55. 42 U.S.C. § 12102(3)(A) (WL, current through Pub. L. 113-9 (excluding Pub. L. 113-4), approved May 1, 2013).
56. *Cordova*, at 2013 WL 1332268 at *6.
57. As a practical matter, there really isn't a statute of limitations for Title III claims since the remedy is instructive relief. That means necessarily that a problem needs to be corrected. Accordingly, an out of compliance Title III situation is essentially a continuing violation until it is remedied. Therefore, the two- or four-year statute of limitations is only likely to be an issue in the Title II area.
58. 42 U.S.C.A. § 12117(a) (WL, current through Pub. L. 113-9 (excluding Pub. L. 113-4), approved May 1, 2013).
59. 42 U.S.C.A. § 1977A(a)(3) (WL, current through Pub. L. 113-9 (excluding Pub. L. 113-4), approved May 1, 2013); *see also* EEOC v. Sears, *supra*.
60. 42 U.S.C.A. at § 1977A(b).

61. Buckhannon Board and Care Home, Inc. v. W. Va. Dep't of Health and Human Resources, 532 U.S. 598, 602 (citing to 42 U.S.C.A. § 12205).
62. *See generally id.*
63. *Id.* at 600.
64. *Id.* at 600–01.
65. *Id.* at 601.
66. *Id.*
67. *Id.* at 602.
68. *Id.* at 603.
69. *Id.* at 603–04.
70. *Id.* at 604.
71. *Id.* at 607.
72. *Id.* at 608–09.
73. Jankey v. Poop Deck, 537 F.3d 1122 (9th Cir. 2008).
74. *Id.* at 1123.
75. *Id.*
76. *Id.* at 1124.
77. *Id.* at 1123.
78. *Id.* at 1123–24.
79. *Id.* at 1124–28.
80. *Id.* at 1128.
81. *Id.* at 1123.
82. *Id.*. at 1129.
83. *Id.* at 1130.
84. *Id.* at 1129–30.
85. *Id.* at 1130.
86. 42 U.S.C.A. § 12203(a) (WL, current through Pub. L. 113-9 (excluding Pub. L. 113-4), approved May 1, 2013).
87. Kramer v. Banc of America Securities, LLC, 355 F.3d 961, 963 (7th Cir. 2004).
88. *Id.* at 964–66.
89. *Id.* at 967–68.
90. Alvarado v. Cajun Operating Co., 588 F.3d 1261 (9th Cir. 2009).
91. Baker v. Windsor Republic Doors, 635 F. Supp. 2d 765, 766 (W.D. Tenn. 2009).
92. *Id.* at 769–71.
93. *Id.* at 769.
94. *Id.*
95. 42 U.S.C.A. § 12133 (WL, current through Pub. L. 113-9 (excluding Pub. L. 113-4), approved May 1, 2013).
96. Howard v. Cherry Hills Cutters, Inc., 935 F. Supp. 1148 (D. Colo. 1996); Lillard v. Sunflower Farmers Market, Inc., 2012 WL 5936543 (D. Colo. Nov. 27, 2012).
97. *See* Doe v. County of Milwaukee, 871 F. Supp. 1072, 1076 (E.D. Wis. 1995).

98. 28 C.F.R. at § 35.107(a).
99. 56 Fed. Reg. 35,694 (July 26, 1991) at discussion of 28 C.F.R. 35.170.
100. Cordova v. Univ. of Notre Dame du Lac, 2013 WL 1332268, *6 (N.D. Ind. Mar. 29, 2013).
101. 28 C.F.R. § 36.501 (WL, current through May 30, 2013; 78 Fed. Reg. 32,362).
102. *Id.*
103. 42 U.S.C.A. § 12188(b)(2) (WL, current through Pub. L. 113-9 (excluding Pub. L. 113-4), approved May 1, 2013).
104. 42 U.S.C.A. § 12188(b)(4) (WL, current through Pub. L. 113-9 (excluding Pub. L. 113-4), approved May 1, 2013).
105. Val D'Aosta Co. v. Cross, 526 S.E.2d 580, 581–82 (Ga. App. 1999).
106. Gross v. FBL Fin. Servs., 557 U.S. 167 (2009).
107. *Id.* at 176–78, 180.
108. Serwatka v. Rockwell Automation Inc., 591 F.3d 957, 962, 962 n.1 (7th Cir. 2010).
109. H.R. Rep. 110-730(I) at discussion of, "Discrimination on the Basis of Disability."
110. *See id.*
111. 42 U.S.C.A. § 12182(a) (WL, current through Pub. L. 113-9 (excluding Pub. L. 113-4), approved May 1, 2013).
112. 42 U.S.C.A. § 12188(a) (WL, current through Pub. L. 113-9 (excluding Pub. L. 113-4), approved May 1, 2013).
113. *Compare* 42 U.S.C.A. § 12132 *with* 29 U.S.C.A. § 794(a) (WL, current through Pub. L. 113-9 (excluding Pub. L. 113-4), approved May 1, 2013).
114. Lewis v. Humboldt Acquisition Corp., Inc., 681 F.3d 312, 315–16 (6th Cir. 2012); *see also*, K.M. v. Tustin United School Dist., *supra*, _ F.3d _, 2013 WL 3988677, *8 (9th Cir. Aug. 6, 2013).
115. *Lewis,* 681 F.3d 312.
116. *Id.* at 315–16.
117. *Id.* at 321.
118. *Id.* at 332 (J. Donald concurring in part and dissenting in part).
119. *See id.* at the separate concurring and dissenting opinions of J. Clay, J. Stranch, and J. Donald at 322.
120. Then again, it might not be better at all. At the national labor and employment conference of the ABA held in Atlanta in 2013, a distinguished panel of attorneys suggested that mixed motive actually did plaintiffs no favors. Since then, I have talked to some other plaintiff attorneys, and they agree. Their reasoning was that mixed motive is very confusing, and it is much easier for a jury to understand "but for," or even necessary cause, than mixed motive.
121. Pearson v. Lawrence Med. Ctr., 2012 WL 5265774 (N.D. Ala. Oct. 24, 2012).
122. *Id.* at *1.
123. *Id.* at *2.

124. *Id.*
125. *Id.*
126. *Id.*
127. *Id.* at *2–3.
128. *Id.* at *3.
129. *Id.* at *4.
130. *Id.*
131. *Id.*
132. *Id.*
133. *Lewis,* at 332 (Donald, J., concurring in part and dissenting in part).
134. Harris v. City of Santa Monica, 294 P.3d 49 (Cal. 2013).
135. *Id.* at 51.
136. *See id.* at 51–53.
137. *Id.* at 51.
138. *Id.* at 53.
139. *Id.*
140. *Id.* at 55.
141. *Id.*
142. *Id.* at 56.
143. Price Waterhouse v. Hopkins, 490 U.S. 228 (1989).
144. *Harris,* 294 P.3d at 57, *citing to* Price Waterhouse v. Hopkins, 490 U.S. 228, 258 (1989) (Brennan, J., plurality opinion).
145. *Id.* at 57.
146. *Id.*
147. *Id.* at 58–59.
148. *Id.* at 59–60.
149. *Id.* at 60.
150. *Id.*
151. *Id.* at 61.
152. *See* 42 U.S.C. 12101(b)(2).
153. *Harris*, 249 P.3d at 66.
154. *See id.* at 56–68.
155. *Id.* at 72.
156. *Id.*
157. *Id.*
158. University of Texas Southwestern Medical Center v. Nassar, 570 U.S. 133 S.Ct. 2517, 2013 WL 3155234 (June 24, 2013).
159. *Id.* at *15.
160. *Id.* at *5.
161. *Id.*
162. *Id.*
163. *Id.*
164. *Id.* at **6-9.
165. *Id.* at **7-8.

166. *Id.*
167. *Id.* at **8-10.
168. *Id.* at **10.
169. *Id.*
170. *Id.* at *11.
171. *See* 42 U.S.C. § 12117(a); *see also* prior discussion earlier in this book of legislative history with respect to what "on the basis," means and with respect to why the term "qualified," was kept in the amendments to the ADA.
172. University of Texas Southwestern Medical Center, 2013 WL 3155234 at *12.
173. *Id.* at *13.
174. *Id.*
175. *Id.*
176. *Id.* at *14.
177. *Id.* at *15.
178. *Id.* at *17 (Justice Ginsburg dissenting).
179. *Id.*
180. *Id.* at *19.
181. *Id.* at *23.
182. *Id.* at *25.
183. *Id.* at *26.
184. Raytheon Co. v. Hernandez, 540 U.S. 44, 53 (2003).
185. *Id.* at 52.
186. *Id.* at 52–53.
187. *See* Ricci v. DeStefano, _ U.S. _, 129 S. Ct. 2658 (2009).
188. *See* my blog entry discussing the current litigation involving the LSAT and the California agency that enforces the Fair Employment and Housing Act, which can be found at http://www.williamgoren.com/blog/2012/10/08/lsat-and-Title-iii-discrimination-excessive-unreasonalbe-documentation-lsat-waiver/.
189. *Raytheon*. 540 U.S. at 52.
190. *Id.*
191. *Id.* at 55.
192. *Id.*
193. *Id.* at 52.
194. In fact, the EEOC charge form has specific questions on it pertaining to how other similar people were treated with regard to the same kind of claim. *See* https://egov.eeoc.gov/eqs/uniformintakequestionnaire09.
195. Golembeski v. Moorestown Twp. Public Schools, 2013 WL 1007672 (D.N.J. Mar. 13, 2013).
196. *Id.* at *1–*2.
197. *Id.* at *2, *5.
198. *See id.* at *5–*6.
199. *Id.* at *6 n.6.

200. *Id.* at *5.
201. *Id.*
202. Melton v. Dallas Area Rapid Transit, 391 F.3d 669, 671 (5th Cir. 2004).
203. Louie v. NFL, 185 F. Supp. 2d 1306, 1308 (S.D. Fla. 2002).
204. Kuketz v. Petronelli, 821 N.E.2d 473, 478 n.23 (Mass. 2005).
205. *Id.*; *see also* Christopher Bidlack, student author, *The Prohibition of Prosthetic Limbs in American Sports: The Issues and the Role of the Americans with Disabilities Act*, 19 MARQ. SPORTS L. REV. 613, 625–26 (Spring 2009).
206. The ADA specifically allows for retaliation claims. *See* 42 U.S.C.A. § 12203(a), (c) (WL, current through Pub. L. 113-9 (excluding Pub. L. 113-4), approved May 1, 2013).
207. *See* Casna v. City of Loves Park, 574 F.3d 420 (7th Cir. 2009).
208. Ill. Supreme Court Rule 434 (WL, current with amendments received through Mar. 1, 2013).
209. *See* 735 ILL. COMP. STAT. 5/2-1105.1 (WL, current through P.A. 97-1173 of the 2012 regular session, and through P.A. 98-6 of the 2013 regular session); 725 ILL. COMP. STAT. 5/115-4(d) 1 (WL, current through P.A. 97-1173 of the 2012 regular session, and through P.A. 98-6 of the 2013 regular session); 705 ILL. COMP. STAT. 405/5-6051 (WL, current through P.A. 97-1173 of the 2012 regular session, and through P.A. 98-6 of the 2013 regular session).
210. Batson v. Ky., 76 U.S. 79 (1986).
211. N.D. CENT. CODE § 27-09.1-07(1)(c) (WL, current through 2011 regular and special sessions of the 62nd and legislative assembly).
212. IND. CODE § 33-28-5-18 (a) (WL, current through P.L. 76 with effective date through Apr. 15, 2013).
213. R.I. GEN. LAWS § 9-9-1.1 (d) (WL, current through chapter 491 of the January 2012 session).
214. COLO. REV. STAT. § 13-71-104(3)(c) (WL, current through laws effective Apr. 1, 2013).
215. Utah judicial administration rule 4-404(5)(B) (WL, current with amendments received through Mar. 1, 2013).
216. Alaska court rule 15(l)(2) (WL, current with amendments received through Aug. 1, 2012).
217. DEL. CODE ANN. tit. 10 § 4509(b)(5) (WL, current through 79 laws 2013, chs. 1–13).
218. MINN. STAT. ANN. § 593. 32 (WL, current with laws of the 2013 regular session through chapter 10).
219. N.J. STAT. ANN. § 2B:20-1(f) (WL, current with laws effective through L. 2013, c. 42 and J.R. No. 3).
220. *See* Freightliner Corp. v. Myrick, 514 U.S. 280, 287 (1995); *see also* Hines v. Davidowicz, 312 U.S. 52, 66–67, 68 n.20, 70 (1941).
221. *Freightliner*, 514 U.S. at 287.
222. *Id.*

223. 42 U.S.C.A. § 12132 (WL, current through Pub. L. 113-9 (excluding Pub. L. 113-4), approved May 1, 2013).
224. 42 U.S.C.A. § 12131(2) (WL, current through Pub. L. 113-9 (excluding Pub. L. 113-4), approved May 1, 2013).
225. *See* Tenn. v. Lane, 541 US 509, 525, 525 n.14.
226. *E.g., compare* 42 U.S.C. § 12132 *with* 735 ILL. COMP. STAT. 5/2-1105.1, 725 ILL. COMP. STAT. 5/115-4(d), and Ill. Supreme Court Rule 434(c) (no reasonable modification requirement appears in the Supreme Court Rule and in the corresponding Illinois statutes).
227. *Lane*, 541 U.S. 509 (1978).
228. *Id.* at 513–14.
229. *Id.*
230. *Id.* at 524.
231. *Id.* at 524–25.
232. *Id.* at 525.
233. *Id.* at 523.
234. *Id.* at 529.
235. In fact, the U.S. Supreme Court in *Lane*, as part of its case of showing a pattern of discrimination in the administration of justice, mentioned two cases where persons with disabilities were excluded from jury service. *Id.* at 525 n.14.
236. *E.g.,* City of Cleburne v. Cleburne Living Center, 473 U.S. 432, 439–41 (1985)
237. *Lane*, 541 U.S. at 530–31.
238. *Id.* at 533–34.
239. *Id.* at 529.
240. *City of Cleburne*, 473 U.S. at 440.
241. *See* Craig v. Boren, 429 U.S. 190, 197–98 (1977).
242. *See* Heller v. Doe, 509 U.S. 312 , 319–21 (1993).
243. Sail'er Inn, Inc. v. Kirby, 5 Cal. 3d 1, 485 P.2d 529 (1971).
244. *Id.* at 543.
245. *Id.* at 540.
246. *Id.*
247. *See Lane,* 541 U.S. at 536–37 (Souter & Ginsburg, J.J., concurring).
248. *Sail'er Inn,* 485 P.2d at 540.
249. *Lane,* 541 U.S. at 523–30.
250. *See Sail'er Inn*, 485 P.2d at 539; *see also Heller,* 509 U.S. at 319.
251. *Lane*, 541 U.S. at 533–34.
252. *See Craig,* 429 U.S. at 198.
253. *See* Board of Trustees Univ. of Ala. v. Garrett, 531 U.S. 356 (2001).
254. Edmondson v. Leesville Concrete Co., Inc., 500 U.S. 614 (1991).
255. *Batson,* 476 U.S. at 96–97.
256. *Id.* at 97.
257. *Harris* 197 F.3d at 874–75.
258. United States v. Watson, 483 F.3d 828 (D.C. Cir. 2007).

259. *Id.* at 829.
260. *Id.*
261. *Id.*
262. *Id.*
263. *Id.*
264. *Id.* at 829–30.
265. *Id.* at 830.
266. *Id.* at 831.
267. *City of Cleburne,* 473 U.S. at 446–50.
268. *Id.* at 456, 458 *(*Marshall, J., concurring and dissenting in part).
269. *Lane,* 541 U.S. at 529.
270. *Watson*, 438 F.3d at 831 (citing to *City of Cleburne* 473 U.S. at 442–44).
271. *Id.* at 446.
272. *See* William D. Goren, Understanding the ADA: An Overview for Lawyers (ABA, 2000) at p. 54.
273. *Watson,* at 832.
274. United States v. Harris, 197 F.3d 870 (7th Cir. 1999).
275. *Id.* at 876.
276. With respect to equal protection category that persons with disabilities fall into regarding employment matters, that case, *Board of Trustees University of Alabama v. Garrett, supra,* was decided by the U.S. Supreme Court in 2001. With respect to the equal protection category that persons with disabilities fall into regarding accessing governmental entities, that case, *Tennessee v. Lane, supra,* was decided in 2004.
277. *Watson,* 483 F.3d at 834.
278. *Id.* at 834–35.
279. Fed. R. Civ. P. 23(a) (WL, current through Amendments received to Feb. 19, 2013).
280. Fed. R. Civ. P. 23(b) (WL, current through Amendments received to Feb. 19, 2013).
281. *See* General Telephone Co. of the Nw., Inc. v. EEOC, 446 U.S. 318, 330 (1980).
282. EEOC v. CRST Van Expedited, Inc., 679 F.3d 657, 671–72 (8th Cir. 2012).
283. Serrano v. Cintas Corp., 699 F.3d 884, 904 (6th Cir. 2012).
284. *CRST Van Expedited*, 679 F.3d at 675.
285. *Id.*
286. *Id.* at 676.
287. *Id.*
288. Wal-Mart Stores, Inc. v. Dukes, 131 S. Ct. 2541 (2011).
289. *Id.* at 2551.
290. *Id.*
291. *Id.*

292. Hohider v. United Parcel Service, Inc., 574 F.3d 169, 191–98 (3d Cir. 2009) (though she did not write the opinion, Justice O'Connor did sit on this panel).
293. Semenko v. Wendy's Int'l Inc., 2013 WL 1568401, *8.
294. *Id.*
295. *Id.*
296. *See* my blog entry of April 15, 2013, which can be found at *http://www.williamgoren.com/blog/2013/04/15/ada-applicable-statute-of-limitations/.*
297. *Id.* at *9.
298. *Id.*
299. *Id.* at *8.
300. *See* Lane v. Kitzhaber, 283 F.R.D. 587 (D. Or. 2012).
301. *Hohider*, 574 F.3d at 195.
302. *See* Powers v. USF Holland, Inc., 667 F.3d 815, 824 (7th Cir. 2011).
303. *See* 42 U.S.C.A. § 12201(h) (WL, current through Pub. L. 113-9 (excluding Pub. L. 113-4), approved May 1, 2013).
304. 42 U.S.C.A. § 12102(3)(A) (WL, current through Pub. L. 113-9 (excluding Pub. L. 113-4), approved May 1, 2013).
305. *See* Nelson v. City of New York, 2013 WL 4437224 *8 (S.D.N.Y. Aug. 19, 2013) (stating that the regarded as disabled clause of the ADA is intended to benefit only those employees erroneously perceived to be disabled *and* who are in fact fully able to perform the essential functions of that job (i.e. is a qualified individual).
306. *Hohider, supra,* assumes without deciding the issue that a pattern or practice theory can be alleged by a private plaintiff. Even so, for the reasons discussed in that case, *Hohider* would make certifying such a class extremely difficult. Note, the "regarded as," of *Powers, supra,* is not really discussed in *Hohider* and certainly not with respect to whether the "qualified," language would apply to "regarded as" claims.

ADA and Sports

12

PROFESSIONAL SPORTS

PROFESSIONAL SPORTS AND THE Americans with Disabilities Act is a topic that I have explored in the previous editions of this book and this one is no exception. This hypothetical is based on a real-life occurrence:

> A professional basketball player develops an irregular heartbeat. The team sends the player for tests and refuses to let him play in the meantime. Six weeks of tests are inconclusive. Further, the NBA's insurance company will not insure the ballplayer. The player also interviews with other teams and takes their physical as a condition of the team pursuing further interest in him. There is no interest there. Finally, the team the player played for in the past tenders him a one-year offer but refuses to let him play unless he takes a genetic test that might reveal whether he has some genetic abnormality that would put him at risk in the future. The basketball player refuses to take the test. Any ADA issues?[1]

Keep in mind that the Genetic Information Nondiscrimination Act, discussed earlier in this book, may also have applicability to this situation.

That said, lets focus this hypothetical on the ADA. Title I of the ADA governs this scenario because an employment relationship is involved. Since there is no exemption for professional sports anywhere in the ADA, and all professional sports teams have at least 15 employees, Title I of the ADA applies here and to the operations of professional sports teams in general.

This hypothetical case raises several ADA issues, including:

- pre-employment and post-employment medical exams;
- job relatedness, business necessity, and whether the person can perform the job with reasonable accommodations;
- the definition of disability;
- essential functions of the job of a pro athlete or coach/manager; and
- defenses that the team may have when an ADA claim is filed.

Turning to the first set of issues, did the other team's interest in our pro basketball player violate the ADA's prohibition on pre-employment medical exams? Whether an illegal pre-employment medical exam has occurred is an issue that operates independently of whether the employee has a disability under the ADA.[2] The pre-employment medical exam issue will arise prior to being drafted and whenever a player is traded or signs on as a free agent.

As noted earlier, the ADA prohibits pre-employment medical exams.[3] A medical exam (any exam that solicits information about a person's health or possible disability) can take place *after* a conditional job offer is made.[4] A conditional job offer can be withdrawn if it is job-related, consistent with business necessity, and the person could not do the essential functions of the job with or without reasonable accommodations.[5]

When a player is traded contingent on passing a physical, does a pre-employment medical exam occur or is the medical exam conducted after a conditional job offer? Clearly, the player has not yet been employed by the team trading for him. On the other hand, the team will hire the player if he can pass the physical. Therefore, it can be argued that these physicals are done pursuant to a conditional job offer and that no illegal pre-employment medical exam occurs. Still, the issue of whether a pre-employment medical exam occurred is very significant because if it did, the ADA was violated. If the exam was made pursuant to a conditional job offer, further analysis under the ADA is needed. Finally, it would seem that the combines that professional leagues conduct prior to drafts and in which all kinds of medical information is gathered and obtained, are particularly at risk of running afoul of the pre-employment medical inquiry prohibition as the combines occur prior to a conditional job offer. Certainly, an employer can ask questions that pertain to assessing whether an individual can perform the essential functions of the job, but the information assessed and obtained at these combines would seem to go far beyond this principle. It is true that layering the ADA onto the combine would fundamentally alter the entire system. However, fundamental alteration is a defense to reasonable accommodation and does not excuse otherwise violating the ADA.

Assume for the sake of argument that these physicals of pro players are done after a conditional job offer.[6] Let's further assume that based on our player's heart condition, the team withdraws the offer to our player. Therefore, the question becomes whether the job offer was withdrawn for reasons related to the job, consistent with business necessity, and the person was unable to perform the essential functions of the job with or without reasonable accommodations. Again, all three requirements must be satisfied before a conditional job offer can be validly withdrawn.

Certainly, whenever a player is traded or signed and a physical is performed, it is certainly job-related and consistent with business necessity. However, if an offer were to be withdrawn after the physical, could the team show that the athlete could not perform the essential functions of the job with or without reasonable accommodations? The first step is to determine the essential functions of the employee's job. In determining the essential functions of the job of an NBA player, for example, the potential exists for confusing tasks with functions. For example, it could be said that jumping, stopping, and running are all tasks associated with the job of the pro basketball player. It also could be said that rebounding, shooting, and playing defense are essential functions of the job. When it comes to determining essential functions of the job, preventive law demands that functions are relevant and tasks are not. For example, shooting, rebounding, and playing defense are essential functions of playing basketball, whereas jumping, running, and stopping are the *tasks* that are used to perform those functions. The reason for the distinction is that people use various means to accomplish the same function, and nowhere is that clearer than on the hardwood. For example, Dennis Rodman (6'9"), now on his second trip to North Korea, used his jumping and blocking-out abilities to rebound, while a player well over seven feet, and there are quite a few of them in the NBA, doesn't have to jump at all.

Did the team even have the right to insist on a post-employment medical exam? The answer is yes because a post-employment medical exam, as we have already discussed, can be done where it is job-related and consistent with business necessity.[7] Certainly, the ability of our player to survive the rigors of an NBA game is related to his job. Also, considering all the dollars the team has potentially wrapped up in this player, it is certainly consistent with business necessity to have the tests done.

The question then becomes what the team does with the results of the testing. Let's say the tests are inconclusive and the player wants to play. The team is scared of the possibilities, especially since it can't get insurance on the player. The team refuses to let the player play. Does the team have any available defenses when an ADA suit is brought against it by an athlete? Three defenses immediately come to mind:

First, the team may allege that the disability is only temporary.[8]

Second, the team may allege that the player is a direct threat to himself or others. In the right case,[9] direct threat could be an excellent defense. For this defense to succeed, it would have to be based on the best available scientific or objective evidence.[10] Answering this question would mean scouring the medical records and hiring medical experts to reach a conclusion as to whether he would be a direct threat. In short, a direct threat defense would be very expensive for the team in this case. Even so, considering the money involved, mounting a direct threat defense might be worth the money for the team to spend.

Finally, the team may argue that accommodating the player would lead to a fundamental alteration in the nature of the business (more on fundamental alteration later in this chapter).

PGA TOUR, INC. V. MARTIN

A discussion of the ADA and Pro Sports cannot be complete without a discussion of the Supreme Court Case of *PGA Tour, Inc. v. Martin*.[11] In *PGA Tour*, Casey Martin, a teammate of Tiger Woods at Stanford, filed for permission to use a cart at the third stage of "Q" school.[12] Q school is one of the ways that a golfer can qualify to play on the Nike or PGA Tours, the Nike tour being one step below the PGA Tour.[13] During the first two stages of Q school, carts are permitted.[14] However, carts are not permitted at the last stage.[15]

Martin since birth suffered from Klippel-Trenaunay-Weber Syndrome, a degenerative circulatory disorder that obstructs the flow of blood from his right leg back to his heart.[16] The disease is progressive, causes severe pain, and atrophies the right leg.[17] In college, he reached a point where he could no longer walk an 18-hole golf course.[18] He then successfully petitioned the NCAA for the right to use a cart.[19]

When he turned pro and successfully completed the first two rounds of Q school, he petitioned the PGA for the right to use a cart and attached extensive medical records.[20] The PGA Tour refused to review the records and denied his request.[21] It should be noted that while the Ninth Circuit agreed with Martin, the Seventh Circuit, in a virtually identical case, held for the golf tour.[22] Thus, it was up to the Supreme Court to resolve the conflict among the circuits.

The Supreme Court had two issues before it: (1) whether the PGA was even subject to the ADA,[23] and (2) if the PGA was subject to the ADA, whether Martin's request to use a cart was a reasonable accommodation.[24] Since all parties agreed that Martin was a person with a disability, the issue of whether Martin had a disability was not before the Court.[25] Turning to the first issue, the Court held that the PGA was subject to the ADA *vis-á-vis* people trying to qualify for its tour and not just people who might watch tour events.[26] In reaching this conclusion, the Court reasoned as follows.

First, Title III of the ADA prohibits discrimination against persons with disabilities in the full and equal enjoyment of the goods, services, facilities, privileges, advantages, or accommodations of any place of public accommodation by any person owning, leasing, or operating a place of public accommodation.[27]

Second, the Court noted that golf courses were explicitly mentioned in the definition of a public accommodation.[28]

Third, the Court referred to the language stating that a lessee could not discriminate against a person with a disability (the PGA Tour being such a lessee for its events).[29]

Fourth, the Court said that one of the privileges offered by this lessee is the chance to play on its tours depending on how well the person does in Q school.[30] Thus, the PGA Tour simply could not, under the ADA, deny a person equal access to its tours on the basis of disability.[31]

The PGA first attempted to persuade the Court that different rules applied depending on whether one was a spectator or a competitor.[32] The Court simply did not buy the argument.[33] The Court believed that watching the tour and competing in the tour were two separate privileges offered by the PGA, both of which had to be accessible to persons with disabilities.[34] To hold otherwise, the Court felt, would be inconsistent with the literal text of the ADA itself as well as with its expansive purpose to read the provisions of Title III broadly.[35]

The second issue the Court was faced with was whether granting Martin's use of the cart would fundamentally alter the nature of the game. In holding that such an accommodation modification would have no such result and therefore was reasonable, the Court reasoned as follows.

First, the Court began by observing that the fundamental character of the game of golf was shot-making.[36]

Second, the Court noted that golf has evolved over the years to include golf bags, caddies, carts pulled by hand, and motorized carts that carry players as well as clubs.[37] The Court went on to note that motorized cars are often encouraged because they speed up play and are a moneymaker.[38]

Third, the court noted that nothing in the rules of golf either prevents the use of a cart or penalizes players for using it.[39] In fact, whether a golfer uses a cart does not even factor into the golfer's handicap.[40]

Fourth, the walking rule cited by the PGA was actually not a rule of golf but buried as an optional condition in the appendix to the rules of golf.[41]

Fifth, the Court stated that the walking rule was not an indispensable feature of tournament golf either.[42] The Court noted that the PGA permits golf carts to be used in the Senior PGA Tour, the open qualifying event for PGA tournaments, the Senior Men and Women's Amateur championships, the first two stages of Q school, and, until 1997, the third stage of Q school as well.[43]

Sixth, the Court said that pure chance may have a greater impact on the outcome of elite golf tournaments than the fatigue resulting from enforcement of the walking rule.[44]

Seventh, the Court noted that the district court had found that the fatigue from walking during one of petitioner's golf tournaments was not significant and that any fatigue incurred by the golfer was the result of psychological factors, such as stress and motivation.[45] Further, even if the rule did promote fatigue, the district court found that Casey Martin, even with a cart, endured more fatigue than the average golfer.[46]

Eighth, the Court stated that the ADA makes no exception for elite athletics.[47]

Ninth, the Court said that the PGA erred in not making an individual inquiry as to whether the requested accommodation would fundamentally alter the nature of the game.[48]

What might be a fundamental alteration in a sport? A case that answers that question is *Kuketz v. Petronelli.*[49] Kuketz, a nationally ranked wheelchair racquetball player, joined the Brockton Athletic Club, which sponsored a racquetball league where men and women competed in divisions organized by gender and ability.[50] The most competitive division was the "A" league, which he wanted to join to help the team prepare for upcoming international wheelchair events.[51] Kuketz paid a nominal fee and requested placement on the men's "A" league roster.[52] As a result of having to use a wheelchair, Kuketz was not competitive at any level of racquetball unless he was permitted to return the ball after the second bounce, which is the case in wheelchair racquetball.[53] He assumed that the club would grant this accommodation and that he would be able to return the ball on the second bounce while his footed opponent would have to return it on the first bounce.[54] Unfortunately for Kuketz, the requested accommodation was denied (though the club did offer him the ability to play in a lower level with the one-bounce rule or to play in a wheelchair league that it would help organize),[55] and he brought suit alleging violation of Title III of the Americans with Disabilities Act.[56]

In finding against Kuketz, the Massachusetts Supreme Court reasoned as follows. First, the court said that allowing for more than one bounce in racquetball is inconsistent with the fundamental character of the game, as the essence of the game, as expressly stated in the rules, is the hitting of a moving ball with the racquet before the second bounce.[57] According to the court, the modification sought by Kuketz would create a new game, with new strategies and new rules.[58] Because the game would have been fundamentally altered by this accommodation, the court did not find it necessary to decide whether the accommodation would give the disabled player an advantage over others.[59]

What we've just discussed is actually an easy question. What about someone who uses prosthetic devices to compete with others—for example, the person who uses prosthetic devices to run track? Could he compete with able-bodied track athletes? If he was denied the right to compete with able-bodied track athletes in the United States, would he be successful in a suit under the ADA?[60] One possible defense for the track governing body if they denied the mobility-impaired track athlete the right to run would be to argue that the track athlete using the prosthetic devices is given an unfair advantage (an issue that *Kuketz* expressly did not decide)[61] over the nondisabled runner.[62] Unfair advantage arguments, as we will also discuss in the next section, would involve very complicated medical testimony and an assessment ultimately by a judge, who probably does not have a disability, as to whether the disabled track athlete would have an advantage over the nondisabled track athlete. A much easier argument to deal with would be whether the game would be fundamentally altered in the sense previously discussed in this section, or whether the person would constitute a direct threat, as discussed earlier in this book. It seems to me that an argument can be made that should an athlete using prosthetic devices fall down on the track, the risk of injury to other athletes might be quite a bit higher than if a nondisabled track athlete fell.[63] The track situation is probably the hardest call. Most such cases can probably be dealt with using the principles of fundamental alteration *a la Kuketz* and the principle of direct threat.

ADA AND COLLEGE OR HIGH SCHOOL SPORTS

Applying the ADA to college or high school sports raises a completely different set of issues. Assuming the high school or college is a public entity, its programs and activities must be accessible in order to comply with Title II of the ADA. What if the college or university takes action against or refuses to accommodate an athlete because the NCAA rules leave it no choice, even though the athlete has a disability under the ADA? It's now pretty clear that the NCAA can be sued for violating the ADA under Title III, because the NCAA exercises sufficient control over athletic programs at member institutions that one could say that a nexus exists between the entity covered by the ADA and the NCAA itself.[64]

Office of Civil Rights Guidance on § 504 Pertaining to Students with Disabilities and Sports

The U.S. Department of Education Office of Civil Rights in January 2013 issued a guidance dealing with its section 504 regulations and how they apply to sporting opportunities for students with disabilities.[65] The specific details mentioned in the guidance focus on elementary and secondary schools, but the Office of Civil Rights also states that students with disabilities at the postsecondary level must also be provided an equal opportunity to participate in sports.[66]

Here are some of the salient points from the Office of Civil Rights (OCR) guidance. First, the school district is required to provide a qualified student with a disability an opportunity to benefit from its programming equal to that of students without disabilities. Just who is a person with a disability? A person with a disability is defined in the same way it is defined by the ADA: a person who has a physical or mental impairment that substantially limits one or more major life activities; has a record of such an impairment; or is regarded as having such an impairment.[67] Just who is a qualified student with a disability? The OCR says a qualified student with a disability is a person of an age during which persons without disabilities are provided such services; of an age during which it is mandatory under state law to provide such services to a person with a disability; or a person to whom the state is required to provide a free appropriate public education under the Individuals with Disabilities Education Act.[68]

Second, it is easy to say (as courts often do) that since the ADA is based on section 504 and amendments to the ADA were meant to apply to section 504, the two laws should be interpreted the same way. However, there are variations between the two laws that just might take you to different places. For example, as mentioned earlier, section 504 when it comes to causation refers to "solely by reason of disability"as the standard,[69] whereas, depending on the ADA title involved, you may see "on the basis of,"[70] or "by reason of,"[71] or even "because,"[72] but you never see the word "solely." Also, OCR is using the word "qualified" in a different way than the term is used in the ADA. Under the ADA, with respect to Title II (the title that applies to accessing governmental services, activities, and programs), a person is otherwise qualified if he can, with or without reasonable modifications to rules, policies, or practices; the removal of architectural, communication, or transportation barriers; or the provision of auxiliary aids and services, meet the essential eligibility requirements for receiving services or participating in programs or activities provided by a public entity.[73] On its face, this means that the ADA has a higher standard for whether a person is qualified than what is being offered by the OCR with respect to its interpretation of section 504 of the Rehabilitation Act.

Third, OCR notes that U.S. Department of Education section 504 regulations also prohibit the following:

A. Denying a qualified student with a disability the opportunity to participate in or benefit from an aid, benefit, or service;
B. Affording a qualified student with a disability an opportunity to participate in or benefit from an aid, benefit, or service that is not equal to that afforded others;
C. Providing a qualified student with a disability with an aid, benefit, or service that is not as effective as what is provided to others and does not afford the student an equal opportunity to obtain the same result, gain the same benefit, or reach the same level of achievement in the most integrated setting appropriate to the student's needs;
D. Providing different or separate aids, benefit, or services to students with disabilities to any class of students with disabilities unless such action is necessary to provide a qualified student with a disability with aid, benefits, or services that are as effective as those provided to others; and
E. Otherwise limiting a qualified individual with a disability in the enjoyment of any right, privilege, advantage, or opportunity enjoyed by others receiving an aid, benefit, or service.[74]

These regulations by themselves aren't particularly problematic, the only issue being that "qualified individual" is used differently than it is under the ADA. On its face, OCR appears to be saying that whether a student is otherwise qualified is not an issue with respect to whether that student can participate in athletic endeavors. I find that very hard to believe, and perhaps OCR should consider clarifying this. You wonder if the omission was inadvertent, because even OCR does say that the school can require a level of skill or ability of a student in order for the student to participate in a selective work, competitive program, or activity so long as the criteria are not discriminatory.[75]

Fourth, in its guidance, OCR says that a school district's legal obligation to comply with section 504 and the regulations supersedes any rule of any association, organization, club, or league that would render the student ineligible to participate, or limit the student's eligibility to participate, in any aid, benefit, or service on the basis of disability.[76] In fact, OCR says that it would violate a school district's obligation under section 504 to provide significant assistance to any organization that discriminates on the basis of disability in providing any aid, benefit, or service to the school district's students.[77] Nothing new here either, as the ADA also prohibits a governmental entity from contracting with entities that discriminate on the basis of disability.[78]

Fifth, in its guidance, OCR says that the school district may not operate its program activities on the basis of generalizations, assumptions, prejudices, or stereotypes about disability generally, or specific disabilities in particular. It also cannot assume what a student with a disability is capable of with respect to athletic competition. Nothing new here, as both the Rehabilitation Act and the ADA require an individual determination about the person with disability's abilities.[79]

Now, let's turn to the examples given by OCR.

1. A student with a learning disability in middle school participates in her school's lacrosse club. As she entered the ninth grade in high school, she tries out and is selected as a member of the high school's lacrosse team. The coach is aware of the student's learning disability and believes that all students with the student's particular learning disability are unable to play successfully in a game given the time constraints and pressures of an actual game. Based on that, the coach decides to never to play the student during games. In the coach's opinion, participating fully in all the team's practice sessions is good enough.

OCR said that it would find the coach's decision in violation of section 504.[80] The problem the coach ran into is that he made an assumption about learning disabilities in general. There is no reason why he could not have simulated a real game experience during practice to see how the person with a learning disability would survive in such a situation. If, after such a simulation, the coach had reservations about how that person would survive in a real game situation, he would certainly be within his rights with respect to playing time. After all, the coach is the one who gets to decide playing time. What the coach should have done is test whether his assumption with respect to that individual player was true.

OCR goes on to talk about ensuring equal opportunity for participation. Ensuring equal opportunity for participation means making reasonable modifications and providing those aids and services necessary to ensure an equal opportunity to participate, unless the school district can show that doing so results in a fundamental alteration to its program.[81] A school district must also afford qualified students with disabilities an equal opportunity to participate in extracurricular athletics in an integrated manner to the maximum extent appropriate to the needs of the student.[82] This makes sense, as the disability discrimination laws are all about integrating persons with disabilities into the mainstream.

What is new is what follows at the end of that discussion. First, OCR states that if a reasonable modification is legally required, the school district must engage in an individualized inquiry to determine whether the modification is necessary.[83] A modification will be necessary unless it would result in a fundamental alteration of the extracurricular athletic activity.[84] What is a fundamental alteration according to OCR? A fundamental alteration alters an essential aspect of the activity or game so that it would be unacceptable even if it affected all competitors equally, or the modification has only a peripheral impact on the activity or game itself but could give the particular player with a disability an unfair advantage over others, and therefore fundamentally alters the character of the competition.[85]

Where is that standard coming from? After all, Title II, 42 U.S.C. § 12201(f) and Title III, 42 U.S.C. § 12182(2)(A)(ii) of the ADA do not speak of unfair advantage at all. Rather, they refer to fundamental alteration. So where is this coming from? For example, in my writings over the years, I have used the starting-line analogy with respect to a person with a disability and reasonable accommodations. Such an analogy presumes that a person with a disability is getting to the same starting line as others and not being given an unfair advantage. The particular phrasing that OCR is relying on comes from *PGA Tour v. Martin*. In particular, the Supreme Court said in its majority opinion that to perceive that using a golf cart would give Martin a competitive advantage was a gross distortion of reality considering his disability.[86] Later on, when discussing fundamental alteration, the Court says that a fundamental alteration of the PGA Tour's golf tournaments could occur in two different ways. First, it could change an essential aspect of the game so that it would be unacceptable even if it affected all competitors equally (for example, changing the diameter of the hole from

3 to 6 inches would be such a modification).[87] Second, a less significant change having only a peripheral impact on the game itself might nevertheless give the disabled player an advantage over others and for that reason fundamentally alter the character of the competition.[88]

In the *Martin* situation, the Supreme Court was not persuaded that a waiver of the walking rule would result in a fundamental alteration in either sense.[89] However, the *Martin* formulation has its own problems. First, in the context of sports, what would be a fundamental alteration of the game so that it would be unacceptable even if it affected all competitors equally? I tend to stay away from law review articles, as they tend to be very theoretical and not practical. However, sometimes you do see a law review article that can be very helpful. In *The Prohibition of Prosthetic Limbs in American Sports: the Issues and the Role of the Americans with Disabilities Act*,[90] Christopher Bidlack, in a student comment, suggests that fundamental alteration in sports occurs if the requested change damages the underlying nature of the game or turns it into an entirely new game.[91] It is a formulation that has a great deal of appeal to it.

How might you be creating a new game with new rules? The *Kuketz* case mentioned earlier, where the Massachusetts Supreme Court said that the ADA did not compel a club to formulate a game where the wheelchair athlete has two bounces and the more traditional athlete only has one bounce with respect to racquetball,[92] is an excellent example. As mentioned above, it needs to be noted that *Kuketz* explicitly said that it was not deciding whether the plaintiff's requests would result in an unfair advantage.[93] Here is the problem—unfair advantage arguments can potentially involve very complicated medical testimony and an assessment by a judge, who most probably does not have a disability, as to whether the athlete with a disability has an advantage over the athlete without a disability. Further, I submit that in most cases the question of unfair advantage is completely unnecessary as most cases could be decided based upon whether the requested change would damage the underlying nature of the game; turn the game into an entirely new game; or result in a direct threat. (A school district is under no obligation to allow a student with a disability to play in the game if doing so would result in a direct threat to himself or others.)[94]

2. The second example referred to by OCR involves a student with a hearing impairment. Interestingly, we don't know from the example the extent of the hearing impairment. At any rate, the student is interested in the 100- and 200-meter dashes and during tryouts for the track team, the start of each race was signaled by a coach's assistant using a visual cue, and the student's speed was fast enough to qualify him for the team in those events. The coach continued to use those accommodations but the district, despite other districts allowing such cues, nevertheless refuses the student's request because the district is concerned that the use of a visual cue may distract other runners and trigger complaints once the track season begins. The coach then tells the student that he can practice with the team but will not be allowed to participate in meets.[95]

OCR says that such a situation violates section 504 because it neither alters an essential aspect of the activity nor gives the student an unfair advantage. Using the formulation posited above, the same conslusion would be reached as the modifcation certainly does not damage the underlying nature of the game nor, as was the case in *Kuketz,* nor does it turn the game into an entirely new game. Nor is there any question of direct threat.[96]

3. High school student born with only one arm wants to participate in the school's swim team. The student has the necessary swimming ability and wants to compete. The school district has a "two-hand touch" finish rule for all swimmers when finishing the race. Therefore, she petitions to have the two hand touch rule waived and be allowed to finish with a, "one-hand touch." The school district refuses the request because it determines that permitting the student to finish with a one-hand touch would give the student an unfair advantage over other swimmers.[97]

Here, OCR says that if the school district could show that she would gain an unfair advantage over others, then the school district would be justified in not waiving the rule. OCR does say that the school district would still be required to determine if other modifications would be available short of fundamentally altering the nature an activity (the ADA would say the same thing).[98]

Here is where unfair advantage becomes terribly problematic in its application. Would this person really be getting an unfair advantage? While it is true that such a person would be allowed a one-hand touch and everybody else would have to use a two-hand touch, that also presumes that everything else was equal. That is, the mechanics of swimming are such that it is hard for me to believe that a person with one hand would be at the same starting line as an athlete with two hands in the first place. Accordingly, it could be argued that even a one-hand touch rule would not give the student an unfair advantage. Of course, putting this all together is going to mean extensive medical testimony at great costs to all sides. It also means the judge, probably a person without a disability, will have to exercise a great deal of subjectivity in analyzing the information.

How would this case play out under the formulation discussed above, which ignores unfair advantage and also allows for greater objective analysis? First, does the requested change damage the underlying nature of the game? Probably not. Second, does it turn the game into an entirely new game? Also, probably not. Is the person a direct threat? Probably not. Thus, under the methodology I am proposing, the proposed accommodation would be allowed. The problem is that athletic competition presumes everyone is at the same starting line, and that whoever wins does so without any inherent unfair advantage. Giving an athlete an unfair advantage violates a sense of fair play. I get that, but how do you figure out unfair advantage? It can get extremely complicated, and a formulation that avoids unfair advantage also avoids unnecessary subjectivity.

4. An elementary school student with diabetes is not eligible for services under the Individuals with Disabilities in Education Act. However, as is the case with many such students, that person is eligible for services under section 504 of the Rehabilitation Act (the scope of coverage between the two laws is very different). The student receives assistance with glucose testing and insulin administeredby trained school personnel, with services provided under section 504. That student wants to participate in a school-sponsored gymnastics club that meets after school, the only eligibility requirement being that the student must attend the school. However, school personnel reject her request on the grounds that the gymnastics club is an extracurricular activity.[99]

OCR finds a section 504 violation here for two reasons. First, the school district has to provide that service during the day under section 504.[100] Second, there would not be a fundamental alteration of the district education program, as the district would have to do it in any event, should the student be eligible for services under the Individuals with Disabilities in Education Act.[101]

I don't see any issues here. On a preventive level, if a student has an Individual Education Program (IEP) or a 504 plan and you know that the student wants to participate in sports, it would behoove the parents to insist that the IEP or 504 plan contain language that the necessary accommodations would be made while participating in sports.

Finally, OCR goes on to talk about offering separate or different athletic opportunities for students with disabilities. The whole idea of the ADA and section 504 is integration of persons with disabilities. However, there may be circumstances in which allowing a student with a disability to participate in an athletic event would result in either a fundamental alteration or where a student is a direct threat to him- or herself or others. In such circumstances, it is possible that by setting up a separate system for students with disabilities, the fundamental alteration problem and the direct threat problem would disappear. OCR says that when the interests and abilities of students with disabilities cannot be fully and effectively met by the school district's existing extracurricular athletic programs, the school district *should* create additional opportunities for those students with disabilities.[102] In those situations, OCR says that the school district *should* offer students with disabilities opportunities for athletic activities separate or different from those offered to students without disabilities, and that those opportunities should be supported equally by the school district.[103] When fielding a team is not possible, the school district could also develop a districtwide regional team for students with disabilities as opposed to an individual school-based team.[104] Male and female students with disabilities can be mixed together on a team, or the district can offer unified sports teams in which students with disabilities participate along with students without disabilities (the latter though could run into problems with fundamental alteration and direct threat).[105]

Here is the issue. This particular section of the OCR guidance turns section 504 into Title IX for persons with disabilities. Title IX has been absolutely critical in giving women the opportunity to participate in athletics, and perhaps OCR is thinking that section 504 regulations can be used in the same way. On a policy level, that has much to commend it. However, a school district not wanting to create separate sports programming might argue that while the ADA and section 504 are all about equal opportunity, that is far different from having to create additional opportunities. For example, an employer does not have to create light-duty positions.[106] Another example: a state without a community integration program in place may not have to create one.[107]

So where does this leave us?

1. *OCR needs to clarify how it deals with the term "qualified individual."* There is a huge difference between OCR referencing "qualified individual" and the way the ADA refers to "otherwise qualified." It would seem that the omission is unintentional, because a reading of the OCR guidance suggests that "otherwise qualified," in the ADA/Rehabilitation Act sense, is still in play. (See, for example, the "eligibility requirement" discussion in the OCR guidance with respect to Example 3.) Nevertheless, it is literally missing from the guidance and, as discussed above, could present problems later.
2. *Unfair advantage is now enshrined as a concept.* As discussed above, that may present unique problems of proof, unnecessarily complicate litigation, and involves a great deal of subjectivity by the fact finder, certainly drives up the costs of litigation. Instead of enshrining unfair advantage, perhaps the better approach is to offer the alternative suggested above. Such an offer may work if you can convince the court that this standard is far more objective than the unfair advantage alternative. You would also argue that the guidance is not entitled to deference, as it did not go through the formal rulemaking procedure.
3. *OCR is now demanding opportunities be created for students with disabilities* in terms of participating in sports, even if the school district has no such programming in place. It is an open question as to whether the ADA and section 504 can be used in that way, and I would look to a school district defending a refusal to do this on the grounds that the ADA and § 504 are not the same kind of statute as Title IX.

ADA AND THE REFEREE

A discussion of the ADA and sports is not complete without a discussion of the people who ensure that a game is played fairly—the referees or umpires. Consider these facts:

> A referee of college football games gains a great deal of weight. As a result, his performance declines. Eventually, he is told to the lose weight or he will lose his job. He does not

> lose the weight, his performance continues to decline, and he is rated last in the conference. He is then terminated. He brings suit under the ADA. How might a court go about analyzing this case?

The first question is who does the referee sue, and under what title of the ADA? Many referees are independent contractors. Consequently, Title I of the ADA, which governs employment, may not apply. However, in some instances, other entities may exercise sufficient control to justify a finding that the referee is employed by that entity.[108] If sufficient control does exist, the question becomes whether the entity being sued has at least 15 employees. That may be more complicated than it seems. For example, a referee association probably wouldn't have that many employees unless you were to count all the referees in the association. The same would not be true with respect to school districts, high school athletic associations, or athletic conferences. Therefore, Title I of the ADA may not be a possibility. That would leave the referee with Titles II and III from which to choose. The problem with utilizing Title II of the ADA is that a governmental entity may not be involved. After all, it is the conference or the referee association that informs the referee that he can no longer work, not a governmental entity. There is a possibility that the referee might be able to sue under Title II of the ADA through a roundabout way. That is, Title II prohibits governmental entities from contracting with any organization that discriminates on the basis of disability.[109] If the referee organization is discriminating on the basis of disability and it has a contract with a governmental entity, then the governmental entity could potentially be exposed to an ADA suit.

The referee could consider suing under Title III of the ADA. However, the problem he faces is that while places of recreation are places of public accommodation under the ADA,[110] it is not the place of recreation itself that is the problem. Rather, it is the ability of the person to referee a game in that place of recreation. For this theory, the referee might draw on *PGA Tour v. Martin*, which said that competitors at a place of public accommodation were subject to the ADA and a referee is a competitor of sorts.[111] The question becomes whether the referee has a disability—a physical or mental impairment that substantially limits one or more of life's major activities. Such a case would raise several questions. For example, is there a physical or mental impairment? What major life activity (eating, neurological) is involved? Is that major life activity substantially limited even under the amendments to the ADA? Morbid obesity, twice recommended weight, has been held to be a disability,[112] but it's hard to believe a referee could be morbidly obese and still do his or her job.

If it can be shown that there is a physical or mental impairment that substantially limits a major life activity, the next question is whether he can perform the essential functions of the job with or without reasonable accommodations—that is, is he otherwise qualified? To determine this answer, the essential functions of a referee's job must be identified. On a basic level, an essential function of the job is to call the game accurately. Obesity certainly limits a referee's movement. If his obesity limits the referee's movement to the point where he can no longer get in the proper position in time to make a call, then he is not able to perform an essential job function. Finally, it is hard to envision what reasonable accommodations could be offered to a referee who, because of his disability, cannot make the calls. Clearly, having other referees do his part of the job is not an option.

To summarize, the referee might find it difficult to sue the proper person, and it also might be difficult for the referee to show that there is a physical or mental impairment that substantially limits a major life activity. Even so, look for more cases in this area, especially if the referee can show that the referee association or athletic conference perceived a disability.

THE DEAF LIFEGUARD

How might you analyze an essential functions situation? I seriously debated talking about the case to be discussed here, involving a deaf lifeguard, in the essential functions chapter. However, I decided to talk about it here because, in addition to discussing essential functions, this particular case also talks about fundamental alterations, and it involves an athletic activity, being a lifeguard.

The case, *Keith v. County of Oakland,* involves a deaf person who wanted to be a lifeguard.[113] In reversing the district court, which had found for the defendant, the Sixth Circuit Court of Appeals reasoned as follows.

First, the ADA mandates an individualized inquiry for determining whether a person is qualified for a particular position.[114] In this case, the county made the individualized inquiries all the way through the training process and even proposed certain accommodations that might work upon hiring him as a lifeguard.[115] However, the physician who did the medical exam jumped to conclusions about whether a deaf person could be a lifeguard and never pursued the matter further.[116] Also, the consultants who worked with the county also jumped to conclusions about whether the plaintiff could perform the essential functions of the job as well and set a 100%-effective rate for the accommodations as the standard.[117] The court said that requiring a 100%-effective rate was not right, because it would be holding persons with disabilities to a higher standard than persons without disabilities, as no lifeguards are ever held to that standard.[118] Finally, the court believed that it just didn't make any sense for an employer to make an individualized inquiry only to defer to the opinions and advice of those who have not, because an employer cannot escape liability under the ADA by mechanically relying on the medical opinions and advice of others.[119]

Second, whether a job function is essential is a question of fact typically not suitable for resolution on a motion for summary judgment.[120] The court went on to say that the plaintiff had raised several points to establish that a question of fact existed. In particular, the court said that the essential communication duties of a lifeguard (protecting and rescuing swimmers in distress, enforcing pool safety rules, activating the emergency action plan, and performing CPR)[121] were all things that the plaintiff could do with or without reasonable accommodations.[122]

The points that the plaintiff raised included that he was: 1) able to follow the 10/20 standard of zone protection (a technique taught to lifeguards whereby they scan their entire zone every 10 seconds and can reach any part of their zone within 20 seconds);[123] 2) able to detect distressed swimmers (an entirely visually based activity);[124] 3) was able to enforce safety rules by relying on his whistle and various physical gestures, which is the way lifeguards do it anyway, since verbal enforcement is usually impractical in a noisy water park;[125] 4) was able to communicate effectively during emergency with a minor modification to the emergency action plan. In particular, lifeguards would signal with a fist in the air, opening and closing their fist in repetition,[126] (interestingly enough, the court said that modifying the emergency action plan in this way turns out to be actually better for the entire lifeguard staff).[127] This is a principle called universal design, which is the belief that by designing systems so that persons with disabilities can use them effectively with or without reasonable accommodation, you actually improve the system for everyone else); and 5) was able to communicate with patrons at the level considered essential for a lifeguard just by carrying a few laminated notecards in the pocket of his swim trunks with basic phrases such as "I am deaf," "I will get someone to assist you," and "wait here."[128] The court noted that attendants were posted throughout the waterpark to assist patrons with basic needs and questions, thereby calling into question whether anything beyond the type of phrases that he would carry in the pocket of his swim trunks would be essential.[129]

The court felt that the most compelling evidence that the plaintiff was otherwise qualified to be a lifeguard came from the experts that he presented who, unlike the ones the county relied on in its decision-making process, did have knowledge, education, and experience regarding the ability of deaf individuals to serve as lifeguards.[130] In fact, the world record for most lives saved by a lifeguard is held by a deaf man (saved over 900 lives in his lifeguarding career).[131] Also, the American Red Cross certifies deaf lifeguards, and Gallaudet University (a college that focuses exclusively on the needs of the deaf) has a lifeguard certification program.[132]

Third, in the Sixth Circuit, in a reasonable accommodation case, it is up to the plaintiff to show that the proposed accommodations were "objectively reasonable."[133] If that can be done, then the employee has the burden of showing that the accommodation would fundamentally alter the nature of the business.[134] With respect to Keith, the plaintiff/appellant, the accommodations, such as the ones discussed above, were objectively reasonable in that they did not fundamentally alter the nature of the business.[135] In fact, as noted above, some of the suggested accommodations may have even made the business better. Also, while the accommodations that the plaintiff needed called for some restructuring of the job's marginal functions, they did not require shifting any essential functions onto any other lifeguards.[136]

Fourth, the ADA specifically includes interpreters among the list of reasonable accommodations.[137] That suggested to the court that provision of an interpreter was generally reasonable, especially when the interpreter was needed only for staff meetings and trainings.[138] The court also noted that several experts had testified that an interpreter was unnecessary to enable a deaf individual to perform the essential functions of a lifeguard.[139] Oakland County didn't even argue, let alone show, that providing accommodations to the plaintiff would constitute an undue hardship on its operations.[140]

Finally, with respect to the district court refusing to hold Oakland County liable for failing to engage in the interactive process, the court said the district court had to revisit the issue.[141] In the Sixth Circuit, failure to engage in the interactive process is not an independent violation of the ADA.[142] However, if the plaintiff can show that a reasonable accommodation is possible, then failing to engage in the interactive process is a violation of the ADA.[143] Here the district court missed the boat, because it incorrectly held that the plaintiff had failed to propose objectively reasonable accommodations.[144] The Sixth Circuit concluded that the accommodations proposed by the plaintiff were objectively reasonable.[145]

So what can we take from this case?

First, what constitutes the essential functions of a job is a question of fact, and, in the Sixth Circuit's view, one not typically suitable for resolution on summary judgment.

Second, it would be helpful for employers if they truly understood what a job's essential functions were. The best way to think of the essential functions of a job is whatever functions are fundamental to the job at hand.

Third, when it comes to essential functions of a job, expert testimony/analysis may be critical.

Fourth, an employer should be very wary of relying on stereotypical conclusions of others without fully engaging in the interactive process.

Fifth, as I have written for years, do not confuse major life activities with the essential functions of a job. As the court notes in great detail in this opinion, being able to hear (a major life activity) is simply not an essential function of the job of being a lifeguard. The analogy that I have used frequently is that seeing balls and strikes is not an essential function of the job of being an umpire; rather, being able to call balls and strikes accurately is the essential function of the job of an umpire. I think this case is even a better example of what happens when you confuse major life activity with essential functions.

Sixth, do not be afraid to reassign marginal functions of a job to others.

Seventh, in looking over the accommodation proposed, do consider whether the proposed accommodations should not be adopted on a general level as something that might make the business better overall (universal design).

Finally, do not hold persons with disabilities to a higher standard than people without disabilities.

Notes

1. This hypothetical is taken from media reports of the situation involving the Chicago Bulls and their center, Eddy Curry. Keep in mind that media reports are not always accurate. There may have been many more critical details that we don't know. Nevertheless, I use this scenario as a way of illustrating various legal principles pertaining to the ADA. Eddy Curry was traded to the Knicks for some players and draft choices. He underwent extensive testing in New York and had those tests reviewed by Knicks doctors and a doctor from the NBA, all of whom cleared him to play, and he did play without incident.
2. 42 U.S.C.A. at § 12112(d)(2)(A). The reader is also referred to the discussion on preemployment medical exams that appeared earlier in this book.
3. 42 U.S.C.A. at § 12112(d)(2)(A).
4. 42 U.S.C.A. at § 12112(d)(3).
5. 29 C.F.R. at § 1630.14(b)(3).
6. It may be a big assumption to assume that physicals of professional players are being done after a conditional job offer. For example, the way the NFL combine occurs strongly suggests that pre-employment medical exams and inquiries are being done prior to a conditional job offers.
7. 42 U.S.C.A. at § 12112(d)(4)(A).
8. *See* 42 U.S.C.A. at § 12102(3)(B). The EEOC is of the view that the clause defining what is a transitory and minor impairment is strictly limited to claims alleging that they were discriminated against because they were regarded as having a disability. Thus, the EEOC believes that a person might have a disability under the ADA even if that disability will last less than six months. *See* Fed. Reg. 48,431–01, 48,446–47). While common sense would dictate that disability be defined in the same way whether it is temporary or not, a literal reading of the ADAAA supports the EEOC view.
9. *See* Knapp v. Northwestern Univ., 101 F.3d 473 (7th Cir. 1996).
10. *Chevron,* 536 U.S. at 86.
11. PGA Tour Inc. v. Martin, 532 U.S. 661 (2001).
12. *Id.* at 669.
13. *Id.* at 665–66.

14. *Id.* at 669.
15. *Id.*
16. *Id.* at 668. Unbelievably, Casey Martin, now the golf coach for the University of Oregon, was recently denied the use of cart when he was at an amateur golf tournament attended by college coaches for the purpose of recruiting prospective players. The sponsoring association claimed there was a mix-up.
17. *Id.*
18. *Id.*
19. *Id.*
20. *Id.* at 669.
21. *Id.*
22. *Id.* at 674.
23. *Id.*
24. *Id.* at 682.
25. *Id.* at 668.
26. *Id.* at 677, 680.
27. *Id.* at 676.
28. *Id.* at 677 n.24.
29. *Id.* at 677.
30. *Id.*
31. *Id.*
32. *Id.* at 678.
33. *Id.* at 679.
34. *Id.* at 680.
35. *Id.*
36. *Id.* at 683.
37. *Id.* at 684–85.
38. *Id.* at 685.
39. *Id.*
40. *Id.* at 686.
41. *Id.* at 685.
42. *Id.* at 685–86.
43. *Id.*
44. *Id.* at 686–87.
45. *Id.* at 687.
46. *Id.* at 690.
47. *Id.* at 689.
48. *Id.* at 690–91.
49. Kuketz v. Petronelli, 821 N.E.2d 473 (Mass. 2005).
50. *Id.* at 474.
51. *Id.*and at n.3.
52. *Id.*
53. *Id.* at 474.
54. *Id.*

55. *Id.* at 475.
56. *Id.*
57. *Id.* at 479.
58. *Id.* at 480.
59. *Id.* at 480 n.30.
60. A very thought-provoking and excellent article on this very issue is the comment by Christopher Bidlack, student author, *The Prohibition of Prosthetic Limbs in American Sports: The Issues and the Role of the Americans with Disabilities Act*, 19 MARQ. SPORTS L. J. 613 (Spring 2009).
61. *Kuketz,* 821 N.E.2d at 480 n.30.
62. *See* Bidlack, *supra* note 60, at 619–22.
63. In the 2012 Olympics, South African Oscar Pistorius used prosthetic devices to compete with able-bodied athletes and no issues arose.
64. *See* Matthews v. NCAA, 179 F. Supp. 2d 1209, 1218–23 (E.D. Wash. 2001).
65. http://www2.ed.gov/about/offices/list/ocr/letters/colleague-201301-504.pdf.
66. *Id.* at 2.
67. *Id.* at 3.
68. *Id.*
69. 29 U.S.C. § 794a.
70. 42 U.S.C. §12112(A) (Title I); 42 U.S.C. § 12184(A) (Title III).
71. 42 U.S.C. § 12132 (Title II).
72. 42 U.S.C. § 12203(a) (retaliation).
73. 28 C.F.R. § 35.104.
74. http://www2.ed.gov/about/offices/list/ocr/letters/colleague-201301-504.pdf at 3-4. *citing to* 34 C.F.R. § 104.4(b)(1)(i)–(iv), (vii), (2), (3).
75. *Id.* at 3.
76. *Id.* at 5.
77. *Id., citing to* 34 C.F.R. § 104.4(b)(1).
78. *See* 28 C.F.R. § 35.130(b)(3).
79. *See* PGA Tour Inc. v. Martin, 532 U.S. 661 (2001) (ADA case); School Board of Nassau County, Fla. v. Arline, 480 U.S. 273 (1987) (Rehabilitation Act case).
80. http://www2.ed.gov/about/offices/list/ocr/letters/colleague-201301-504.pdf at 5–6.
81. *Id.* at 6.
82. *Id.*
83. *Id.* at 7.
84. *Id.*
85. *Id.*
86. *PGA Tour*, at 672.
87. *Id.* at 682.
88. *Id.* at 683.
89. *Id.*

90. Christopher Bidlack, student author, *The Prohibition of Prosthetic Limbs in American Sports: The Issues and the Role of the Americans with Disabilities Act*, 19 MARQ. SPORTS L. J. 613 (Spring 2009).
91. *Id.* at 632.
92. *Kuketz,* 443 Mass. at 364.
93. *Id.* at 365 n.30.
94. *See generally* Chevron v. Echazabal, 536 U.S. 73 (2002).
95. http://www2.ed.gov/about/offices/list/ocr/letters/colleague-201301-504.pdf at 8.
96. *Id.* at 9.
97. *Id.*
98. *Id.* at 9–10.
99. *Id.* at 10.
100. *Id.*
101. *Id.* at 11.
102. *Id.*
103. *Id.* at 12.
104. *Id.*
105. *Id.*
106. Foreman v. Babcock & Wilcox Co., 117 F. 3d 800, 809 (5th Cir. 1997).
107. *See* Olmstead v. L.C. By Zimring, 527 U.S. 581, 612 (Kennedy, J., concurring).
108. *See* Covington v. Int'l Ass'n of Approved Basketball Officials, 710 F.3d 114, 118–20 (3d Cir. 2013).
109. *See* 42 U.S.C.A. at § 12182(b)(ii).
110. 42 U.S.C.A. at § 12181(7)(L).
111. *PGA Tour*, 532 U.S. at 679–80.
112. *See* Cook v. State of Rhode Island, 10 F.3d 17 (1st Cir. 1993).
113. Keith v. County of Oakland, 703 F.3d 918, 919 (6th Cir. 2013).
114. *Id.* at 923.
115. *Id.* at 920–21.
116. *Id.* at 920.
117. *Id.* at 920–21.
118. *Id.* at 924.
119. *Id.*
120. *Id.* at 926.
121. *Id.*
122. *Id.* at 926–27.
123. *Id.* at 926.
124. *Id.*
125. *Id.*
126. *Id.*
127. *Id.*
128. *Id.*
129. *Id.*

130. *Id.* at 927.
131. *Id.*
132. *Id.*
133. *Id.*
134. *Id.*
135. *Id.* at 928.
136. *See id.*
137. *Id.*
138. *Id.* at 929.
139. *Id.* at 928 n.2.
140. *Id.* at 929.
141. *Id.*
142. *Id.*
143. *Id.*
144. *Id.*
145. *Id.* at 927–29.

13 Areas on the Cutting Edge

NEGLIGENCE AND NEGLIGENCE PER SE ACTIONS AS AN ALTERNATIVE OR AS AN ADDITIONAL CAUSE OF ACTION TO TITLE III CLAIMS

A mobility-impaired person uses a motel. It turns out that motel does not meet the ADA guidelines for architectural accessibility. As a result, the person suffers personal injuries. Or, a person goes to a theater and asks for help from theater personnel but does not receive any. The theater also does not meet ADA architectural accessibility standards, and the person suffers severe personal injuries. Can both of these individuals bring a cause of action for personal injuries alleging that the motel and theater were negligent because they did not meet the ADA architectural standards? The answer in both of these cases is yes, though they get there in different ways using different theories.

The motel case is *Val D'Aosta v. Cross.*[1] Georgia law requires that any facility used by the public constructed or renovated after 1995 must meet Americans with Disabilities Act Architectural Guidelines (ADAAG) standards for accessibility.[2] If construction or renovation occurred after July 1, 1984, but before July 1, 1987, that construction or renovation has to comply with the American National Standards Institute (ANSI) specifications A117.1-1980 or A117.1-1986 for making buildings and facilities accessible to and usable by people with disabilities.[3] If construction or renovation occurs after July 1, 1987, but before July 1, 1995, the construction or renovation has to comply with the ANSI specification A117.1-1986 for making buildings and facilities accessible to and usable by people with disabilities.[4] Violation of these standards is a misdemeanor.[5] Georgia also has a negligence per se statute that allows an injured party to recover damages for breach of legal duty whenever the law requires a person to perform an act for the benefit of another.[6]

In *Val D'Aosta*, the Georgia Court of Appeals held that the plaintiff could proceed with a negligence per se claim because: 1) the accessibility standards were mandatory and imposed a continuing obligation at the risk of criminal penalties for noncompliance on the owner, and therefore the owner would be deemed to have superior knowledge over the plaintiff about whether the accessibility standards were violated; 2) the statute and regulations created a factual question as to whether these particular statutes and regulations were intended to protect the class of persons from certain risk of injury; and 3) a factual question existed as to whether the violation of the statute and regulations pertaining to accessibility constituted the proximate cause or a concurrent proximate cause of any injury and damages.[7] The superior knowledge piece of this opinion is a bit confusing, as the case that the majority cites to, *Alterman Foods, Inc. v. Ligon*,[8] is clearly distinguishable since it dealt with a foreign substance and not with premises liability. Nevertheless, whether the owner has superior knowledge in a case like this is clearly an important consideration in Georgia, as pointed out by the vigorous dissent in *Val D'Aosta* of Judge Andrews when he cites to *Parks-Nietzold v. J.C. Penney, Inc.*[9]

So how do you make sense of the Georgia situation?

First, it bears noting that negligence per se may vary from state to state. In some states, it is possible that if you can show a violation of the statute, that the statute was meant to protect the person from certain risk of injury, and that the violation was the proximate cause of the injury, the plaintiff automatically wins. In other states, such as Nevada, all this would do is get you a presumption that the defendant can't rebut if he or she can show a good reason why the statute or regulation was not complied with in this case.[10] Therefore, you should check your state law to see how it deals with negligence per se.

Second, in Georgia you might be able to argue that superior knowledge is part and parcel of the negligence per se case. You also might be able to argue that superior knowledge just goes to causation and not to whether the duty was breached at all. Complicating matters further is Georgia Code § 51-11-7, which provides, "If the plaintiff by ordinary care could have avoided the consequences to himself caused by the defendant's negligence, he is not entitled to recover. In other cases the defendant is not relieved, although the plaintiff may in some way have contributed to the injury sustained."[11]

Therefore, in Georgia, if a person suffers injury as a result of the accessibility standards not being complied with, the person bringing a personal injury cause of action will have to show a myriad of things: 1) knowledge of noncompliance that is not superior to the owner; 2) violation of the statute or its regulations and its proximate cause of injuries; 3) the statute or regulations were meant to protect the plaintiff from the injuries resulting from that violation; and 4) plaintiff exercised ordinary due care to avoid the injury. The superior knowledge requirement and the plaintiff being required to exercise ordinary care would seem to go a long way toward preventing the person with a disability with superior knowledge of ADA architectural standards from recovering for personal injuries should she be injured by a facility that is not in compliance with the ADA standards. Nevertheless, in Georgia anyway, a plaintiff who suffers injuries as a result of ADA noncompliance with the architectural standards will have a cause of action for personal injuries under Georgia law, but proving it up will not be an easy task.

There is another possibility, which is the approach taken by the District of Columbia Court of Appeals in the theater case mentioned above, *Theater Management Group, Inc. v. Dalgliesh.*[12] In that case, the approach the D. C. Court of Appeals took was to say that the architectural standards can be used not to show negligence per se but to show the standard of care.[13] Depending upon how your jurisdiction goes about the concept of negligence per se, the distinction may be theoretical rather than practical. Thus, if you are in a Theater Management Group, Inc. type of jurisdiction, the analysis for proving negligence may go like this:

1. Was there a duty owed (ADA architectural standards)?
2. Was there a breach of duty (were the ADA architectural standards not complied with)?
3. Was the breach of duty the proximate cause of the injuries (actual and legal cause)?
4. Were there damages?

In short, call it what you want, but it would seem that under traditional negligence per se concepts and under the Theater Management Group, Inc. approach, you would generally get to the same place, though the concepts being used are not precisely the same.

Finally, you might argue that a good policy reason exists as to why personal injury plaintiff attorneys should pursue the kind of cases. That is, through principles of spreading the loss, such suits would increase accessibility for persons with disabilities because the owners of the facilities would be at risk of facing damages suits rather than just the injunctive relief (which can be prevented by simply fixing the problem), and attorneys fees, per Title III of the ADA. Also, personal injury plaintiff attorneys are used to dealing with things on a contingency fee basis.

ADA AND MENTAL ILLNESS

Mental illness is likely to be a hot area for ADA litigation in the years to come for two reasons: First, mental illness often is not understood by employers. Second, the concepts of undue hardship and undue burden are very much focused on physical disabilities, as they often require some kind of equipment or auxiliary services. But what about the person with a mental illness?

Most of the accommodations in the mental illness area cost very little, although at some point a fundamental alteration in the business may come into play. For example, a reasonable accommodation for a person with an anxiety disorder could be to allow that person to take a five-minute break to regain his or her composure when the anxiety becomes overwhelming. The cost to the company is nominal.

Another accommodation may be a job coach who is paid, directly or indirectly, through a state vocational rehabilitation agency. In short, many accommodations for mental illness do not involve an additional outlay of funds. Also, when dealing with the concept of mental illness, it must be remembered that the ADA does not permit discrimination if the work force is simply disrupted; the workplace must be fundamentally altered or suffer or the organization must suffer an undue hardship/undue burden, a far higher standard than simple disruption.

INTELLECTUAL DISABILITIES

With respect to intellectual disabilities (formerly called mental retardation), there are several areas of exposure that occur across Titles I, II, and III of the ADA. Many employers like to think their jobs require a certain degree of mental acuity. However, in truth, many jobs don't require much intellectual ability at all. If an employer were to use a prospective employee's low intelligence as the reason for not hiring that individual, the employer could, according to the EEOC, run the risk of ADA liability where it can be shown that intellectual acuity is simply not required for the particular job.[14]

The issue of a governmental entity violating Title II of the ADA with regard to persons with intellectual disabilities takes on various forms. For instance, a group home is audited in such a way that the disabilities of the residents are not taken into account. This can have disastrous consequences for the members of the home and for the provider, as it could lead to wrongfully decertifying the facility—a violation of Title II of the ADA.

Another area of exposure is prescribing medication to the intellectually disabled as a means of behavior control. This is commonplace[15] and is a controversial medical practice. If there is no other reason for prescribing the medication than the person's disability, the practice could well violate the ADA, either Title II or Title III, depending on the circumstances.

The final area is the state practice of "warehousing" persons with mental illness and mental retardation in state institutions. The ADA uses very strong language in Title II and in its implementing regulations to suggest that failing to place a person with a disability in the most integrated setting appropriate to his or her needs is an ADA violation.[16]

The U.S. Supreme Court in *Olmstead v. L.C. by Zimring,* which involved a suit by persons with disabilities claiming that it was a violation of Title II of the ADA to unnecessarily warehouse them in institutions squarely addressed this warehousing issue.[17] What is interesting is that the Supreme Court decided to hear the *Olmstead* case even though no other circuit had even reached the issue of the ADA's stance on the placement of persons with mental retardation and/or mental illness. It's hard to say why the Supreme Court decided to hear the case, because the justices had a difficult time reaching consensus. The case generated four different opinions: one opinion for the Court (in which not all of the justices joined all the parts), a concurrence by Justice Stevens, a concurrence by Justice Kennedy, and a dissent by Justice Thomas.

The opinion for the Court, written by Justice Ginsburg, tried to stake out a middle ground between the two possible extremes: that the ADA did not apply to this situation at all or that the ADA mandated community integration of persons with mental illness and/or mental retardation. Instead, the Court decided that the ADA does require community integration when:

1. The state's treatment professionals have determined that community placement is appropriate.
2. The transfer to the less restrictive setting is not opposed by the affected individual.
3. The placement can be reasonably accommodated, taking into account the resources available to the state and the needs of others with mental disabilities.[18]

Elements 1 and 2 are very straightforward, but it is much harder to understand what Justice Ginsburg meant by element number 3. Other aspects of the opinion for the Court are confusing as well. For example, as we have already discussed, a public entity does not have to accommodate a person with a disability if doing so would constitute an undue burden or a fundamental alteration to the nature of the program or activity of the public entity.

I have always thought of undue burden and fundamental alteration as two different concepts. "Undue burden" signifies financial hardship, and "fundamental alteration" has to do with the way the program or activity operates. Yet Justice Ginsburg appears to use the term *fundamental alteration* as a synonym for *undue burden* when she specifically rules out looking at the entire mental health budget as the yardstick for measuring whether a particular reasonable accommodation is appropriate.[19] Justice Ginsburg says that a state utilizing the fundamental alteration defense should be allowed to show that in the allocation of available resources, immediate relief for the plaintiffs would not be fair, given the responsibility of the state for the care and treatment of a large and diverse population of persons with mental disabilities.[20]

Justice Ginsburg's discussion of what the state needs to show with a fundamental alteration defense is broad enough to wonder whether the state would not always prevail using such a defense, given how a state government often locks itself into set bureaucracies that are difficult to change. However, Justice Ginsburg appears to qualify these remarks at the conclusion of the opinion, which was not joined by all the justices, when she addresses how the state can satisfy its obligation to make reasonable accommodations for a person with a disability. Justice Ginsburg said that one way a state could demonstrate that it has made the appropriate reasonable modifications is to show that it has a comprehensive, effective plan for placing qualified persons with mental disabilities in less restrictive settings and a waiting list that moved at a reasonable pace not controlled by the state's desire to keep institutions fully populated.[21] Thus, from the majority opinion, we know that unnecessary segregation of persons with mental disabilities in institutions is prohibited by the ADA, but it is unclear at what point the state has a sufficient defense to refuse to place a person with mental disabilities in a community program.[22]

Justice Stevens would have gone much further than Justice Ginsburg by simply voting to affirm the lower court decision.[23] Justice Stevens also mentions that there were not five votes for simply affirming the lower court's opinion.[24] Justice Stevens' mention of the difficulty of getting five votes for affirmance may go a long way toward explaining why certain aspects of Justice Ginsburg's opinion are hard to understand, as the opinion may have been written with consensus rather than bright lines in mind.

Justice Kennedy also filed a concurring opinion. Of particular note is his statement that a state without a community integration program in place is not required to create one.[25] Nevertheless, Justice Kennedy does say how he would go about deciding whether a state's community integration program passes muster under the ADA. He states that such a program would *not* pass under the ADA if (1) the state provides treatment to individuals suffering from medical problems of comparable seriousness; (2) as a general matter, such treatment is provided in the most integrated setting appropriate for those problems after taking into account medical and other practical considerations; *but* (3) without adequate justification, fails to do so for a group of mentally disabled persons.[26]

Even this paradigm for deciding when a state's community integration program passes muster is confusing at times. For example, what does Justice Kennedy mean by "practical considerations"? What does he mean by "as a general matter"? And what does "adequate justification" mean? Perhaps there will be other decisions to come before the Court that will address those questions.

Finally, Justice Thomas filed a dissenting opinion in which the chief justice and Justice Scalia joined.

OLMSTEAD EVOLVES

Sheltered Workshops

Recently, Oregon was warned by the Department of Justice that its system of not giving people in sheltered workshops the opportunity to develop skills so that they could work in the community instead of in sheltered workshops was in violation of the ADA. In May of 2012, a district court judge in Oregon, in *Lane v. Kitzhaber*, relying on the reasoning in *Olmstead,* held that a state could be in violation of the ADA if its system did not give opportunities for persons in sheltered workshops to participate in integrated activities.[27] That is, there must be employment services offered to persons with disabilities other than sheltered workshops. To say it another way, it is a violation of the ADA to unnecessarily segregate persons with disabilities into sheltered workshops.[28] So, what is a state to do?

A state will want to ensure that persons in sheltered workshops are individually assessed to see whether they may be able to function in integrated settings. The state will also want to ensure that programs are in place so that individuals currently in sheltered workshops who can function in integrated settings (it is possible the number of such persons is not that high) are given the opportunity to take advantage of those programs. The governor of Oregon recently issued an executive order doing exactly this.[29]

Budget Cuts

The state of Washington ran into some serious budget issues. The agencies were directed to cut 6.3% from the budget.[30] As a result, the personal care program, which is designed to keep people with disabilities out of institutions, was significantly reduced.[31] The question is whether a state is at risk of violating the ADA by making a decision to reduce services that may lead to increased institutionalization of persons with disabilities. A panel of the Ninth Circuit in *M.R. v. Dreyfus*[32] held that it was. The state of Washington then petitioned for an en banc hearing of the Ninth Circuit.[33] There were not sufficient votes to rehear the case en banc, so the panel decision stands. However, there was a vigorous dissent with regard to the denial of the en banc hearing filed by Judge Bea, which was joined by eight other members of the full Ninth Circuit.[34]

Does *Olmstead* really say that a state could lose an ADA lawsuit when, due to insufficient funds, it decides to cut its budget? While it is true that *Olmstead* mandates that persons with disabilities be integrated into the community, one thing about that case that has been ignored over the years is that there was no majority view as to when the obligation of the state to integrate persons with disabilities into the community kicks in. When might a state have a defense for not integrating persons with disabilities into the community? On that point, only a plurality existed in *Olmstead*.

Under Title II of the ADA, there is a defense if the modification would create an undue burden (financial) or fundamentally alter (operational) the nature of the program. With undue burden, the question has always been whether you would measure it against the entire operations of the governmental entity or perhaps against the budget of a particular program. Justice Ginsburg in *Olmstead* said that to measure it against the entire state budget would mean that the fundamental alteration defense would be no defense at all.[35] Rather, the allocation of available resources given the responsibility the state has undertaken for the care and treatment of a large and diverse population of persons needed to be considered.[36] Justice Ginsburg also said that the state would be able to successfully defend such a suit if it could demonstrate that it had a comprehensive, effectively working plan for placing qualified persons with mental disabilities in less restrictive settings as well as a waiting list moving at a reasonable pace not controlled by the state's attempts to keep the institution fully populated.[37] Finally, Justice Ginsburg turned to § 504 regulations, which deal with employment, to say that undue hardship (undue burden and undue hardship are the same concepts except that undue hardship applies to Title I and undue burden applies to Titles II and III of the ADA) does not refer to overall budget but a case-by-case analysis weighing a variety of factors, including the overall size of the program in terms of the number of employees, number and type of facility, and size of budget; the type of recipients operation, including the composition and structure of the workforce; and the nature and cost of the accommodation needed.[38]

What does this mean? First, it is unfortunate that fundamental alteration and undue burden seem to be confused, since in "ADA speak," the cases and regulations have referred to "undue burden" as pertaining to cost and "fundamental alteration" as pertaining to operations. This distinction also allows for two different phrases to reflect different concepts; otherwise, why have different phrases at all? Second, it is simply very unclear whether Justice Ginsburg, who was joined by Justice O'Connor (no longer on the Court) and Justice Souter (no longer on the Court) with respect to this section, would say that *Olmstead* could be used as a sword to prevent budget cuts. In particular, Justice Ginsburg's reference to "overall resources" suggests that the state may have some leeway in how it decides to parcel out its resources, particularly, in light of the other points discussed above, if the state has other ways of ensuring that persons with disabilities do not face unnecessary institutionalization.

Justice Kennedy and Justice Breyer, while agreeing with the majority in terms of result, did not agree with the section of Justice Ginsburg's opinion that talked about fundamental alteration/undue hardship. In particular, Justice Kennedy says that no state has unlimited resources and that each state must make hard decisions on how much to allocate to the treatment of diseases and disabilities.[39] He goes on to say that if funds for care and treatment of the mentally ill, including the severely mentally ill, are reduced to support programs directed to the treatment and care of other disabilities, that decision may be unfortunate, but it is a political one and not within the reach of the ADA.[40] Justice Kennedy continues by saying that grave constitutional concerns would be raised when a federal court is given the authority to review the states' choices on basic matters such as establishing or declining to establish new programs.[41] That is, it is simply not reasonable to read the ADA to permit court intervention on those kinds of decisions.[42] From these statements, it is hard to believe that Justice Kennedy, whose opinion was joined by Justice Breyer, would allow the Americans with Disabilities Act to be used to prevent budget cuts.

Justice Thomas wrote an opinion joined by Justice Scalia. Much of that opinion doesn't really apply to the situation here. However, he does say that constitutional principles of federalism place limits on the federal government's ability to direct state officers or to interfere with the functions of state government.[43] That statement by itself, especially considering the jurisprudence of Justice Thomas and Justice Scalia over time, strongly indicates that they would not support using the ADA as a sword to stop budget cuts.

In short, it seems that using the ADA to stop budget cuts in light of the decision in *Olmstead* would face very tough going at the Supreme Court. While the Ninth Circuit and the Fourth Circuit both have panels now on record as supporting this use of the ADA,[44] I seriously doubt that all the other circuits will follow suit. Ultimately, it will head to the U.S. Supreme Court, where, if this analysis is any guide (and it may not be), there would seem to be five votes, and perhaps more, against using the ADA to prevent budget cuts (of course, I am assuming that there would not be any evidence that the budget cuts were done out of animus toward persons with disabilities).

SERVICE DOGS V. THERAPY DOGS

There is a great deal of confusion over the difference between a service dog, therapy dog, emotional support dog, etc., and why it matters. With respect to Title I, which is governed by the EEOC regulations, it may not matter much. However, with respect to Titles II and III, which are governed by Department of Justice regulations, it matters a great deal. Also, in addition to the ADA, there may be other laws you need to be aware of as well. For example, the Fair Housing Act regulations may apply and may differ considerably from the Department of Justice regulations that implement Title II and Title III of the ADA.

The applicable regulations, 28 C.F.R. § 35.104 and 28 C.F.R. § 36.104 (the sections of the federal regulation that apply to service animals for public entities (Title II) and for places of public accommodations (Title III) both define service animal in the same way. Under those regulations, a service animal is any dog trained to do work or perform tasks for the benefit of an individual with a disability, whether a physical, sensory, psychiatric, intellectual, or other mental disability.[45] The work or task performed by the service animal must be directly related to the handler's disability.[46] According to the regulations, such work or tasks may include assisting individuals who are blind or have low vision with navigation and other tasks; alerting individuals who are deaf or hard of hearing to the presence of people or sounds; providing nonviolent protection or rescue work; pulling a wheelchair; assisting an individual during a seizure; alerting an individual to the presence of allergens; retrieving items such as medicine or the telephone; providing physical support and assistance with balance and stability to individuals with mobility disabilities; and helping persons with psychiatric and neurological disability by preventing or interrupting impulsive or destructive behaviors.[47] It is important to note that the regulations state the following:

> The crime deterrent effects of an animal's presence and the provision of emotional support, well-being, comfort, or companionship do not constitute work or tasks for the purposes of this definition.[48]

It should also be noted that while not specifically listed in the definition of a service animal, in a separate section of the regulations, miniature horses get treated much the same way as service animals.[49]

The next question is what inquiries can a Title II or III entity make when encountering a service dog? 28 C.F.R. § 35.136(f) and 28 C.F.R. § 36.302(c)(6) both limit the inquiries that can be made when someone shows up with an animal at a public entity or a place of public accommodation. Inquiries can be made as to whether the animal is required because of a disability and what work or task the animal has been trained to perform.[50] However, those inquiries cannot be made if it is readily apparent that an animal is trained to do work or perform tasks for an individual with a disability.[51]

Here's the problem: Under the ADA, service dogs must be allowed into a place of public accommodation or into a public entity. However, as the Department of Justice sees it, dogs that are there merely to keep the person with a disability calm are not protected by this regulation, because those animals are providing emotional support, well-being, comfort, or companionship rather than working or performing a task for the handler. The other problem is that the ADA is not the only law in play. For example, the Fair Housing Act and its regulations do allow for emotional support animals.[52]

All of this leads to the following. If a person shows up with a dog and wants to take it into a public entity or a place of public accommodation and it is not obvious that the dog is performing work or a task for the handler, the public entity or place of public accommodation can make the inquiries noted above. However, because the allowed inquiries are limited, making them may not be terribly helpful. For example, if the person with a disability is knowledgeable enough about the distinction between service dogs and dogs providing emotional support, that person may very well phrase a response in terms of the dog performing work or a task. At that point, the public entity or place of public accommodation is in a difficult position. In such a situation, will the public entity or place of public accommodation really pick up the phone and ask the appropriate person, preferably legal counsel, whether the response meant the dog was, in fact, performing work? Maybe someone would, but it is certainly not practical. All this does is state the need for training of personnel when dealing with these situations.

To summarize: Service dogs and therapy dogs are not the same thing. Also, it would be wise for a public entity and a place of public accommodation to conduct training so that staff members are aware of the difference and know how to handle situations when a dog shows up. Also, that training would need to discuss permissible inquiries and how to deal with the information gleaned from those inquiries. Finally, especially if you are responsible for "dwellings" as the term would be understood by the Fair Housing Act,[53] don't assume that you can stand behind the service animal definition under the ADA. Other laws, such as the Fair Housing Act, may go considerably further.

Title II And III Regulations on Service Dogs: Kosher?

The Department of Justice regulations on service dogs create a bit of a mess. That is especially so since the EEOC in its Title I regulations does not adopt any kind of approach to service dogs, and other laws, such as the Fair Housing Act, specifically allow for animals that provide therapy and comfort. Further, as discussed above, whether a dog is actually working per the criteria set forth in the DOJ regulations can be a very fine line indeed. All this raises the question as to whether the DOJ regulations would withstand a challenge under the Administrative Procedure Act or under the Fourteenth Amendment to the U.S. Constitution.

For a regulation that has gone through proper rulemaking to be thrown out by the courts, it must be found to be arbitrary, capricious, or manifestly contrary to the statute.[54] "Manifestly contrary to the statute" is the easier term, but what does it mean for a regulation to be arbitrary and capricious? An agency action is arbitrary and capricious if the agency relies on factors that Congress did not intend for it to consider, offers an explanation for its decision that runs counter to the evidence before it, fails to consider an important aspect of the problem, or is so implausible that it cannot be ascribed to a difference in view of or the product of agency expertise.[55]

Does the Department of Justice meet this burden so that this regulation would not be found arbitrary, capricious, or manifestly contrary to the statute?[56] It probably did. Whenever a final regulation comes into place, the agency is required to do a section-by-section analysis in response to public comments. As can be expected, the DOJ received extensive comments with respect to service dogs v. therapy dogs. These comments were so extensive that the Department literally devotes more than seven pages to discussing the particular rules pertaining to service dogs, the comments submitted, and why the DOJ decided to do what it did.[57] In the end, the Department says that it wants to make sure that any such dog is working (recognition and response) rather than providing comfort, and as long as that is the case, it doesn't matter what the disability is.[58]

The harder question is whether such a distinction is contrary to the statutory intent of the ADA. As we know from our in-depth discussion of *Olmstead*, the ADA requires that people with disabilities be integrated into the community. Is the Department of Justice through this regulation violating that intent? In order to show that, the plaintiff would have to show that the choice the DOJ made in insisting that a dog engage in recognition and response rather than just comfort is a choice that Congress would not have sanctioned.[59] If that choice was a reasonable accommodation of conflicting policies committed to the agency's care by statute, then the court will not disturb it.[60] Which one is it? Recognition and response v. comfort certainly seems like a reasonable distinction. However, that distinction may be narrower than it seems. For example, a person with anxiety may need just some kind of a cue to redirect herself. Would simply looking at the dog do the trick, or would the dog need to do something, however subtle, to redirect the person? That may depend on the person. Would "however subtle" be enough to meet the recognition-and-response language of the DOJ? If not, an argument might be made that the regulation is contrary to statutory intent because it is not allowing for the service animal to perform cognitive behavior therapy techniques (anything that redirects the person so the attack doesn't continue). In short, it is hard to believe that the DOJ regulation could be considered arbitrary and capricious considering its extensive response to all the comments that were submitted, and considering the recognition-and-response standard that it came up with, which seems on its face to be reasonable. That said, there is a concern that the standard is not broad enough to allow for cognitive behavior therapy techniques. (That name sounds a little scary, but it is really quite simple. For example, when a person recognizes that an attack is imminent, he or she might do breathing exercises or react to a visual or physical cue either from someone else or an animal.)

What about the Equal Protection Clause? The problem there is that we never know what category of equal protection jurisprudence persons with disabilities fit into. With respect to employment, we know, per our discussion of *Board of Trustees of the University of Alabama v. Garrett*, that persons with disabilities fall into the rational basis class.[61] With respect to accessing the courts, we know from our prior discussions that persons with disabilities fall into the intermediate scrutiny class or higher.[62] We also know from our prior discussions that per *Tennessee v. Lane*, the classification of persons with disabilities with respect to equal protection jurisprudence depends entirely on the facts.[63]

What class would persons with disabilities fit into with respect to a Department of Justice regulation? If they would fit into the rational basis class, then the regulation would stand, as it is a rational way to carry out the ADA. If they fit into the intermediate scrutiny class, then the DOJ would have to show that the regulation was based on very good reasons. Could it show that? Possibly it could, though the narrowness of the definition of recognition and response for persons with psychiatric disabilities may be an issue. If the person with disabilities for these purposes was in the highest class—the suspect class—then the Department would have to show a compelling reason for its definition. While it would be unlikely, though not a given, that the DOJ could meet such a standard in this situation, it would also seem unlikely that persons with disabilities would fall into a suspect class for purposes of the DOJ regulations. We know from *Lane* that there is an extensive history of the states' discriminating against persons with disabilities.[64] However, as this is a federal regulation, we would need to know the history of the federal government with respect to discriminating against persons with disabilities before we could begin to decide what equal protection class they would fit into in terms of this fact pattern. If the person with a disability could show that the DOJ regulation involves basic constitutional guarantees, basic rights, class of cases implicating judicial services, or fundamental rights,[65] then the DOJ regulations would be easier to challenge.

In short, a challenge to this regulation under the Administrative Procedure Act will be really tough. The best approach will be to try to show that the service dog regulation is not consistent with the ADA's statutory intent. In regard to the Equal Protection Clause, due to the thoroughness of the response to comments from the DOJ, any equal protection challenge will be extremely difficult as it would seem to be unlikely that persons with disabilities in this instance would receive either intermediate or strict scrutiny.

INTERNET AND TITLE III OF THE ADA

Consider:

> A former client of yours is very impressed with the work you did for her. She has a friend who she believes can also use your expertise. Your law firm has a website. However, it is not accessible to the blind, and this friend of your client is blind. To be accessible to the blind, your website would have to be encoded to allow the blind person to use his screen-reader software so that he could use a keyboard instead of a mouse to navigate the site. When the blind friend tries to access your Internet site, he is unable to use it and becomes very frustrated. If he or she sues you for violating Title III of the Americans with Disabilities Act, does he or she have a case?

Restated, the question is whether Title III of the ADA, which applies to places of public accommodations,[66] applies to physical spaces only or to electronic space as well. To hold that physical structure is the key would mean giving businesses that operate solely on the Internet *carte blanche* to discriminate against persons with disabilities when selling their goods and services. Such a holding is hardly equitable, but is there law to support such an inequitable result?

The case law breaks down into four views. First, there is the view that the Internet is simply not a place of public accommodation, a view seen in *Access Now, Inc. v. Southwest Airlines, Co.*[67] In *Access Now*, the Southern District of Florida held that Southwest Airlines did not have to make its Internet site accessible to persons with disabilities because Title III of the ADA restricted its coverage to physical places.[68] Second, the opposite view was stated by Judge Posner of the Seventh Circuit in *Doe v. Mutual of Omaha Insurance Company*.[69] While admittedly the statement that follows may well not have been critical to the disposition of *Doe*, since accessing the Internet was not before the court at all, it is nevertheless noteworthy because of how convinced Judge Posner seems to be of his view of the scope of Title III of the ADA's nondiscrimination provision. Relying on *Carparts Distribution Center, Inc. v. Automotive Wholesaler's Association of New England*,[70] Judge Posner said:

> The core meaning of this provision [Title III of the ADA's nondiscrimination provision], plainly enough, is that the owner or operator of a store, hotel, restaurant, dentist's office, travel agency, theater, Web Site, or other facility (whether in physical space or in electronic space) [citation to *Carparts* omitted] that is open to the public cannot exclude disabled persons from entering the facility and, once in, from using the facility in the same way that the nondisabled do.[71] (Emphasis added.)

Third, there is a middle ground mentioned by the Ninth Circuit in *Weyer v. Twentieth Century Fox Film Corporation*.[72] That ground essentially relies on a two-step approach: 1) Determine if a place of public accommodation as defined by Title III of the ADA is somehow involved; and 2) if the answer to the first question is in the affirmative, assess whether a nexus exists between the event complained of and the place of public accommodation.[73] However, *Weyer* did not deal with the Internet. Thus, *Weyer* leaves open how the test might apply to the Internet.

We now have an idea how a court might apply *Weyer* to a case where the inaccessibility of the Internet was at issue. In *National Federation of the Blind v. Target Corp.*,[74] the Northern District of California was faced with a motion to dismiss by Target.[75] The National Federation of the Blind had sued Target because the blind could not access Target's website as it had not been encoded for the blind to do so.[76] In rejecting Target's motion to dismiss, the Northern District of California reasoned as follows:

First, the court noted the ADA said that the person with a disability had a right to access the services *of* a place of public accommodation and not services *in* a place of public accommodation.[77] (Emphasis added.)

Second, the court noted that the purpose of the ADA is far broader than physical access, as it seeks to bar actions or omissions that impair a disabled person's full enjoyment *of* the services or goods of a place of public accommodation. (Emphasis added.)[78]

Third, the court distinguished three other cases that would appear to dictate a different conclusion if the court were to have followed them. They distinguished *Rendon v. ValleyCrest Productions, Ltd.*[79] (where persons with disabilities sued because the screening process to get on "Who Wants to be a Millionaire" discriminated against them), because that case focused on distinction between tangible and intangible barriers.[80] The court then distinguished *Access Now*, discussed above, in which *Weyer*'s nexus approach was mentioned,[81] by saying no allegations of a physical place of public accommodation were presented in that case.[82] The court also distinguished *Stoutenborough v. National Football League* (where a person with a disability sued to have the blackout rule lifted as a violation of the ADA)[83] on the grounds that *Stoutenborough* involved a separate party leasing the public space, which was not the situation the *National Federation of the Blind* court was faced with.[84]

Finally, the *National Federation of the Blind* court noted that the challenged service was heavily integrated with Target's brick and mortar stores and operated in many ways as a gateway to the stores.[85]

For the reasons just mentioned, the court held that Target's motion to dismiss had to be denied.[86] However, it also noted that to the extent the plaintiffs were complaining about information and services offered on Target.com that were not connected to Target stores—i.e., did not affect the enjoyment of goods and services offered by Target stores—the plaintiff did not state a claim for discrimination under the ADA.[87]

What can we take from the *National Federation of the Blind* case? Based on the holding in the case, it seems fair to take as a standard that the ADA will apply to the Internet whenever it can be shown that the challenged services are heavily integrated with brick and mortar places of public accommodations and operate in many ways as a gateway to those places of public accommodations.[88] Thus, if *National Federation of the Blind* is the controlling law, then our law firm would most certainly have to make its website accessible to persons with disabilities, because the website is most probably heavily integrated with the firm's physical place and is operating as a gateway to that law firm.

Finally, there is now a fourth view of how the ADA works with respect to the Internet. That view is represented by *National Association of the Deaf v. Netflix, Inc.*, where a deaf person, the National Association of the Deaf, and the National Association of the Deaf's Massachusetts affiliate brought suit against Netflix alleging that its streaming, which was not closed captioned, violated the Americans with Disabilities Act.[89] The defendant responded that the ADA was not violated and that the act was preempted by the 21st-Century Communication Video Accessibility Act of 2010.[90] The court was having none of these arguments.

First, the court said that the ADA was meant to evolve with technology.[91]

Second, the court read the categories of places of public accommodation and assumed they applied in the context of the Internet regardless of how the product of the business is consumed, because the ADA covers the services "of" a place of public accommodation and not services "at" or "in" a place of public accommodation (*National Federation of the Blind*, as mentioned above, made the same argument).[92] For example, Netflix could well be a service establishment because it provides customers with the ability to stream video programming through the Internet.[93] It could also be a place of exhibition or entertainment because it displays movies, television programs, and other content.[94]

Finally, it could be a rental establishment because it engages customers to pay for the rental of video programming.[95]

In other words, there is no reason why these categories could not apply in electronic space.

A business entity that is sued for not being accessible as a place of public accommodation under the ADA must also be the entity that owns the place that is being sued.[96] Netflix claimed that it was not such an entity. However, Netflix did admit that it was working to provide captioning for the content on its streaming service, and that was enough for the court to say that Netflix had some degree of control over the situation.[97]

Finally, the defendant tried to claim that the 21st Century Communications and Video Accessibility Act of 2010 precluded claims under the ADA and/or conflicted with the act.[98] The court was having none of this either. Nothing in the 21st Century Communications Act suggested that it preempted the Americans with Disabilities Act.[99] Further, the court saw no conflict between the two acts because the scope of the 21stCentury Communications Act is fairly narrow.[100] That act requires captioning of things originally shown on TV that make their way to the Internet after a certain date. Much of that may not even be applicable to the *Netflix* situation.[101]

Before moving on to a summary of what the *National Association for the Deaf* decision means, it should be noted that Netflix, instead of appealing the decision, entered into a consent decree committing Netflix to closed caption its streaming.[102]

So what does this fourth approach mean? It means that disability rights advocates have now been given the green light to think beyond the three traditional lines of thought that had previously existed on whether an Internet site could be subject to the ADA. It also means that defendants must be aware that their exclusively online businesses, even if they don't fit the traditional lines of thought that existed previously, may now be subject to the ADA. This case is significant because of the new approach that it takes; businesses are places of public accommodations if they are exclusively on the Internet doing what places of public accommodations listed in the ADA would be doing if they were in physical space.[103]

To summarize, if *Access Now* is the law, our law firm probably has nothing to worry about, as that court was quite clear the ADA applied to physical spaces only. On the other hand, if *Doe*, *National Federation of the Blind*, or *National Association of the Deaf* is the law, then our firm should have its Internet site accessible to persons with disabilities (1) because electronic space is involved, (2) because the site would be integrated with the law firm and operate as a gateway, or (3) because it is operating a business subject to Title III of the ADA. The firm might be able to argue that to embed its Internet site would be an "undue burden," but that would necessitate determining just how expensive the embedding would be and then assessing the firm's overall financial resources.[104]

The question of how Title III of the ADA applies to the Internet is not going to go away, especially as e-commerce takes over all of our lives. The ultimate question will have to be decided by the U.S. Supreme Court, and I would not want to hazard a guess as to how it might decide this question. In the meantime, based on *Doe, National Federation of the Blind*, and *National Association of the Deaf*, good preventive lawyering, especially in the Seventh Circuit and in Massachusetts, would suggest that unless your law firm is operated from your house and you see no clients there (which would call into question the existence of a public accommodation under all of the approaches prior to *National Association of the Deaf v. Netflix*), encoding your law firm's website so that it is accessible to persons with visual impairments would be a step well worth considering.

LOVE BOAT

Ever taken a cruise? While I have yet to do so, a few facts about cruises are well known.

Various companies own and operate cruise lines, such as Norwegian, Carnival, Royal Holland, etc. These ships, essentially floating resorts,[105] sail from U.S. ports containing mainly U.S. passengers, more than 7 million by one count,[106] and go to various ports of call,[107] often in foreign countries. Ever notice the country's flag flying on the ship? For whatever reason, even though these ships are basically U.S.-centered ventures, it is most assuredly not the United States flag.[108] Should a ship carrying mainly U.S. passengers from U.S. ports of call and ending in U.S. ports of call be subject to the ADA if the flag it flies is not that of the United States? That was exactly the issue before the U.S. Supreme Court in *Spector v. Norwegian Cruise Line.*[109]

In *Spector*, the plaintiff and others claimed that the Norwegian Cruise Line required disabled passenger to pay higher fares and special surcharges that non-disabled passengers did not have to pay; maintained evacuation programs and equipment in locations not accessible to disabled individuals; required disabled individuals but not the non-disabled to waive any potential medical liability; required disabled individuals to travel with a companion; and reserved the right to remove from the ship any disabled individual whose presence endangered the comfort of other passengers.[110] Spector and others also claimed in a more general way that the cruise line failed to make reasonable modifications to policies, practices, and procedures necessary to ensure their full enjoyment of all the services offered.[111]

In a plurality opinion, a majority of the Court found that the ADA did apply to such vessels, even though they carried a foreign flag of convenience, as long as the internal affairs (the Court also used the term "internal order and discipline") of the ship were not compromised.[112] They could not, however, agree on what "internal affairs" meant.[113] In fact, Justice Kennedy in his opinion admitted that "internal affairs" is a category that is not always well defined and that may require future judicial elaboration.[114]

The justices had varying views on what "internal affairs" might mean. Justice Kennedy, for example, believed that when it came to physical barriers for persons with disabilities on the ship, such a problem could well go to the internal affairs of the ship, as different countries might have different architectural requirements.[115] Justice Thomas clearly believed that the ADA would not be applicable to structural modifications, as that would go to the ship's "internal affairs."[116] Justices Ginsburg and Souter believed that "internal affairs" only came into play where the ADA would conflict with international obligations.[117]

So where does *Spector* leave us with respect to the ADA? It's confusing to try to piece together how the opinion breaks down among the justices. We can say this: If structural modifications are not involved, the disabled plaintiff has a much better shot at winning an ADA suit against a cruise line. Of course, with the unpredictability of decisions on the ADA by the Supreme Court and with Justice Sotomayor now being on the Court, this all bears close watching.

What might be such a situation involving internal affairs of the ship? P & O, whose sister company is Cunard, instituted a rule saying that wheelchairs and scooters must be stored in the passenger cabin and not in the hallways due to safety concerns.[118] This means that persons with disabilities who use scooters may have to book more expensive cabins because not every cabin has room for a scooter. Nevertheless, assuming this company can justify its safety concerns, the situation would seem to have a strong probability of falling within the "internal affairs" language of *Spector*.

ASSOCIATION DISCRIMINATION

One thing we have not discussed yet is that the ADA prohibits the exclusion or denial of equal jobs or benefits to a qualified individual because of the known disability of another individual with whom the person is known to have a relationship or association.[119] Association cases generally break down into three types: expense (a spouse has a disability that is costly to the employer because the spouse is covered by the company's health plan); disability by association (the employer fears that the employee may become infected by his or her companion or develop a genetically based condition suffered by a relative); and distraction (employee is inattentive at work because his or her child has a disability that requires his or her attention, but no accommodation is needed).[120] Association cases can be proven by either direct or indirect evidence.[121] What is more complicated is trying to figure out how a prima facie case is proven, as the answer depends on the circuit you are in.

In the Tenth Circuit, to make a prima facie case for association discrimination, the plaintiff must show that 1) the plaintiff was qualified for the job at the time of the adverse employment action; 2) the plaintiff was subject to adverse employment action; 3) the plaintiff was known by his employer at the time to have a relative or associate with a disability; and 4) the adverse employment action occurred under circumstances that raise a reasonable inference that disability of the relative or associate was a determining factor in the employer's decision.[122]

In the Seventh Circuit, the formulation is slightly different: 1) the plaintiff was qualified for the job at the time of the adverse employment action; 2) the plaintiff was subject to adverse employment action; 3) the plaintiff was known by his employer at the time to have a relative or associate with a disability; and 4) the case falls into one of the three relevant categories (expense, distraction, or association) mentioned above.[123] Thus, when taking on an association discrimination case, check your jurisdiction to see what the requirements are for making a prima facie case.

Finally, it's hard to say whether we will see more association discrimination cases in the future, especially in light of the Genetic Nondiscrimination Act, which we discussed earlier. To date, association discrimination has not been frequently litigated.[124]

Notes

1. Val D'Aosta v. Cross, 526 S.E.2d 580 (Ga. App. 1999).
2. Ga. Code § 30-3-3 (current through the 2012 Regular Session).
3. *Id.*
4. *Id.*
5. Ga. Code § 30-3-8 (current through the 2012 Regular Session).
6. Ga. Code § 51-1-6 (current through the 2012 Regular Session).
7. *Val D'Aosta,* 526 S.E.2d at 584–85.
8. Alterman Foods, Inc. v. Ligon, 272 S.E.2d 327 (Ga. App. 1980).
9. Parks-Nietzold v. J.C. Penney, Inc., 490 S.E.2d 133 (Ga. App. 1997).
10. Barnes v. Delta Lines, Inc. 669 P.2d 709, 710–11 (Nev. 1983).
11. Ga. Code § 51-11-7 (current through the 2012 Regular Session).
12. Theater Mgmt. Group, Inc. v. Dalgliesh, 765 A.2d 986 (D.C. App. 2001).
13. *Id.* at 991.
14. In an informal discussion letter, the EEOC makes precisely this point. It posits in the letter that requiring a high school diploma may, depending on the job, run afoul of the ADA. In a blog entry, I discuss that letter and whether the EEOC may have gone too far. That blog entry can be found at http://www.williamgoren.com/blog/2012/02/19/has-the-eeoc-gone-too-far/.
15. *See* Heller v. Doe, 509 U.S. 312 (1993).
16. *See* Pa. Prot. and Advocacy, Inc. v. Pa. Dep't of Public Welfare, 402 F.3d 374 (3d Cir. 2005).
17. L.C. By Zimring v. Olmstead, 138 F.3d 893, 895 (11th Cir. 1998); *see also* discussion of U.S. Supreme Court decision in this case *supra* and *infra*.
18. Olmstead v. L.C. By Zimring, 527 U.S. 581, 607 (1999).
19. *Id.* at 603–04.
20. *Id.* at 604.
21. *Id.* at 605–06.
22. The courts are struggling as to when a state has a sufficient financial defense under *Olmstead vis-á-vis* what are now final federal rules requiring the integration of persons with disabilities into the community. For example, one court adopted several different parts of *Olmstead* to decide that the state of Pennsylvania had not presented as a matter of law a sufficient fundamental alteration defense. *See* Pa. Prot. and Advocacy,

Inc. v. Pa. Dep't of Public Welfare, 402 F.3d 374 (3rd Cir. 2005). Cases such as this one bear very close watching to see just how far a state's Title II obligations will extend with respect to the integration of persons with disabilities into the community.

23. *Olmstead, supra*, 527 U.S. at 607–08 (J. Stevens concurring).
24. *Id.* at 608.
25. *Id.* at 612 (J. Kennedy concurring).
26. *Id.* at 612.
27. Lane v. Kitzhaber, 841 F. Supp. 2d 1199, 1205–06 (D. Or. 2012).
28. *Id.*
29. *See* http://www.oregon.gov/gov/docs/executive_orders/eo_13-04.pdf.
30. M.R. v. Dreyfus, 697 F.3d 706, 723 (9th Cir. 2011, panel opinion).
31. *Id.* at 723–24 (panel opinion).
32. *Id. at* 734–36 (panel opinion); *see also* Pashby v. Delia, _F.3d_, 2013 WL 791829, *10 (4th Cir. Mar. 5, 2013).
33. *M.R.*, 697 F.3d at 709 (9th Cir. 2012) (J. Bea dissenting from denial of rehearing en banc). Similarly, there was also a vigorous dissent in *Pashby*, filed by J. Agee. *Pashby* at *20.
34. *M.R.*, 697 F.3d at 708.
35. *Olmstead*, 527 U.S. at 603.
36. *Id.* at 604.
37. *Id.* at 605–06.
38. *Id.* at 606 n.16.
39. *Id.* at 612 (Kennedy, J., concurring).
40. *Id.*
41. *Id.* at 612–13.
42. *Id.* at 613.
43. *Id.* at 624.
44. *M.R.* 697 F.3d at 734–36 (panel opinion); *see also Pashby*, _F.3d_, 2013 WL 791829, at *10.
45. 28 C.F.R. § 35.104 and 28 C.F.R. § 36.104.
46. *Id.*
47. *Id.*
48. *Id.* (emphasis added)
49. *See* 28 C.F.R. § 35.136(i) and 28 C.F.R. § 36.302(c)(9) (DOJ regulations pertaining to the inclusion of miniature horses with respect to Title II and Title III entities, respectively).
50. 28 C.F.R. § 35.136(f) and 28 C.F.R. § 36.302(c)(6).
51. *Id.*
52. *See* United States v. Univ. of Neb. at Kearney, 2013 WL 1694603 (D. Neb. Apr. 19, 2013).
53. *Id.*
54. Chevron, USA, Inc. v. Natural Resources Defense Council, Inc., 467 U.S. 837, 844 (1984).

55. Air Transport Ass'n of Am., Inc. v. Nat'l Mediation Board, 719 F. Supp. 2d 26, 30 (D.C. Cir. 2010).
56. For a situation in which a regulation might be found to be arbitrary as well as exceeding the enforcement powers of the Fourteenth Amendment as incorporated into the Fifth Amendment, see my blog entry of Aug. 28, 2013, "Affirmative action and persons with disabilities part two and did OFCCP set up a constitutional challenge to torpedo all of it." This blog entry can be found at http://www.williamgoren.com/blog/2013/08/affirmative-action-and-persons-with-disabilities-part-two-constitutional-challenge-regulations.
57. *See, e.g.,* Appx. A to Part 35—Guidance to Revision to ADA Regulation on Nondiscrimination on the Basis of Disability in State and Local Government Services at discussion of "service animal."
58. *Id.*
59. *Chevron,* 467 U.S. at 845.
60. *Id.*
61. *Garrett,* 531 U.S. at 366.
62. *Lane,* 541 U.S. U.S. at 529.
63. *Id.* at 530.
64. *Id.* at 524–25.
65. *Id.* at 509, 522, 524, 529, 531, 534.
66. *See* 42 U.S.C. § 12181(7). In particular, under section F of § 12181(7), professional offices are places of public accommodations.
67. Access Now, Inc. v. Southwest Airlines Co., 227 F. Supp. 2d 1312 (S.D. Fla. 2002).
68. *Id.* at 1319–21.
69. Doe v. Mutual of Omaha Ins. Co., 179 F.3d 557 (7th Cir. 1999).
70. Carparts Distrib. Center, Inc. v. Automotive Wholesaler's Ass'n of New England, 37 F.3d 12, 19 (1st Cir. 1994).
71. *Doe*, 179 F.3d at 559.
72. Weyer v. Twentieth Century Fox Film Corp., 198 F.3d 1104 (9th Cir. 2000).
73. *Id.* at 114–15.
74. Nat'l Federation of the Blind v. Target Corp., 452 F. Supp. 2d 946 (N.D. Cal. Sept. 6, 2006).
75. *Id.* at 950.
76. *Id.* at 949–50.
77. *Id.* at 953.
78. *See id.* at 955.
79. Rendon v. Valleycrest Productions, Ltd., 294 F.3d 1279 (11th Cir. 2002).
80. *Id.* at 1283.
81. *Access Now*, *supra*, note 66, at 1321.
82. *Nat'l Federation of the Blind,* 452 F. Supp. at 954.
83. Stoutenborough v. Nat'l Football League, 59 F.3d 580, 581 (6th Cir. 1995).

84. *Nat'l Federation of the Blind*, 452 F. Supp. at 954–55.
85. *Id.*
86. *Id.* at 956.
87. *Id.*
88. If one compares the holding of *National Federation of the Blind* at *24 with how the court fully distinguishes *Stoutenborough*—see notes 81–82, *supra*—it would be a fair way for the holding to be stated as a positive rather in the negative as it exists at *24.
89. Nat'l Ass'n of the Deaf v. Netflix, Inc., 869 F. Supp. 2d 196, 199 (D. Mass. 2012).
90. *Id.*
91. *Id.* at 200–01.
92. *Id.* at 201.
93. *Id.*
94. *Id.*
95. *Id.*
96. *Id.* at 202.
97. *Id.*
98. *Id.* at 203.
99. *Id.* at 203–05.
100. *Id.* at 205–08.
101. *Id.* at 208.
102. http://www.nad.org/news/2012/10/netflix-and-national-association-deaf-reach-historic-agreement-provide-100-closed-capti.
103. Judge Posner's approach and the approach taken in the *National Association of the Deaf* case are slightly different, though they may get you to the same place. Judge Posner says that the ADA applies to electronic space, while the *National Association for the Deaf* case says that the ADA applies in electronic space *providing* the business meets one of the general categories of places of public accommodation. While the two approaches get to the same place, they are using different concepts.
104. *See* 28 C.F.R. at 36.104.
105. Spector v. Norwegian Cruise Line, Ltd., 545 U.S. 119, 126 (2005).
106. *Id.* at 132.
107. *Id.* at 126.
108. *Id.*
109. Spector v. Norwegian Cruise Line, Ltd., 545 U.S. 119 (2005).
110. *Id.* at 133–34.
111. *Id.*
112. *Id.* at 136–42.
113. The plurality in this case is complicated. One has to closely study what part of the opinion a majority of justices agreed with. It then becomes apparent that there was agreement only as to the "internal affairs" language but not as to what it meant.

114. *Id.* at 142. (This particular statement comes from a section of the opinion for which there was no majority, though a reading of all the opinions would suggest that a majority of the justices would not disagree with the statement.)
115. *Id.* at 137.
116. *Id.* at 149 (Thomas, J., concurring and dissenting).
117. *Id.* at 144 (Ginsburg and Souter, JJ., concurring in part and concurring in the judgment).
118. http://www.telegraph.co.uk/travel/cruises/cruise-news/9997482/Mobility-rule-angers-cruisers.html .
119. 42 U.S.C.A. §12112(b)(4) (WL, current through Pub. L. 113-9 (excluding Pub. L. 113-4), approved May 1, 2013).
120. Larimer Int'l Bus. Machs. Corp., 370 F.3d 698 (7th Cir. 2004).
121. *See* Dewitt v. Proctor Hosp., 517 F.3d 944, 948 (7th Cir. 2008).
122. Trujillo v. Pacificorp., 524 F.3d 1149, 1154 (10th Cir. 2008).
123. *Dewitt*, 517 F.3d at 948.
124. While the ADA was signed into law in 1990 and went into effect in 1992, the Seventh Circuit did not get an association discrimination claim until 2004. *See Larimer,* 370 F.3d at 700. Also, a Westlaw search using "[("association with" /4 disability) "association discrimination" /p "Americans with Disabilities Act"]" turned up 38 cases, which is not a lot considering the ADA has been in effect, at the time of this writing, for just about 21 years.

14

Rocking and Rolling with Your ADA Case: Checklists and Forms

ARE YOU READY TO ROCK AND ROLL WITH YOUR ADA CASE?

WHAT FOLLOWS ARE THREE CHECKLISTS for practitioners to use as they develop their ADA cases and prepare for trial. These checklists will help format discovery requests and serve as a reference point as the case develops. They are divided into three categories: employment, operations of governmental entities, and places of public accommodation. The lists are not meant to be exhaustive, nor are they necessarily in any order of priority, but they serve as a starting point. Also included in this chapter are sample ADA forms. Those forms are offered by way of example and illustration and are not meant to substitute for the judgment of the litigator/individual attorney.

CHECKLISTS

Checklist 1: Employment (Title I)

- ❑ Have you established that the plaintiff has a physical impairment?
- ❑ Have you established that the plaintiff has a mental impairment?

- ❑ Have you established that the plaintiff has a major life activity that is substantially limited?
  - Does your case arise prior to January 1, 2009, or after?
    - o If before, have you reviewed *Sutton* and *Toyota Motor*?
    - o If after, have you reviewed how the amendments to the Americans with Disabilities Act define major life activity?
- ❑ If a plaintiff is alleging working as the affected major life activity and you represent the plaintiff, are you absolutely sure there is no other major life activity that could have been relied upon?
- ❑ Have you examined all applicable records to see if the plaintiff has a record of a disability?
- ❑ If the case arises prior to January 1, 2009, have you analyzed the case to see if the plaintiff is perceived as having a physical or mental impairment *and* that the employer also perceives the plaintiff as being substantially limited in a major life activity?
- ❑ If the case arises after January 1, 2009, have you analyzed the case to see if the plaintiff was perceived by the employer as having a physical or mental impairment while ignoring whether the employer also perceived the plaintiff as being limited in a major life activities?
- ❑ If on the defense side, can you structure the case so that working becomes the major life activity that plaintiff relies upon?
- ❑ Does the plaintiff use mitigating measures?
  - If the case arises after January 1, 2009, excepting eyeglasses, have you been sure not to factor mitigating measures into the equation as to whether the person has a physical or mental impairment that substantially limits a major life activity?
  - If the case arises before January 1, 2009, have you determined after factoring in mitigating measures whether the person has a physical or mental impairment that substantially limits a major life activity per *Sutton* and *Toyota Motor*?
- ❑ If a "regarded as" claim, have you determined whether the plaintiff's disability is "transitory and minor" (actual or expected duration of six months or less)?

A. If plaintiff and dealing with an actual disability of short duration, are you prepared to argue that the transitory and minor clause only applies to regarded as claims?

B. If plaintiff and dealing with a regarded as claim, are you prepared to argue that the defense must show that the disability was both transitory *and* minor?

- ❑ Have you determined that the plaintiff has the requisite skills, experience, and education for the position he/she holds or desires?
- ❑ Have you established that the plaintiff can perform the essential functions of the job he/she holds or desires with or without reasonable accommodations?
- ❑ Have you assessed whether the plaintiff is a direct threat to him-/herself or others?
  - ❑ Have you come to that conclusion based on objective medical or other factual evidence?
  - ❑ Have you determined whether the risk can be reduced to less than that of a direct threat by reasonable accommodations?
  - ❑ Have you determined if the safety of others is one of the essential functions of the job?
- ❑ Have you received a right-to-sue letter from the EEOC?
- ❑ Have you accurately determined the essential functions of the job(s)?
- ❑ Have you made sure in assessing the essential functions of the job(s) that the essential functions have not been confused with job tasks or with major life activities?
- ❑ In the course of analyzing the job's essential functions, have you determined what actually transpires?
- ❑ If the plaintiff affirmatively disclosed a disability in a prehire interview, have you determined the nature of the follow-up questions, if any, that were asked? Did those follow-up questions relate to an essential function of the job?
- ❑ If on the defense side, can you show instances of negotiating in good faith with the plaintiff to find a suitable reasonable accommodation? Can the client demonstrate a record of creativity in the quest to find a reasonable accommodation for the plaintiff?

- ❑ Have you assessed whether providing the reasonable accommodation would fundamentally alter the nature of the business? (Logistical undue hardship)
- ❑ Have you assessed whether the employer can afford the accommodation without undue hardship?
- ❑ If on the defense side, are you sure the client understands that undue hardship does not equal inconvenience?
- ❑ If on the defense side, have you established that in the reasonable accommodation process the lines of communication were always kept open?
- ❑ Have you established that the plaintiff affirmatively disclosed to the employer in some way that he/she had a disability or that the employer had reason to know of the disability?
- ❑ Have you determined whether the plaintiff is using illegal drugs or alcohol?
- ❑ Have you determined whether the plaintiff has ever been in an alcohol or drug rehabilitation program?
- ❑ Have you determined whether the plaintiff has a record of using drugs that went beyond casual use?
- ❑ Have you determined whether the plaintiff was asked any pre-employment disability-related questions?
- ❑ Have you determined whether the defendant insisted on a full release to return to work?
- ❑ Have you analyzed the terms of the collective bargaining agreement or the company's seniority system to see how it addresses accommodating a person with a disability?
- ❑ If representing a union, are you satisfied that the union's interest and the union member's interests are aligned? If not, have appropriate steps been taken to satisfy fair representation obligations?
- ❑ Have you determined whether an impermissible medical exam occurred?
- ❑ Regardless of whether the person underwent a pre-employment medical exam, have you analyzed whether that exam contained any pre-employment medical or disability-related inquiries?
- ❑ If a post-employment medical exam is involved, have you determined whether the medical exam was job-related and consistent with business necessity?

- ❑ Have you evaluated the medical exam or inquiries to ensure compliance with the Genetic Information Nondiscrimination Act?
- ❑ If employer is a religious entity, have you assessed whether plaintiff would be deemed a minister under any of the tests disclosed in *Hossana-Tabor Evangelical Lutheran Church School v. EEOC*, 1325 S. Ct. 694 (2012). *See also* my blog entry of April 26, 2012, on this case, which can be found at www.williamgoren.com/blog/2012/04/26/the-ADA-Rehabilitation-Act-and-the-ministerial-exception.
- ❑ Have you analyzed the collective bargaining agreement to determine the circumstances it allows for drug testing?
- ❑ Have you determined if there was a conditional job offer? If so, and the offer was withdrawn, can it be shown that 1) the reason for the withdrawal was job-related; 2) the reason for the withdrawal was consistent with business necessity; and 3) the medical exam revealed that the plaintiff cannot perform the essential functions of the job with or without reasonable accommodations?
- ❑ Have you reviewed the personnel file and the confidential medical information file? Have you determined whether medical information about the person's disability appears in the personnel file?
- ❑ If a Title I case, does the defendant have 15 or more employees?
- ❑ If it appears the company has less than 15 employees, have you applied "the control test" to see if individuals not considered employees by the company are in fact employees under the case law?
- ❑ If on the defense side, have you determined whether the plaintiff applied for Social Security benefits, long-term disability benefits, or short-term disability benefits? If so, have you reviewed the statements made in those applications to see if they jeopardize the plaintiff's request for an accommodation under the ADA?
    - ❑ Have you established who told the plaintiff to apply for such benefits? Was it the employer?
    - ❑ Do you have copies of the long-term and short-term disability benefits policies?

  - ❑ Do you have copies of the representations made by the plaintiff during the course of seeking disability benefits?
  - ❑ Have you read the U.S. Supreme Court opinion in *Cleveland v. Policy Management Systems Corp.*?
  - ❑ If a plaintiff, have you considered bringing suit under ERISA? If a defendant, is the plaintiff's ADA claim somehow preempted by ERISA?
- ❑ Have you analyzed the relationship between the ADA, the FMLA, and worker's compensation as it applies to your case?
- ❑ Have you considered that professional sports teams are employers under the ADA?
- ❑ Is your case a disparate impact case or a disparate treatment case, and are you aware of how each type of case is proven?
- ❑ Have you checked to see if the plaintiff has signed any arbitration agreement? If so, is the agreement written to include the ADA?
- ❑ If an employment matter is involved and the defendant is a state entity, has your state waived sovereign immunity?
- ❑ At trial, have you used *Batson* challenges to ensure that persons with disabilities are not excluded from the jury pool?
- ❑ If on the plaintiff's side, have you maximized your chances for obtaining attorneys' fees per the case law?
- ❑ Have you considered whether other federal laws and/or regulations trump the ADA?
- ❑ If plaintiff in a reasonable accommodation is not involved, have you pleaded both "regarded as" and actual disability prongs of what is a disability under the ADA?
- ❑ If suing a governmental entity for employment discrimination and the governmental entity defends on the ground that accommodations were not feasible, have you:
  - determined when the building was built;
  - determined whether any alterations or modification occurred since 1992; and
  - reviewed the self-evaluation and transition plans?

Checklist 2: Operations of a Governmental Entity (Title II)

- ❑ Have you established that the plaintiff has a physical impairment?

- ❑ Have you established that the plaintiff has a mental impairment?
- ❑ Have you established that the plaintiff has a major life activity that is substantially limited?
  - Does your case arise prior to January 1, 2009, or after?
    - o If before, have you reviewed *Sutton* and *Toyota Motor*?
    - o If after, have you reviewed how the amendments to the Americans with Disabilities Act define major life activity?
- ❑ Have you examined all applicable records to see if the plaintiff has a record of a disability?
- ❑ If a service dog or therapy dog is involved, have you assessed whether the dog is engaged in recognition and response?
- ❑ If the case arises prior to January 1, 2009, have you analyzed the case to see if the plaintiff is perceived as having a physical or mental impairment and that the governmental entity also perceived the plaintiff as being substantially limited in a major life activity?
- ❑ If the case arises after January 1, 2009, have you analyzed the case to see if the plaintiff was perceived by the governmental entity as having a physical or mental impairment while ignoring whether the governmental entity also perceived the plaintiff as being limited in a major life activity?
- ❑ Does the plaintiff use mitigating measures?
  - If the case arises after January 1, 2009, excepting eyeglasses, have you been sure not to factor mitigating measures into the equation as to whether the person has a physical or mental impairment that substantially limits a major life activity?
  - If the case arises before January 1, 2009, have you determined after factoring in mitigating measures whether the person has a physical or mental impairment that substantially limits a major life activity per *Sutton* and *Toyota Motor*?
- ❑ Assuming federal funds are received by the entity, have you also filed suit to enforce § 504 of the Rehabilitation Act?
- ❑ Have you determined if a governmental entity is involved?
- ❑ If a zoning issue is involved, have you studied the zoning regulations, their purpose, and whether a waiver might be in order?

- ❏ If on the plaintiff's side, have you obtained a copy of the ADA internal grievance procedure, the self-evaluation plan, and the transition plan?
- ❏ Have you determined just what governmental program was denied to the plaintiff?
  - ❏ If plaintiff, have you defined "program" as broadly as possible?
  - ❏ If defendant, have you defined "program" as narrowly as reasonable?
- ❏ Have you determined whether the plaintiff can, with or without reasonable modifications to rules, policies, or practices; the removal of architectural, communication, or transportation barriers; or the provision of auxiliary services and aids, meet the essential eligibility requirements for the receipt of services or the participation in programs or activities provided by the governmental entity?
- ❏ Have you determined the essential eligibility requirements of the program at issue? Do these requirements screen out persons with disabilities? Have you involved the subject matter experts during the process of determining a program's essential eligibility requirements.
- ❏ If on the defendant's side, can you establish that the accommodations asked for would fundamentally alter the nature of the program? (See *Easley v. Snider.*)
- ❏ If on the plaintiff's side, if public entity claims undue burden, do you have a copy of the public entity's certification?
- ❏ If on the plaintiff's side, have you determined whether services are being provided in as integrated a setting as possible? (See *Olmstead v. L.C.*)
  - ❏ Is state overrelying on sheltered workshops?
  - ❏ Have state budget cuts resulted in an increased risk of institutionalization?
- ❏ Is an activity involved rather than a program? If on the defense side, where the activity is not accessible, can you show that the activity is just part of a larger program that is accessible?
- ❏ Have you determined the essential eligibility requirements of the activity?
- ❏ If on the plaintiff's side, have you amassed evidence to show that an adverse zoning decision was the result of stereotypical

attitudes toward persons with disabilities or involved other forms of disability discrimination?

- ❑ Have you considered the applicability of other state laws and other federal laws, such as, but not limited to, the Federal Fair Housing Act to your case?
- ❑ If on the plaintiff's side, and your client is in "special education," have you exhausted all of the IDEA processes? If so, have you considered adding ADA/Rehabilitation Act causes of action to your case when you file in court?
- ❑ Have you made sure that punitive damages have not been alleged?
- ❑ If suing a state entity for discrimination outside of the employment context, have you researched the question of whether the discrimination at issue involved fundamental rights, basic rights, basic constitutional guarantees, or the administration of justice (assuming the state has not waived sovereign immunity)?
- ❑ At trial, have you used *Batson* challenges to ensure that persons with disabilities are not excluded from the jury pool?
- ❑ If on the plaintiff's side, have you maximized your chances for obtaining attorneys' fees per the case law?
- ❑ Have you determined whether the state has waived sovereign immunity?
- ❑ If suing a governmental entity for lack of access and the governmental entity defends on the ground that accommodations were not feasible, have you:
    - determined when the building was built;
    - determined whether any alterations or modification to the building occurred since 1992; and
    - reviewed the self-evaluation and transition plans?

Checklist 3: Places of Public Accommodation

- ❑ If the building was built after January 26, 1992, have you determined whether the facility satisfies ADA architectural standards?
- ❑ Have you assessed whether the facility, new or otherwise, meets state disability accessibility standards, where applicable?
- ❑ If a service dog is involved, is the dog engaged in recognition and response?

- ❑ Have you determined whether any alterations were performed on the facility after January 26, 1992? If so, was the path of travel regulations complied with?
- ❑ Have you determined the nature of the business? Does it fit into one of the categories the ADA refers to as places of public accommodation? If not, is the business leasing out a place of public accommodation for its event?
- ❑ Has the business begun to make readily achievable modifications to a facility built before January 26, 1992, as set forth in the Department of Justice regulations?
- ❑ If plaintiff, have you considered suing for architectural malpractice or personal injury using negligence or negligence per se principles?
- ❑ Have you investigated where your state stands on indemnity clauses with respect to the ADA?
- ❑ Are auxiliary aids or services involved?
- ❑ If on the defense side, are you prepared to show an undue burden? Have you assessed what are the essential elements of the business?
- ❑ If on the defense side, are you prepared to show that the requested accommodation would fundamentally alter the nature of the business operation?
- ❑ Have you assessed whether the business is controlled by a religious entity?
- ❑ If the business itself is not a place of public accommodation, have you assessed whether a portion of the business is a place of public accommodation?
- ❑ Have you considered the applicability of federal and state fair housing acts?
- ❑ If a building was built after January 26, 1992, and does not meet ADA accessibility regulations, have you considered suing the architect on two grounds: (1) directly for malpractice (plaintiff or defense side), and (2) under Title III of the ADA (plaintiff's side)?
- ❑ Have you obtained a copy of the lease between the business and the landlord?

- ❑ Have you considered bringing suit under Title III of the ADA even when the plaintiff was not physically on the premises when denied access to the business?
  - ❑ If so, have you considered whether the business is strictly on-line or does it have a physical place of business that people can access?
  - ❑ If the activity complained of is online:
    Have you determined your jurisdiction's treatment of such situations?
    Does your jurisdiction demand either a nexus or a gateway between an entity in one of the categories and the discriminatory action complained of? (*National Federation of the Blind v. Target or depending upon jurisdiction*)
    Does your jurisdiction demand a showing that the business in electronic space falls into one of the public accommodation categories? (*National Association of the Deaf v. Netflix*)
    Does your jurisdiction say that the ADA applies to electronic space? (*Doe v. Mutual of Omaha*)
    Does your jurisdiction say that the ADA has no applicability to the Internet? (*Access Now v. Southwest Airlines*)
- ❑ Have you drafted your lease to account for complying with the ADA?
- ❑ If on the plaintiff's side, have you maximized your chances for obtaining attorneys' fees per the case law?
- ❑ Have you considered other laws that may be involved, such as (but not limited to) the Air Carrier Access Act, laws of negligence, state antidiscrimination laws, etc.

LITIGATION FORMS (THE PLAINTIFF'S VIEW)

TITLE I (COMPLAINT)

Keep in mind, as mentioned in the book, that pure notice pleading may no longer be sufficient.[1] Attorneys may want to think about whether enough facts are alleged to give a reasonable person notice of the claim (e.g., this standard is essentially the pleading standard that is used in the state of Illinois.

Nature of Action

This is an action under Title I of the Americans with Disabilities Act of 1990 as amended (ADA) to redress unlawful disability-based employment practices and to make plaintiff, (name of plaintiff), whole. Defendant, (names of defendants), discharged plaintiff, a qualified individual with a disability, (state disability), from his position as (state title of position) on the basis of his disability. [Also, if desired, include state law supplemental claims here and throughout.]

Jurisdiction and Venue

1. Jurisdiction of this court is proper under 28 U.S.C. 451, 1331, 1337, and 1343. This action is instituted under Section 12117(a) of the ADA, 42 U.S.C. § 12117—incorporating by reference Sections 706(f)(1), (3) of Title VII of the Civil Rights Act of 1964 (Title VII), 42 U.S.C. § 2000e–5(f)(1), (3). (*If alleging violation of Civil Rights Act, cover that as well. Also, if the defendant receives federal funding, consider alleging violations of Section 504 of the Rehabilitation Act of 1973.*) Venue is proper in this district under 28 U.S.C. § 1391.
2. The alleged unlawful employment practices took place and are taking place in the ____________ District of _________, ___________ Division.

Parties

3. Plaintiff (name of plaintiff) is an individual with a disability in that Plaintiff has a physical or mental impairment, (state impairment), that substantially limits the major life activity of _________________ (state major life activity)

1. *See* Ashcroft v. Iqbal. _ U.S. _, 129 S. Ct. 1937, 1949–1954 (2009). *See also* Chapter 11 of this book.

4. Plaintiff is an otherwise qualified (Rehabilitation Act) or qualified (ADA) individual with a disability in that Plaintiff was able to perform all of the essential functions of the job of ____________ (state position) with or without reasonable accommodations.
5. Plaintiff was employed by Defendant (names of defendants) from ______ to _____.
6. Plaintiff is expressly authorized under Section 12117(a) of the ADA, 42 U.S.C. 12117—incorporating by reference Sections 706(f)(1), (3) of Title VII of the Civil Rights Act of 1964 (Title VII), 42 U.S.C. 2000e-5(f)(1),(3)—to bring this action.
7. At all relevant times, (names of defendants) has been a corporation doing business in (state and city), and at all relevant times (names of defendants) has had at least 15 employees.
8. At all relevant times, (names of defendants) has been engaged in an industry affecting commerce within the meaning of Section 101 (5) of the ADA, 42 U.S.C. 12111(5).
9. At all relevant times, (names of defendants) has been a covered entity under Section 12111(2) of the ADA, 42 U.S.C. 12111(2).

Statement of Claims

10. On ________________ (date of EEOC filing), (name of plaintiff) filed a charge with the Equal Employment Opportunity Commission (note, charges can also be filed with an equivalent state agency), alleging violations of Title I of the ADA by (names of defendants). Plaintiff received his/her Right to Sue Notice on (date of the notice). Consequently, Plaintiff has exhausted all available administrative remedies prior to the filing of this complaint
11. On the following occasions, plaintiff requested accommodations for his disability: (list each occasion and what accommodations were requested).
12. Since at least (date), (names of defendants) has engaged in unlawful employment practices in violation of ADA sections (list specific sections of Title I of the ADA that were violated) at (place where the ADA violations occurred). These practices include, but are not limited to, denial of accommodation, denial of promotions, denial of employment benefits,

failure to engage in the interactive process, and/or discharge of (name of plaintiff), an individual with a disability able to do the essential functions of the job with or without reasonable accommodations. [Plead disability and perceived disability in the alternative. Also, if you plead perceived disability and your case precedes the ADAAA , you will have to show that the defendant perceived a substantial limitation in a major life activity and thus, you might want to plead that as well. If the ADAAA applies to your case and you are pleading perceived disability, be cognizant of the "transitory and minor" language with respect to whether the person has a disability.

13. As a result of the disability discrimination alleged herein, the effect of the practices complained of above has been to deprive (name of plaintiff) of equal employment opportunities and otherwise adversely affect his status as an employee.
14. The unlawful employment practices complained of herein were and are intentional.

Prayer for Relief

WHEREFORE, Plaintiff respectfully requests that this court:

A. Grant a permanent injunction enjoining (names of defendants), its owners, officers, management personnel, employees, agents, successors, assigns, and in participation with them, from engaging in any employment practices that discriminate on the basis of disability;

B. Order (names of defendants) to institute and carry out policies, practices, and programs that provide equal employment opportunities to qualified individuals with disabilities and eradicate the effects of past and present unlawful employment practices;

C. Order (names of defendants) to make (name of plaintiff) whole by providing him or her with appropriate lost earnings and insurance premiums, with pre-judgment interest, in amounts to be proved at trial, and other affirmative relief necessary to eradicate the effects of its unlawful employment practices, including, but not limited to, reinstatement of (name of plaintiff) to the position of (title of position held by plaintiff);

D. Order (names of defendants) to make (name of plaintiff) whole by providing compensation for pecuniary losses, including, but not limited to, costs to be incurred for health and life insurance premiums and costs of seeking new employment, in amounts to be determined at trial;

E. Order (names of defendants) to remit payment to (name of plaintiff) for future prospective loss of pay for a period of time following the filing of the complaint;

G. Grant such further relief as the Court deems appropriate;

H. Grant Plaintiff his/her fees and costs in this action.

Note: In an employment case under Title I of the ADA, the Civil Rights Act of 1991 prohibits punitive damages against a governmental entity. Where a governmental entity is not involved in an employment matter under Title I of the ADA, the attorney may want to consider asking for punitive damages where appropriate.

Jury Demand

Plaintiff demands trial by jury.

TITLE II (COMPLAINT)

(Denial of Access to Governmental Services, Programs, and Activities)

Nature of Action

This is an action under Title II of the Americans with Disabilities Act of 1990 (ADA) and under Section 505 of the Rehabilitation Act of 1973, which enforces Section 504 of the Rehabilitation Act of 1973 (Rehabilitation Act), to redress unlawful disability-based practices and to make plaintiff, (name of plaintiff), whole. Defendant, (names of defendants), denied (name of plaintiff) access to (names of defendants and names of defendants's program, activity, or service) on the basis of his disability.

[If architectural accessibility is involved, you may also have violation of state building codes.]

Jurisdiction and Venue

1. Jurisdiction of this court is proper under 28 U.S.C. §§ 451, 1331, 1337, and 1343. This action is brought under Sections 12132 and 12133 of the ADA, 42 U.S.C. §§ 12132 and 12133—incorporating by reference the remedies, procedures,

and rights under the Rehabilitation Act, 29 U.S.C. § 794 and 794a, and under Section 505 of the Rehabilitation Act, which enforces Section 504 of the Rehabilitation Act, 42 U.S.C. § 794 and 794a—incorporating the remedies, rights, and procedures set forth in Section 717 of the Civil Rights Act of 1964, including the application of Sections 706(f) through 706(k), 42 U.S.C. § 2000e-5(f)–(k).

2. The alleged unlawful practices were and are taking place in the __________ District of ________, _________Division.
3. [If injunctive relief is being requested] As a result of (describe how the plaintiff is likely to return and use the governmental entity's programs and activities in the future but for the barriers; see section of book in Chapter 11 discussing standing), plaintiff has standing to pursue this action.

Parties

4. (Name of plaintiff) is an individual with a disability in that Plaintiff has a physical or mental impairment (state impairment) that substantially limits the major life activity of (state major life activity).
5. Plaintiff is an otherwise qualified (Rehabilitation Act) or qualified (ADA) individual with a disability in that Plaintiff is qualified to access defendant's program or activity.
6. Plaintiff was denied access to (names of defendants) (names of defendants's program or activity) on or about (date).
7. Plaintiff is expressly authorized under the ADA, 42 U.S.C. §§ 12132 and 12133,incorporating by reference the remedies, procedures, and rights under the Rehabilitation Act, 29 U.S.C. § 794 and 794a—and under Section 505 of the Rehabilitation Act, which enforces Section 504 of the Rehabilitation Act, 42 U.S.C. § 794 and 794a—incorporating the remedies, rights and procedures set forth in Section 717 of the Civil Rights Act of 1964, including the application of Sections 706(f) through 706(k), 42 U.S.C. § 2000e-5(f)–(k), to bring this action.
8. At all relevant times, (names of defendants) has been a public entity as defined in Section 12131(1) of the ADA, 42 U.S.C. § 12131(1), in that it is a state or local governmental entity or

agency thereof.

9. At all relevant times (names of defendants) has received federal funds. (Allege if also pursuing a Rehabilitation Act claim.)
10. Since at least (date), (names of defendants) has engaged in unlawful practices in violation of ADA sections (list specific sections of Title II of the ADA that were violated) and in violation of Section 504 of the Rehabilitation Act, 42 U.S.C. § 794. These practices include but are not limited to denying (name of plaintiff)—an individual with a disability who, with or without reasonable modifications to rules, policies, or practices; the removal of architectural, communication, or transportation barriers; or the provision of auxiliary aids and services, meets the essential eligibility requirements for the receipt of services or the participation in programs or activities provided by (names of defendants)—access to the (name of program, service, or activity) of (names of defendants).
11. The effect of the practices complained of has been to deprive (name of plaintiff) equal access to a public entity's services, programs, and activities and to otherwise adversely affect his/her status as a member of the public interested in accessing (names of defendants)'s programs and activities.
12. The unlawful practices complained of were and are done with deliberate indifference.

Prayer for Relief

WHEREFORE, Plaintiff respectfully requests that this court:

A. Grant a permanent injunction enjoining (names of defendants), its owners, officers, management personnel, employees, agents, successors, assigns, and in participation with them, from engaging in discrimination based on disability in the programs, services, and activities of (names of defendants).

B. Order (names of defendants) to formulate and implement services, programs, and activities that provide equal access to otherwise qualified individuals with disabilities and to eradicate the effects of past and present unlawful practices in the carrying out of (names of defendants)'s programs, services, and activities.

C. Order (names of defendants) to make (name of plaintiff) whole by providing plaintiff with appropriate remuneration incurred in obtaining suitable programming, services, and activities, with prejudgment interest, in amounts to be proved at trial, and other affirmative relief necessary to eradicate the effects of its unlawful practices, including the making of reasonable modifications and the provision of auxiliary aids and services so that (name of plaintiff) can access the programs, services, and activities of (names of defendants).

[Note: Punitive damages against a governmental entity are not going to be available for Title II/Rehabilitation Act cases per *Barnes v. Gorman*, 536 U.S. 181 (2002).

D. Grant such further relief as the Court deems appropriate.

E. Grant Plaintiff his/her fees and costs in this action.

Jury Demand

Plaintiff demands trial by jury.

TITLE III COMPLAINT

(Seeking injunctive relief for discrimination by a place of public accommodation)

Nature of Action

This is an action under Title III of the Americans with Disabilities Act of 1990 as amended (ADA) to enjoin unlawful disability-based discrimination. Plaintiff, (name of plaintiff), was discriminated against on the basis of disability so that he was denied the full and equal enjoyment of the goods, services, facilities, privileges, advantages, or accommodations of a place of public accommodation owned, leased, or operated by the defendants, (names of defendants).

Jurisdiction and Venue

1. Jurisdiction of this court is proper under 28 U.S.C. §§ 451, 1331, 1337, and 1343. This action is brought under Section 12188(a) of the ADA, 42 U.S.C. §12188(a)—incorporating by reference the remedies and procedures found in 42 U.S.C. § 2000a–3, Section 204 of the Civil Rights Act of 1964. [If architectural accessibility is involved, you may also want to consider pleading state law claims. It is not unusual for states to have even stricter architectural standards than those required by the ADA. Also, as mentioned in Chapter 13 of this book,

plaintiff should consider suing the architect of the building directly for designing a building out of compliance with ADA architectural standards or filing a Department of Justice claim alleging as much. Personal injury claims using the principles of negligence or negligence per se are another possibility. The defendant may also want to consider suing the architect for malpractice.]

2. The alleged unlawful practices were and are now being committed in the _______ District of _____________, _____________ Division.
3. As a result of (describe how the plaintiff is likely to return and use the facility in the future but for the barriers; see section of book discussing standing), plaintiff has standing to pursue this action.

Parties

4. (Name of plaintiff) is a person with a disability, (state nature of disability), who was denied the full and equal enjoyment of the goods, services, facilities, privileges, advantages, or accommodations of a place of public accommodation owned, leased, or operated by the defendant.
5. (Name of plaintiff) is expressly authorized under Section 308 of the ADA, 42 U.S.C. § 12188(a)—incorporating by reference the remedies and procedures found in 42 U.S.C. § 2000a–3, Section 204 of the Civil Rights Act of 1964—to bring this action.
6. At all relevant times (names of defendants A) has been the owner/lessor of (location of the place of public accommodation).
7. At all relevant times (names of defendants B) has been the operator of (name of the place of public accommodation).
8. (Name of the place of public accommodation) at all relevant times has been a place of public accommodation under (select applicable type of public accommodation as set forth in 42 U.S.C. § 12181(7); include its corresponding statutory reference).

Statement of Claims

9. Since at least (date), (names of all defendants) have engaged in unlawful practices in violation of ADA Sections (list specific sections of Title III of the ADA that were violated and the facts

supporting same). These practices include but are not limited to (list the incidents of discrimination by each defendant).

10. The effect of the practices complained of has been to deprive (name of plaintiff) the full and equal enjoyment of a place of public accommodation and to otherwise adversely affect his/her status as a member of the public interested in accessing the place of public accommodation owned, leased, and/or operated by the defendants, (names of defendants).

Prayer for Relief

WHEREFORE, Plaintiff respectfully requests that this court:

A. Grant a permanent injunction enjoining (names of defendants), its officers, management personnel, employees, agents, successors, assigns, and in participation from engaging in discrimination based on disability.

B. Order (names of defendants) to make (name of place of public accommodation) readily accessible to and usable by individuals with disabilities.

C. Order defendants to provide the auxiliary aids or services, modify policies, or provide an alternative method so that (name of plaintiff) can obtain the full and equal enjoyment of the place of public accommodation, (name of place of public accommodation), owned, operated, or leased by defendants.

D. Grant the plaintiff his/her costs and reasonable attorneys' fees in this action.

NOTICE TO PRODUCE

Key

In a jurisdiction that adheres to the Revised Discovery Rules, much of what follows below is covered in the initial disclosures. In such jurisdictions, a lawyer commonly writes to his or her adversary before the scheduling conference listing the documents he or she expects in the disclosures. If the other side fails to furnish those documents, the lawyer then seeks judicial sanctions. Also, the notices to produce contained here are not meant to be specific to any of the titles of the ADA.

Plaintiff's Request to Produce

Pursuant to Rule 34, Plaintiff requests that the following documents be produced at the offices of ________, located at ___________ on ___________ ___________, for the purpose of inspection and copying by the Plaintiff.

Definition: Depending upon how your notice to produce is structured, the attorney may want to include in the definition section of such notice the meaning of the terms as they now exist under the amendments to the Americans with Disabilities Act, such as: The definition of a disability, definition of major life activity and what it includes, and the definition of auxiliary aids and services.

1. Any and all records analyzing the job tasks of the position held by the Plaintiff.
2. Any and all personnel records of Plaintiff.
3. Any and all records of Plaintiff kept in confidential files in accordance with federal law, such as pursuant to the Americans with Disabilities Act of 1990.
4. Any and all tests that Plaintiff took as part of the pre-employment hiring process, including the actual test questions themselves.
5. The employment application filled out by Plaintiff.
6. The financial and annual reports of Defendant. (Note: This may not be discoverable unless the Defendant alleges that the accommodation would be an undue hardship.)
7. Defendant's employee handbook.
8. Defendant's 504/ADA Grievance Procedure.
9. Defendant's self-evaluation plan.
10. Defendant's transition plan.
11. Defendant's organizational chart.
12. Defendant's EEO reports for relevant years.
13. Any certifications by the head of the public entity citing an undue burden.
14. Any and all notes, documentation, or questions used during the exam performed on Plaintiff at Defendant's behest either while Plaintiff was in Defendant's employ or subsequent to a conditional job offer. Include the results and conclusions of said exam. (Be aware that the employer may not have anything other than conclusions.)
15. Plaintiff's job description.
16. Copies of the long- and short-term disability policies offered by the Defendant, and the actuarial data used to decide the limitation at issue.
17. Copies of the collective bargaining agreement, relevant griev-

ance files, amendments to the collective bargaining agreement, and the letter of agreement between the collective bargaining unit and the Defendant.

18. Any materials that describe the nature and scope of (name of program/activity/service at issue). Include any data or information indicating the nature of the population served by the program/activity or service at issue, and the contact information for the person(s) in charge of same.
19. Any materials detailing the criteria for admission to the (list name of program/activity or service at issue), and the contact information for the person(s) in charge of same.
20. Transcripts and minutes of the meeting of (date) in which the zoning of (state names of defendants's business) was discussed. Include the list of witnesses appearing at that meeting.
21. The architectural plans/blueprints for the building housing the place of public accommodation at issue.
22. Any architectural records, materials, documents sent to (name of state in which place of public accommodation is located) in accordance with (name of state in which place of public accommodation is located) equal access laws.
23. The architectural plans for the alterations performed at (location of place of public accommodation and place of public accommodation itself).
24. Any materials describing the nature and scope of the (name of place of public accommodation) business.
25. Copies of the lease between (name of place of public accommodation and its lessor).
26. The records of Defendant pertaining to the investigation of Plaintiff's physical/mental condition and the determination of coverage or noncoverage under (name of Defendant or Defendant's administrator of the disability plan) benefit/disability plans.
27. Any written materials, records, or documents kept by Defendant in its benefits department pertaining to any medical care received by Plaintiff while employed by Defendant.
28. Any and all records pertaining to Defendant's investigation of Plaintiff's physical/mental impairment.
29. The job description of the persons holding Plaintiff's position prior to and subsequent to plaintiff.

INTERROGATORIES

It may not be possible to ask all of these interrogatories, as jurisdictions limit the number of interrogatories, the specific number varies from place to place, that can be asked. Also, there may be standard language used for interrogatories. Finally, it is, of course, ultimately the decision of the litigating attorney to decide on the formulation and scope of what is asked in the interrogatories.

Plaintiff's Interrogatories

The Plaintiff requests that the following interrogatories be answered under oath by Defendant.

Definition: Depending upon how your interrogatories are structured, the attorney may well want to include in his or her definition section the meaning of various terms (such as disability, major life activity, auxiliary aids and services, etc.) as they now exist under the amendments to the Americans with Disabilities Act.

1. The name, title, and address of the officers of Defendant involved in the decision to restructure the company's health insurance plan.
2. The name, title, and address of the officers of Defendant that were responsible for compiling/overseeing any and all actuarial data justifying the distinction in benefit levels among disabilities.
3. Detail completely the investigation made by Defendant as to Plaintiff's physical/mental condition and coverage under the Defendant's benefits plan.
4. At any time, did the Defendant or its officers, employees, or agents receive any information as to the Plaintiff's physical/mental condition?
5. If Defendant did receive information about the Plaintiff's physical/mental condition, please state the nature of that information, its source, when that information was received, and where that information was kept.
6. Did the Defendant or its officers, employees, or agents receive any information as to the Plaintiff's physical/mental condition

at any time during the course of Plaintiff's employment with Defendant? If so, please state the nature of that information and its source. Also, describe where that information was stored by the Defendant.

7. Detail completely the investigation made by Defendant as to Plaintiff's physical/mental condition.
8. Identify the person answering these interrogatories.
9. Identify all individuals (part-time and full-time) who have worked under Plaintiff's supervisor for three years prior to and subsequent to Plaintiff's employ with defendant. Please provide the names and addresses of such persons.
10. Identify by name and address the individual hired into the vacancy sought by Plaintiff.
11. Describe in detail the reasons for selecting the individual hired for the vacancy sought by Plaintiff.
12. Describe in detail just how the Defendant determined the essential functions of Plaintiff's position/position sought by Plaintiff.
13. State whether any person employed by Defendant has received any comment, criticism, or complaint concerning the Plaintiff's conduct or job performance.
14. If an employee of Defendant has received any comment, criticism, or complaint concerning the Plaintiff's conduct or job performance, provide the name, title, and address of such person.
15. If an employee of Defendant has received any comment, criticism, or complaint concerning the Plaintiff's conduct or job performance, state the specifics of the comment, complaint, or criticism.
16. If an employee of Defendant has received any comment, criticism, or complaint concerning the Plaintiff's conduct or job performance, identify the person making the comment, criticism, or complaint by name, employment, job title, and last known address.
17. If an employee of Defendant has received any comment, criticism, or complaint concerning the Plaintiff's conduct or job performance, identify the occasion for the making of such com-

ment, criticism, or complaint.

18. Please describe whether the safety of the public, other employees, or the self was a fundamental aspect of the position held by Plaintiff while in Defendant's employ.
19. State the name, title, and address of all persons participating in the process of hiring the Plaintiff and describe the roles played by each.
20. Describe all instances where Defendant offered to make accommodations for Plaintiff's disability. Include in that description the name, Title, and address of the person offering the accommodation. Also, include the date(s) the accommodation was offered and the specific accommodation offered, as well as whether such accommodations were accepted by Plaintiff.
21. Describe the purpose of the department Plaintiff worked in while in Defendant's employ and how that department relates to Defendant's company achieving its goals. Also, state the various locations where this department conducts operations.
22. Describe the operations of the department Plaintiff worked in while in Defendant's employ. Provide the name, title, and address of each person in that department.
23. Describe the pre-employment hiring process. Include in that description the nature of any tests that applicants take in that process as well as the test and the test questions themselves.
24. Describe the medical exam performed on Plaintiff on ___________ (date) while plaintiff was employed by Defendant. Include in that description the scope of such exam and the reasons for Defendant insisting on such an exam.
25. Did anyone in Defendant's employ encourage Plaintiff to seek SSDI, long- or short-term disability benefits? If so, state the name, title, and address of such person.
26. Describe the ___________ program/activity/service (Title II or III matter assumed). In that description, describe the purpose of the program/activity, the number of employees in that program/activity, the population served by the program/activity, the locations where the program/activity occurs, and whether such programs/activities are integrated with the nondisabled.
27. Describe the eligibility requirements for the program/activity

[state the program/activity involved].

28. (public entity assumed) Does Defendant claim that accommodating Plaintiff would result in an undue burden? If so, please state when the head of Defendant certified as such (Title II case being assumed).
29. Describe the process for which an adverse zoning decision against Plaintiff was made.
30. When was Defendant's facility built?
31. Has Defendant's facility been altered or renovated since 1/26/92?
32. Is Defendant a religious entity? If so, describe. Also [assuming employment mater against a religious entity] describe the religious duties, if any, expected of plaintiff's position.
33. Is Defendant's place of business under lease? If so, state the name and address of the lessor.
34. If a public entity is involved, has Defendant conducted a self-evaluation of its operations?
35. If a public entity is involved, state who the ADA/504 coordinator is.

REQUEST TO ADMIT

Request to Admit can be a very useful tool to narrow the issues of contention. As for what to ask in a Request to Admit, refer to the Checklists, the Interrogatories, and the Notices to Produce. It is possible that useful Requests to Admit could be formulated based on that material. A detailed request to admit may also help with summary judgment motions.

LITIGATION FORMS (THE DEFENDANT'S VIEW)

Answer (Title I)

Defendants _______________, by and through their attorneys, ____________________, as their Answer to Plaintiff's complaint in the above-captioned cause, hereby deny each and every allegation contained in the complaint and as delineated below.

Notice of Action
This is an action under Title I of the Americans with Disabilities Act of 1990 as amended (ADA) to redress unlawful disability-based employment practices and to make plaintiff, (name of plaintiff), whole. Defendant, (names of defendants), discharged plaintiff, a qualified individual with a disability, (state disability), from his position as (state title of position), on the basis of his disability.

Answer: Defendant admits that this is an action filed under Title I of the Americans with Disabilities Act of 1990 (hereafter ADA). Defendant denies committing unlawful employment practices or taking adverse action against plaintiff on the basis of a disability, as defined by the ADA, or that any alleged disability of plaintiff was a motivating factor in the adverse employment decision. Defendant also denies that plaintiff was a qualified individual with a disability at the time the adverse action was taken. *Defendant further denies that plaintiff was a person with a disability as defined by the ADA.

*For this particular denial, you will need to assess whether the cause of action arises under the ADA before the effective date of the ADAAA. If the cause of action arises before the advent of the ADAAA, this may be a possible defense. If the cause of action arises after the advent of the ADAAA, the chances are not good that this defense could be successful. (This paragraph applies whenever you see an * throughout these forms).

Jurisdiction and Venue

1. Jurisdiction of this court is proper under 28 U.S.C. 451, 1331, 1337, and 1343. This action is instituted under Section 107(a) of the ADA, 42 U.S.C. 12117—incorporating by reference Sec-

tions 706(f)(1), (3) of Title VII of the Civil Rights Act of 1964 (Title VII), 42 U.S.C. 2000e–5(f)(1), (3).
Answer: *Defendant admits the allegations contained in paragraph 1 of plaintiff's Jurisdiction and Venue section of this complaint.*

2. The alleged unlawful employment practices took place and are taking place in the ____________ District of _________, ___________ Division.
Answer: *Defendant denies that any unlawful employment practices have taken place or are taking place. Defendant admits that it does conduct business in the ___________ District of ______, _____________ Division.*

Parties

3. (Name of plaintiff) is an otherwise qualified individual with a disability who was employed by (names of defendants) from ______ to _____.
Answer: *Defendant denies that plaintiff is an otherwise qualified (Rehabilitation Act) or qualified (ADA) individual with a disability. *Defendant further denies that plaintiff has a disability as defined in the ADA. [Alternatively, defendant lacks sufficient information or knowledge as to whether plaintiff has a disability as defined by the ADA and therefore: a) demands that plaintiff be put to his/her proof, and/or b) denies same.] [Check your jurisdiction to see whether a simple "denied" is consistent with Federal Rule 8(b)(1)(B) and consider doing that unless you have to parse out the admitted and denied parts. This comment applies to several responses below.]*
4. Plaintiff is expressly authorized under Section 107(a) of the ADA, 42 U.S.C. 12117—incorporating by reference Sections 706(f)(1),(3) of Title VII of the Civil Rights Act of 1964 (Title VII), 42 U.S.C. 2000e–5(f)(1),(3)—to bring this action.
Answer: *Defendant admits [or denies, see paragraph 8 below].*
5. At all relevant times, (names of defendants) has been a corporation doing business in (state and city), and at all relevant times (names of defendants) has had at least 15 employees.
Answer: *Defendant admits. [If true; plaintiffs sometimes make errors in designation of defendant.]*

6. At all relevant times, (names of defendants) has been engaged in an industry affecting commerce within the meaning of Section 101(5) of the ADA, 42 U.S.C. 12111(5).
   Answer: *Defendant admits. [Defendant denies that it is engaged in an industry affecting commerce.]***
   ***Hard to believe that this could be a possible defense, especially with the Internet thrown into the equation, but it is mentioned here as at least a theoretical possibility.*
7. At all relevant times, (names of defendants) has been a covered entity under Section 101(2) of the ADA, 42 U.S.C. 12111(2).
   Answer: *Defendant admits. [Defendant denies.]*

Statement of Claims

8. (Name of plaintiff) has exhausted his/her administrative remedies by timely filing a charge with the Equal Employment Opportunity Commission alleging violations of Title I of the ADA by (names of defendants) and obtaining a right to sue letter from the EEOC. All conditions precedent to the institution of this lawsuit have been fulfilled.
   Answer: *Defendant admits. [If right-to-sue letter has not been issued, then deny. Also may wish to deny, if plaintiff is under a collective bargaining agreement and the terms of that agreement have not been exhausted.]*
9. Since at least (date), (names of defendants) has engaged in unlawful employment practices in violation of ADA sections (list specific sections of Title I of the ADA that were violated) at (place where the ADA violations occurred). These practices include but are not limited to discharge of (name of plaintiff), an individual with a disability able to do the essential functions of the job with or without reasonable accommodations.
   Answer: *Defendant denies that it has engaged in unlawful employment practices in violation of the ADA. Defendant denies that it committed any of the alleged practices complained of in paragraph number 9 of plaintiff's complaint. Defendant denies that plaintiff was able to perform the essential functions of his position with or without reasonable accommodation. [In this situation, this may be a section where the Defendant would make the first sentence denial and then state that the allega-*

tions of alleged practices were too vague for Defendant to admit or deny, setting up a Motion for More Definite Statement.]

10. As a result of the unlawful disability discrimination, the effect of the practices complained of above has been to deprive (name of plaintiff) of equal employment opportunities and otherwise adversely affect his status as an employee.

    Answer: *Defendant denies that plaintiff has been deprived of equal employment opportunities or otherwise adversely affected as an employee as a result of his alleged disability. Defendant further alleges that plaintiff's alleged disability was not a motivating factor in any alleged adverse employment decision against the plaintiff.* If a Title I case, defendant might not want to assume motivating factor is in play, depending on the judge. That is, while *University of Texas Southwestern Medical Center v. Nassar*, 133 S. Ct. 2517 (2013), to my mind clearly compels the conclusion that motivating factor is the rule in Title I suits, it has not been explicitly decided as such by the U.S. Supreme Court. Thus, defense may want to consider the phrase "cause in fact," rather than "motivating factor," especially if the defense will be litigating causation. If a retaliation claim (Title V) is being pled, then defense would be better served with the "cause in fact" language per *University of Texas Southwestern Medical Center.*

11. The unlawful employment practices complained of herein were and are intentional.

    Answer: *Defendant denies that any unlawful employment practices complained of occurred. Defendant further avers that if any such practices did occur, such practices were not intentional.*

Defenses

12. Plaintiff has failed to state a claim upon which relief may be granted. [While this may be pleaded as a defense, you might note that it will only be timely considered if presented as a motion, and that the motion must be included in or filed before the Answer.]

13. Defendant asserts that plaintiff was terminated for reasons related to job performance and not to disability. Plaintiff's disability was not a factor considered in terminating plaintiff's employment. [Paragraphs 14 through 22 of this section should

be included only if there has been a reasonable inquiry satisfying the requirements of Fed. R. Civ. P. 11, and if the defendant has concluded there is a strategic advantage to including them in the pleading or they constitute an affirmative defense.]

14. Defendant asserts that plaintiff was not a person with a disability as defined by the ADA.*
15. Defendant asserts that plaintiff was not an otherwise qualified (Rehabilitation Act) or qualified (ADA) individual with a disability at the time of termination.
16. Even if plaintiff has a disability as defined by the ADA, defendant asserts that it in good faith attempted to reasonably accommodate plaintiff's disability and that plaintiff did not accept the proffered accommodations. Alternatively or in combination, defendant also alleges that plaintiff failed to engage in reasonable accommodation efforts in good faith.
17. Defendant asserts that to accommodate plaintiff would have created a logistical undue hardship by fundamentally altering the nature of its business operations.
18. Defendant asserts that plaintiff presented a direct threat to the health and safety of him-/herself or to others at the time the plaintiff was terminated, denied promotion, demoted, etc. (Also refer to Chapter 1 of the text.)
19. Defendant asserts that plaintiff's admissions in his/her application for disability benefits has estopped plaintiff from proceeding with his/her claim under the ADA. [Note: Be sure to read the Supreme Court opinion in *Cleveland v. Policy Management Systems Corp.*]
20. Defendant asserts that to accommodate plaintiff would constitute an undue hardship.
21. Defendant alleges that it is in receipt of evidence obtained after plaintiff was terminated. That evidence, if known to defendant at time of termination, would have resulted in plaintiff's termination in any event. Therefore, any damages suffered by plaintiff as a result of the alleged discrimination should be limited accordingly.

Attorneys' Fees

22. Defendant is entitled to recover attorneys' fees pursuant to 42 U.S.C. 2000e-5(k).

Prayer for Relief

WHEREFORE, defendant, by and through its attorney, ____________, prays that this Court dismiss the complaint filed in this cause and the Court grant the defendant such relief, equitable or at law, as the Court should so decide.

Answer (Title II)

Defendant ________________, by and through its attorneys, ____________________, as its answer to plaintiff's complaint in the above-captioned cause, hereby denies each and every allegation contained therein except as expressly delineated below.

Nature of Action

This is an action under Title II of the Americans with Disabilities Act of 1990 (ADA) as amended and under Section 505 of the Rehabilitation Act of 1973, which enforces Section 504 of the Rehabilitation Act of 1973 (Rehabilitation Act), to redress unlawful disability-based practices and to make plaintiff, (name of plaintiff), whole. Defendant, (names of defendants), denied (name of plaintiff) access to (names of defendants and names of defendants's program, activity, or service) on the basis of his disability.

Answer: *Defendant admits that this is an action under Section 505 of the Rehabilitation Act of 1973 and Title II of the Americans with Disabilities Act of 1990 (ADA). Defendant denies that plaintiff was denied access to its programs and activities because of unlawful disability discrimination or that plaintiff suffered unlawful disability discrimination.*

Jurisdiction and Venue

1. Jurisdiction of this court is proper under 28 U.S.C. 451, 1331, 1337, and 1343. This action is brought under Sections 202 and 203 of the ADA, 42 U.S.C. 12132 and 12133—incorporating by reference the remedies, procedures, and rights under the Rehabilitation Act, 29 U.S.C. 794 and 794a—and under Section 505 of the Rehabilitation Act, which enforces Section 504 of the Rehabilitation Act, 42 U.S.C. 794 and 794a—incorporating the remedies, rights, and procedures set forth in Section 717 of the Civil Rights Act of 1964, including the application of Sections 706(f) through 706(k), 42 U.S.C. 2000e-5(f)–(k).

Answer: *Defendant admits that this action is brought under Title II of the ADA and Section 505 of the Rehabilitation Act of 1973.*

2. The alleged unlawful practices were and are taking place in the __________ District of ________, _________Division.
3. As a result of (facts indicating standing), plaintiff has standing to bring this suit.

   Answer: *Defendant denies that the practices alleged in plaintiff's complaint are unlawful. Defendant admits that it does conduct business in the _________District of _____________, _____ Division. Especially if injunctive relief is involved, if possible, defendant should deny standing. Keep in mind, that it may not be possible at the answer stage, for the defendant to deny standing. That said, with respect to federal matters, standing is a constitutional matter and cannot be waived. Accordingly, if defendant cannot deny standing at the answer stage, the defendant should be prepared to contest standing at a later time.*

Parties

4. (Name of plaintiff) is an otherwise qualified (Rehabilitation Act) or qualified (ADA) individual with a disability, (state disability), who was denied access to (names of defendants) (names of defendants's program or activity) on or about (date).

   Answer: *Defendant denies that plaintiff is an otherwise qualified (Rehabilitation Act) or qualified (ADA) individual with a disability. Defendant further avers that it does not possess sufficient facts to state whether plaintiff is a person with a disability as defined by the ADA and therefore denies same. Therefore, defendant demands plaintiff be put to his proof.** [*Alternative: Defendant denies that plaintiff is a person with a disability as defined under the ADA.*]
5. Plaintiff is expressly authorized under Sections 202 and 203 of the ADA, 42 U.S.C. 12132 and 12133—incorporating by reference the remedies, procedures, and rights under the Rehabilitation Act, 29 U.S.C. 794 and 794a, and under Section 505 of the Rehabilitation Act, which enforces Section 504 of the Rehabilitation Act, 42 U.S.C. 794 and 794a—incorporating the remedies, rights, and procedures set forth in Section 717 of the Civil Rights Act of 1964, including the application of Sections

706(f) through 706(k), 42 U.S.C. 2000e-5(f)–(k), to bring this action.

Answer: *Defendant admits* [*or denies if the plaintiff's status as an aggrieved person is denied*].

6. At all relevant times, (names of defendants) has been a public entity as defined in Section 201 of the ADA, 42 U.S.C. 12131(1).

   Answer: *Defendant admits.*

7. At all relevant times (names of defendants) has received federal funds.

   Answer: *Defendant admits* [*theoretically possible but extremely unlikely that a public entity would not receive federal funding. However, in such a rare occurrence, you can go ahead and deny if defendant doesn't receive federal funding*].

8. Since at least (date), (names of defendants) has engaged in unlawful practices in violation of ADA Sections (list specific sections of Title II of the ADA that were violated) and in violation of Section 504 of the Rehabilitation Act, 42 U.S.C. 794. These practices include but are not limited to denying (name of plaintiff)—an individual with a disability who, with or without reasonable modifications to rules, policies, or practices; the removal of architectural, communication, or transportation barriers; or the provision of auxiliary aids and services, meets the essential eligibility requirements for the receipt of services or the participation in programs or activities provided by (names of defendants)—access to the (name of program, service, or activity) of (names of defendants).

   Answer: *Defendant denies the allegations that it has engaged in unlawful practices in violation of Title II of the ADA or in violation of Section 504–505 of the Rehabilitation Act of 1973. Defendant denies that plaintiff can, with or without reasonable modifications to rules, policies, or practices; the removal of architectural, communication, or transportation barriers; or the provision of auxiliary aids and services, meet the essential eligibility requirements for the receipt of services or the participation in programs or activities that defendant is alleged to have denied plaintiff access to. Defendant further avers that admitting plaintiff to defendant's (name of program or activity) would result in a fundamental alteration in the nature of the* *program/activity.* [*This is another spot where the defendant might consider saying it can neither admit nor deny if the plaintiff's pleading is not sufficiently specific. It may be the case, and in fact is quite likely, that the defendant has engaged in some discriminatory activity when the plaintiff's claim is broad and non-specific. Rather than a denial that is wrong, the defendant might move for a more specific statement.*]

9. The effect of the practices complained of has been to deprive (name of plaintiff) equal access to a public entity's services, programs, and activities and to otherwise adversely affect his/her status as a member of the public interested in accessing (names of defendants)'s programs and activities.
   Answer: *Defendant denies that plaintiff has been denied equal access to defendant's programs and activities.* [*Same comment as paragraph 8.* Also, keep in mind, as discussed in this book, that Title II causation may or may not require a plaintiff to show "but for" causation.]

Defenses

1. Plaintiff has failed to state a claim upon which relief may be granted. [Same comment as Title I.]
2. Defendant denies that plaintiff is a person with a disability as defined by the ADA. [Same comment as Title I.]
3. Defendant denies that plaintiff can, with or without reasonable modifications to rules, policies, or practices; the removal of architectural, communication, or transportation barriers; or the provision of auxiliary aids and services, meet the essential eligibility requirements for the receipt of services or the participation in defendant's (name of programs or activities).
4. Defendant alleges in the alternative that if plaintiff is a person with a disability, to admit plaintiff to defendant's (name of program or activity) would fundamentally alter the nature of the program or activity.
5. Defendant avers that its executive director certified that the requested accommodation was an undue hardship [inserted here as a theoretical defense, though it is unlikely to occur in practice].
6. Defendant avers that plaintiff was offered numerous modifications and refused those modifications.

7. Defendant denies that it receives federal funding [inserted here as a theoretical defense, though it is unlikely to occur in practice].
8. Defendant denies that plaintiff has construed defendant's program correctly. Rather, plaintiff was denied access to ________ (state defendant's view of program). Alternatively, defendant avers that plaintiff was denied access to an activity that is part of a larger program, which is readily accessible to plaintiff.

Attorneys' Fees

9. Defendant is entitled to recover attorneys' fees pursuant to 42 U.S.C. 2000e-5(k).

Prayer for Relief

WHEREFORE, defendant, by and through its attorneys, ____________, prays that this Court dismiss the complaint filed in this cause and the Court grant the defendant such relief, equitable or at law, as the Court should so decide. [Same comment as Title I.]

TITLE III (ANSWER)

(Seeking injunctive relief for discrimination by a place of public accommodation)

Nature of Action

This is an action under Title III of the Americans with Disabilities Act of 1990 (ADA) as amended to enjoin unlawful disability-based discrimination. Plaintiff, (name of plaintiff), was discriminated against on the basis of disability so that he was denied the full and equal enjoyment of the goods, services, facilities, privileges, advantages, or accommodations of a place of public accommodation owned, leased, or operated by the defendants, (names of defendants).

Answer: *Defendants admit that this is an action under Title III of the Americans with Disabilities Act of 1990 (ADA). Defendants deny that plaintiff has suffered discrimination on account of disability as defined by the ADA.*

Jurisdiction and Venue

1. Jurisdiction of this court is proper under 28 U.S.C. 451, 1331, 1337, and 1343. This action is brought under Section 308 of

the ADA, 42 U.S.C. 12188(a)—incorporating by reference the remedies and procedures found in 42 U.S.C. 2000a–3, Section 204 of the Civil Rights Act of 1964. [If there are not sufficient allegations to show standing (as discussed in this book), consider denying jurisdiction.]

Answer: *Defendants admit.*

2. The alleged unlawful practices were and are now being committed in the _______ District of _____________, _____________ Division.
3. As a result of (facts indicating standing), plaintiff has standing to bring this suit.

   Answer: *Defendants deny that any unlawful practices were or are now being committed. Defendants admit that they conduct business in the _________________ District of ______________, _____________ Division. If possible, defendant should deny standing. Keep in mind that it may not be possible at the answer stage for the defendant to deny standing. That said, with respect to federal matters, standing is a constitutional matter and cannot be waived. Accordingly, if defendant cannot deny standing at the answer stage, defendant should be prepared to contest standing at a later time.*

Parties

4. (Name of plaintiff) is a person with a disability, (state nature of disability), who was denied the full and equal enjoyment of the goods, services, facilities, privileges, advantages, or accommodations of a place of public accommodation owned, leased, or operated by the defendants.

   Answer: *Defendants lack sufficient information to determine whether plaintiff is a person with a disability as defined by the ADA and therefore leave plaintiff to his/her proof. Defendants further deny that plaintiff was denied the full and equal enjoyment of defendants' facilities.*
5. Name of plaintiff is expressly authorized under Section 308 of the ADA, 42 U.S.C. 12188(a)—incorporating by reference the remedies and procedures found in 42 U.S.C. 2000a–3, Section 204 of the Civil Rights Act of 1964, to bring this action.

   Answer: *Defendants admit.*

6. At all relevant times, (names of defendants A) has been the owner/lessor of (location of the place of public accommodation).
   Answer: *Defendant admits that it has been the owner/lessor of (name of business). Defendant denies that it operates a place of public accommodation as defined by Title III of the ADA. (If access to the Internet is involved, the defense will most definitely want to make the case that it is not a place of public accommodation).*
7. At all relevant times, (names of defendants B) has been the operator of (name of the place of public accommodation).
   Answer: *Defendant admits that it has operated (name of business) but denies that it is a place of public accommodation.*
8. (Name of the place of public accommodation) at all relevant times has been a place of public accommodation under (select applicable type of public accommodation as set forth in 42 U.S.C. 12181(7). Include its corresponding statutory reference.).
   Answer: *Defendants deny that it is a place of public accommodation. [It is of course possible that the facts of the case are such that it is clear a place of public accommodation is involved, and if so, admit.]*

Statement of Claims

9. Since at least (date), (names of all defendants) have engaged in unlawful practices in violation of ADA Sections (list specific sections of Title III of the ADA that were violated). These practices include but are not limited to (list the incidents of discrimination by each defendant).
   Answer: *Defendants deny that they have engaged in unlawful practices in violation of the ADA and that any of its practices violated the ADA.*
10. The effect of the practices complained of has been to deprive (name of plaintiff) the full and equal enjoyment of a place of public accommodation and to otherwise adversely affect his/her status as a member of the public interested in accessing the place of public accommodation owned, leased, and/or operated by the defendants, (names of defendants).

Answer: *Defendants deny that plaintiff has lost the full and equal enjoyment of a place of public accommodation and deny otherwise adversely affecting plaintiff's status as a member of the public interested in accessing the defendants' place of business/facility.*

Defenses

1. Plaintiff has failed to state a claim under which relief can be granted.
2. Defendants deny that they operate a place of public accommodation as defined by Title III of the ADA. [Should be included only where there has been a reasonable inquiry satisfying the requirements of Federal Rule of Civil Procedure 11, and if the defendant has concluded there is a strategic advantage to including them in the pleading or they constitute an affirmative defense. Also, in most situations, whether the entity is a place of public accommodation is going to be relatively straightforward. Remember, when dealing with this issue, the categories listed as places of public accommodations in Title III are exclusive but the examples are not. If the entity is entirely in electronic space, then the defense attorney is definitely going to want to deny that they represent a place of public accommodation.]
3. *Defendants deny that plaintiff has a disability as defined by the ADA.
4. Even if plaintiff has a disability under the ADA, defendant avers that the modifications requested by plaintiff would not be readily achievable.
5. Even if plaintiff has a disability under the ADA, defendant avers that the auxiliary aids and services requested by plaintiff would, if provided, constitute an undue burden on defendants.
6. Even if plaintiff has a disability under the ADA, defendant avers that providing the auxiliary aids and services requested by the plaintiff would result in a fundamental alteration in the nature of defendants' business.
7. Defendants aver that the facility plaintiff complains of being denied access to is a facility on the National Register of Historic Places.

8. Even if plaintiff has a disability under the ADA, defendant avers that the modifications requested by plaintiff would either result in an undue burden on the defendant or fundamentally alter the nature of the defendant's business.

Attorneys' Fees

9. Defendant is entitled to recover attorneys' fees pursuant to 42 U.S.C. 2000e-5(k).

Prayer for Relief

WHEREFORE, defendants, by and through their attorneys, _____________, pray that this Court dismiss the complaint filed in this cause and the Court grant the defendants such relief, equitable or at law, as the Court should so decide.

DEFENDANT'S REQUEST TO PRODUCE

Pursuant to Rule 34, Defendant requests that the following documents be produced at the offices of ________, located at ___________ on _________________________, for the purpose of inspection and copying by the Defendant.

1. Any and all medical records involving Plaintiff's alleged disabilities, including but not limited to (list physical or mental impairment being complained of) (list physical/mental impairments which you are aware of that Plaintiff has or had).
2. Any and all medical records involving Plaintiff's use of mitigating measures used in relation to each and every one of Plaintiff's alleged disabilities. *(If the cause of action arises after the advent of the ADAAA, one has to question the relevance of this Request for Production).*
3. Any and all records kept by the entity supplying the Plaintiff with his or her prosthetic device, medications, or other mitigating measures. *(If the cause of action arises after the advent of the ADAAA, one has to question the relevance of this Request for Production).*
4. Any and all records regarding Plaintiff's educational background. *(This request should be tailored to the particular Plaintiff. In some cases educational background might be of only marginal relevance.)*
5. Copies of any applications, statements, or written materials made by the Plaintiff in the course of applying for short-term

and/or long-term disability benefits or made in the course of applying for Supplemental Social Security Income (SSI), Supplemental Social Security Disability Income (SSDI), or state disability programs.

6. Any and all medical records of the Plaintiff. Include both hospital and physician records.
7. Any and all psychiatric records of Plaintiff.
8. Any and all prescription records of Plaintiff. [Requests 6 to 8 are broad enough to incorporate items 1 and 2, which makes 1 and 2 redundant]
9. Any and all employment records of Plaintiff prior to and subsequent to the time Plaintiff was in defendant's employ. [*This request should be tailored to the particular Plaintiff and claim as employment history may not be of much relevance.*]
10. Copies of any lease or other contract between (owner of place of public accommodation or governmental entity and the lessor of same).
11. "All written requests for a reasonable accommodation."
12. "All documents that evidence an oral request for a reasonable accommodation."
13. "All written responses to any request for reasonable accommodation."
14. "Any documents not more specifically requested that evidence a request for a reasonable accommodation."
15. All documents that identify what Plaintiff contends are the essential functions of his/her job. [Alternative: "Every document that contains a description of your job or any part of your job."]
16. All documents submitted by Plaintiff to the Equal Employment Opportunity Commission regarding his/her Charge of Discrimination filed on or about [date].
17. All documents that show the Plaintiff tried or has been trying to find a job at any time since [date].
18. All paystubs for paychecks received by Plaintiff since [date].
19. All W-4 forms issued to Plaintiff for compensation received after [date].
20. All bank deposit records for each of Plaintiff's bank accounts since [date].

21. All check stubs for checks received from any person since [date].
22. Any letters, memos, or other written communications that mention payments to Plaintiff after [date].
23. All 1099 forms issued to Plaintiff showing income since [date].
24. Any federal tax document not specifically requested above showing income, whether or not taxable, received after [date].
25. Any notes, memos, or other documents reflecting your receipt of money since [date].
26. A copy of every claim for worker's compensation you have filed since [date].
27. A copy of every response, notice, or other document connected to your claim(s) for worker's compensation.
28. All documents itemizing, supporting, or referencing any of Plaintiff's claimed damages in this lawsuit. [Based upon the pleaded claim, considering breaking this up. Thus, you also could consider asking these questions: "If you claim past lost wages as damages, produce all of your paystubs, W-4 forms and income tax returns showing wages paid to you after ______." "If you claim medical expenses as damages, produce all medical records, including bills and payment records, for such expenses." "If you claim pain and suffering or mental anguish as damages, produce any document that evidences the extent of your claimed suffering or mental anguish." If you claim front pay as damages, produce all of your paystubs, W-4 forms, and income tax returns for the period for which you claim front pay.]
29. Produce any document that includes evidence supporting your claim that the reasonable accommodation described in (<u>list paragraph of complaint</u>), would enable you to perform the essential functions of the job. (Title I)
30. Produce any document that includes evidence supporting your claim that the reasonable accommodation described in (<u>list paragraph of complaint</u>), would enable you to meet the essential eligibility requirements for receiving services or for participating in the program or activity provided by the public entity. (Title II)

Defendant's Interrogatories

The Defendant requests that the following interrogatories be answered under oath by Plaintiff. As with plaintiff interrogatories, the formulation and scope of interrogatories is a matter for litigation counsel.

Definitions:

Disability—A person has a disability if he/she has a physical or mental impairment that substantially limits one or more of life's major activities, has a record of such an impairment, or is perceived as having such an impairment.

Physical/Mental Condition—The plaintiff's physical or mental status.

1. Describe in detail all physical/mental impairments that you had while employed at Defendants. Include but do not limit the description to those physical/mental impairments that you claim as the basis for disability discrimination and those physical/mental impairments that you claim may have been aggravated by your employment with Defendants.
2. State the name of each practitioner who has treated your physical/mental impairments. As to each such practitioner, state: A) the name, address, and specialty; B) the date of each examination or treatment; C) the physical/mental impairment for which each examination or treatment was performed.
3. Describe how the physical/mental impairments referenced in #1 above substantially limit a major life activity. Depending on whether your case is preamendments or post amendments, the substantial limitation on a mjaor life activity, depending on the life activity involved, may be obvious and therefore the utility of using available interrogatory for this may want to be considered.
4. Since leaving Defendants' employ, has Plaintiff been hospitalized for any physical/mental impairment? If so: A) state the name and location of each hospital where the plaintiff was hospitalized; B) the date of each hospitalization; C) the conditions treated during each hospitalization; D) the nature of the treatment rendered during each hospitalization.
5. Is the Plaintiff still under the care of a medical practitioner? If so, state: A) the name and address of each practitioner; B) the nature of each condition being treated by the practitioner; C) the medi-

cal specialty of each practitioner; D) which of the conditions are related to the physical/mental impairments that Plaintiff had while in the employ of Defendants, and whether any of those conditions are a part of Plaintiff's claim of having a disability.

6. State for each medical expense stemming from treatment of Plaintiff's mental or physical impairment: A) the amount; B) the name and address of the person or entity paid or owed for the service; C) the date of each expense.
7. State whether Plaintiff has filed for: A) Supplemental Social Security Income (SSI); B) long-term disability benefits; C) short-term disability benefits. Also, state whether said application(s) was granted.
8. If Plaintiff has applied for short- or long-term disability benefits, state the name of the company administering the short-term or long-term disability benefits program.
9. List each job or employment held by Plaintiff since termination from Defendant's employ. State the following: A) name and address of employer; B) dates worked at each employer; C) nature of employment and duties; D) name, address, and title of immediate supervisor; E) rate of pay or compensation; F) reason for leaving/termination.
10. List each job or employment held by Plaintiff for the five years before becoming employed by Defendant. State: A) name and address of employer or entity hiring the person for a job; B) date of employment or length of the job; C) place of employment or where the job took place; D) nature of employment and duties performed; E) name and address of immediate supervisor; F) rate of compensation; G) reason for leaving/termination.
11. Does the Plaintiff claim that, as a result of termination from Defendant's employ, he/she has lost opportunities for advancement or promotion in his/her line of work? If so, state what opportunities would have been available had the alleged discrimination not occurred.
12. Does the Plaintiff take any medication for his/her disability? If so, state: A) the name of each medication taken and its dosage; B) whether there are any side effects to Plaintiff from taking

the medication, and describe same; C) how the medication so taken impacts on Plaintiff's daily living activities.

13. Describe Plaintiff's job search after termination from Defendant's employ, including all jobs applied for, addresses of entities to which resumés were sent, and all employment agencies contacted.
14. Does the Plaintiff wear any prosthetic devices, take any medication, or engage in any other mitigating measures related to his/her physical or mental impairments? If so, state: A) the nature of each prosthetic device, medication, mitigating measure, how the prosthetic device is built or constructed, and how it operates; B) any side effects Plaintiff suffers as the result of the use of such device, medication(s), or other mitigating measure; C) how the prosthetic device, medication(s), or other mitigating measure impacts on Plaintiff's daily living activities. *(If the cause of action arises after the advent of the Americans with Disabilities Act Amendments Act, this Interrogatory is of dubious utility unless eyeglasses are involved.)*
15. Describe Plaintiff's educational history. [Same comment as the request for production.]
16. Identify what Plaintiff/Defendant believes to be the essential elements of the position Plaintiff held while in Defendant's employ. Describe how your conclusion was reached.
17. Identify all reasonable accommodations that you contend would enable you to perform the essential functions of your job.
18. Explain how each of the reasonable accommodations that you identified in Interrogatory No. ___ would enable you to perform the essential functions of your job.
19. Explain how each of the reasonable modifications that you identified in interrogatory No. _ would enable you to meet the essential eligibility requirements for receiving services or for participating in programs or activities provided by the defendant. (Title II)

Epilogue

I hoped to accomplish several goals with this book. The book needed to be comprehensively updated, as the law is always evolving. I wanted to make the ADA, as it exists today (September 2013), understandable. Thus, think of this book as a primer on how the ADA actually works—an ADA road map, if you will, that also shows the reader just how broad the ADA really is.

One of my goals was to cover some of the recurring problems I have seen over the years, decipher them in a manner that can be readily understood, and suggest ways to deal with the issues so that larger problems can be averted. I also wanted to discuss ways that the ADA might evolve so that businesses can better plan for the future and give the reader a sense of how other laws relate to the ADA. Finally, I wanted people, after reading this book, to say to themselves, "I can work with this law," and not to succumb to anti-ADA feelings that often exist. Of course, the book is no substitute for competent legal counsel.

Before signing off, let me say that writing the fourth edition of this book has been a pleasant, though time-consuming, obsession for me. As has been the case in the past, I have to thank my wife for suggesting and then encouraging me to undertake this. Once again, she was right; it was worth it. I do hope the reader shares my assessment that the rather ambitious goals I have set for this book have been accomplished. If not, I hope the reader has at least achieved a level of comfort in working with the ADA. The ADA as amended is a good law, and now that readers are able to understand it and have some ideas of how to work with it, perhaps it can achieve its promise of making the world a more accessible and better place for persons with disabilities.

William D. Goren, J.D., LL.M.
Decatur, Georgia

Table of Authorities

CASES

ACTS OF CONGRESS

CODE OF FEDERAL REGULATIONS

EEOC GUIDELINES

UNITED STATES CODE

STATE COURT RULES

STATE LAWS

Index

A

E

F

G

H

I

J

L

M

R

Z